# Traveling
## *Solo*

"Berman has done the single traveler a tremendous service with this guide. . . . tells single travelers what they really want and need to know."
—*Library Journal*

"A comprehensive guide for anyone contemplating a solo vacation. Berman, a firm believer that 'alone' need not mean lonely, outlines a range of rewarding group vacations for all ages."
—*New York* magazine

"Earns our respect for a job well done . . . If you're about to plan a vacation on your own, read this first."
—*Modern Maturity*

# Traveling *Solo*

{ Advice and Ideas
for More Than 250 Great Vacations }

*Eleanor*
# BERMAN

The
Globe
Pequot
Press

Old Saybrook, Connecticut

Cover and text design by Bill Brown Design
Cover illustration by Pam Meier

**Library of Congress Cataloging-in-Publication Data**
Berman, Eleanor, 1934–
    Traveling solo: advice and ideas for more than 250 great vacations /
Eleanor Berman. —1st Globe Pequot ed.
    p. cm.
    Rev. ed. of: Traveling on your own. 1st ed. c1990
    Includes bibliographical references and index.
    ISBN 0–7627–0044–0
    1. Travel.    I. Berman, Eleanor, 1934–    Traveling on your own.
II. Title.
    G151.B483    1997
    910'.2'02—dc21                                              97–1531
                                                                  CIP

Manufactured in the United States of America
First Globe Pequot Edition/First Printing

# Contents

## Section I:
## Great Group Vacations
## for Solo Travelers

## Section II:
## Solo Travel Know-how

# Introduction

The first time I traveled by myself, I was newly divorced and scared to death. I never dreamed at that point that travel writing was to become my profession, almost forcing me to become adept at getting around on my own. I was just a travel lover determined that lack of a companion was not going to keep me at home. Happily, I discovered that the excitement of my first visit to San Francisco overcame my qualms. I did meet people along the way—not every day or for every meal, but enough to keep me from feeling totally alone. I discovered to my surprise that there were unique pleasures to being completely on my own. And I had a wonderful time.

That was a long time ago, but I still remember my initial fear, and I have special empathy when someone asks me plaintively, "But where can I go alone"?

Having now traveled extensively for both business and pleasure, I've learned that there are many happy answers to that question; that, in fact, solo travel can have special advantages simply because you can tailor it exactly to your own tastes.

The purpose of this book is to point out some of the myriad possibilities for rewarding solo vacations, as well as offer some of the know-how that makes for more confident travel on your own. My aim is to help you discover that you don't always need a traveling companion to have a wonderful time—that alone need not mean lonely.

No one asked or paid to be included in this book. I chose programs and tours strictly because they represented a wide range of activities that seemed to offer an opportunity for comfortable and exciting singular vacations. I tried to stay with those that have been around long enough to have a proven record. The basic information was provided by the operator of each program, as were the names of most of the references quoted. The comments were requested because the trips I could experience personally were necessarily limited (you will find my remarks under E.B.). Wherever possible, I wanted to hear from travelers who could give firsthand reports.

The best way to ensure that any vacation is successful is to gather as much information as possible before you make a choice. That is doubly true when you are planning a trip alone, without a companion to help cushion disappointments. Use the listings in this book as a guide and a starting point only, to be followed up by research with travel agents, friends, and specialized magazines. If you're considering a particular group trip or activity, ask for current information and *references,* and phone directly to clear up unanswered questions before you sign on. You might follow my example and ask for names of past solo participants who can tell you whether they felt comfortable as part of such a group.

I've tried to give the cons as well as the pros for some of these trips in the hopes that they will be of value to you in making a choice. Inevitably, these are personal assessments, and my tastes may not always match your own.

The pages that follow present only a sampling of trips, and I may have omitted some equally rewarding possibilities for solo travel. If you know of any, please write to me care of The Globe Pequot Press and share them for a future edition.

If this book gives you new ideas, encourages you to overcome your fears of traveling by yourself, and helps you to make the right choices for *you,* my mission will have been accomplished.

*The information provided in this guidebook was confirmed at press time. We recommend, however, that you call establishments before traveling to obtain current information.*

*The Globe Pequot Press assumes no liability for accidents happening to, or injuries sustained by, readers who engage in the activities described in this book.*

# Your Own: The Rewards

**N**OT VERY LONG AGO IN NEW YORK CITY, A LECTURE WAS HELD that packed the auditorium. The topic: vacations for singles.

The turnout was not surprising. We are living in a world where the number of single people is increasing dramatically. According to the U.S. Census Bureau, the number of never married adults over age 18 more than doubled from 1970 to 1994, rising from 21 to 44 million, and the 30 to 34 age range tripled in size. Adding those who are divorced or widowed, unmarried adults now comprise 39 percent of the over-18 population.

And solo travelers comprise a growing number of vacationers. In their quarterly forecast for the summer of 1996, the United States Travel Data Center, the research arm of the Travel Industry Association of America, reported that 9 million people were planning summer vacation trips on their own in this one season alone. And this does not count the large number of solo business travelers who will extend their stays for a few days of vacation pleasure.

Yet information for those who want to plan a vacation alone has been hard to come by. Most people know about Club Med and some of the tours designed for single travelers. But there is also a world of exciting travel to be enjoyed on your own that is not labeled "For singles only."

Many people are at a loss when it comes to finding these vacations because information is scattered. The occasional lecture or article may not be available when you really need it. Few guidebooks look at travel issues from the point of view of a single traveler. Travel agents also are limited by this lack of reference material.

The aim of Traveling Solo is to fill that gap, to bring together in one sourcebook the wide range of rewarding vacations that can be enjoyed without a traveling companion.

Today no one, young or old, needs to stay at home for lack of company. The exciting possibilities for travel are as varied as the ages, budgets, and interests of those millions of singles. And while that old stickler, the single supplement, still makes it more expensive to travel alone, for those who need to economize there are ways to match up with compatible roommates to share the costs.

One chapter ahead will include the range of programs exclusively for singles, but most of the options in this book are not limited by marital status. They are choices based on personal interests, places, and programs where you can feel equally comfortable with or without a partner. Many of them include family-style meals, eliminating the need to eat alone, a prospect that is daunting to many travelers.

The first chapters are divided into various categories of vacation experiences, from shaping up your body to stretching your mind, from active adventure to relaxing in the sun. There is something here for everyone, from travelers in their 20s to adventure-seekers over age 50.

Many of these ideas can be found in other guides. The difference here is that the information was compiled with the single traveler in mind— single in this case meaning simply traveling alone.

The data supplied by the organizer of each trip is supplemented wherever possible by firsthand accounts from past solo travelers—including myself. If there are no reports, it is because no references were made available. Big tour companies and cruise lines in particular were generally unwilling to give out names of past clients.

Exact prices change rapidly, so the trips here are designated by general price categories as follows:

I = $150 a day or less including meals
M = $150–$200 daily
E = $200–$250 daily
EE = More than $250 per day

Transportation is not included in these estimates except for tours or unless it is specifically mentioned.

For your information, "single supplement" refers to the common practice of adding a surcharge for solo travelers. Though it is a source of expense and annoyance to everyone who travels alone, the supplement has a practical reason; it is an attempt to make up for the lost revenue of a second person in the room. Some wise hoteliers and tour operators have realized that single travelers are valuable customers and have minimized or eliminated the supplement. Many offer guaranteed "shares," which means that they will provide you with another single person of your sex as a roommate or they will waive the supplement if they cannot find someone to share the room.

The term "homestay" means an arrangement of accommodations in another person's home.

The last section of the book is for those who want to travel completely on their own, with ideas and guidance for doing so safely and comfortably.

One issue should be stressed from the start. This is not a book about how to find Mr. or Ms. Right on your vacation. Cupid is notoriously unreliable about where and when he aims his arrows, and there is no surer way to doom your trip than to base its success on whether or not you find romance on your travels.

The trips here encourage you to look at solo travel not as a way to find someone else, but as a time to find yourself. That is the secret of a truly successful solo vacation.

Certainly there are challenges in traveling by yourself. Dining alone is a big one, and successful solo travel requires more advance research, more careful planning, and more resourcefulness than a trip for two. All these topics will be covered in the pages ahead.

But what stops most people from traveling alone is less logistics than attitude. If you've never traveled by yourself, it may seem frightening. It's easy to feel nervous, shy, self-conscious, and even self-pitying when you seem to be one in a world of twos. The tendency is to imagine that people will look at you and say, "Poor thing—all alone."

In truth, traveling alone says nothing about you whatever except that you have a spirit of independence and adventure. Who's to say you don't have a wonderful friend at home who can't get away for this particular trip?

Furthermore, rather than feeling sorry for you, many of the couples you are envying may be jealous of your spirit and your freedom. Travel shared can be wonderful—but it can sometimes pose its own problems. Neither friends nor lovers are always in harmony in their enthusiasm or energy levels. If she loves Gothic cathedrals but he'd rather scuba dive, tensions can loom. Nothing is more frustrating than a companion who wants to use up all of your free time shopping—unless it is a travel mate who taps a foot impatiently every time *you* want to browse in a store. Travel partners sometimes lack your stamina, or, even worse, may keep up a pace that wears you out.

So, travel with a partner means compromises. Solo travel, on the other hand, can be the ultimate self-indulgence, the chance to tailor a vacation strictly to your own tastes, energies and timetable, to go where you please, do exactly what you want when you want, and meet interesting new people of all ages and both sexes, married and single, in the process.

Without the insulation of a partner, you may find that you are more open to experiencing a new environment. You notice more, impressions are more vivid, you can take time to linger—and reactions are completely your own, uncolored by someone else's opinions.

By yourself you can feel freer to broaden your horizons and try out new roles, to live out a few fantasies perhaps, like riding a horse or rafting a river or painting a sunset—activities you might hesitate to attempt in front of the folks back home.

Because there is far more incentive to meet other people when you are by yourself, you tend to become more outgoing, to seek out new friends—and to find them.

What's more, many travelers who set out a bit shaky about traveling solo return feeling very good about themselves, with a stronger sense of competence, self-assurance, and independence for having proved that they can make it on their own.

Traveling alone has its challenges, but it can also be a wonderful opportunity. In the pages ahead you'll find a world of ideas for rewarding adventures. Make the most of them by selecting those that are uniquely right for you.

## Making Choices

In planning a successful solo vacation, the first and most important tip to keep in mind is a simple one: Know yourself.

You may consider literally thousands of possibilities or vacations, from tennis camps and museum tours to cruising the Nile or trekking in

Nepal. Or you may choose to explore a great city on your own. One of the pitfalls of planning a trip alone is the temptation to choose what you think other single people are doing rather than doing the research to find something suited to your own tastes.

Yes, lots of people go on rafting trips by themselves, but if you hate camping and would be terrified by swirling rapids, it makes little sense to head for a river. Remember that the greatest advantage to traveling by yourself is the freedom to do exactly what you like best.

And while trips for "singles" may seem more comfortable than being a single among couples, it is a mistake to limit yourself only to this category. Consider these trips, certainly, but if you sign up for a trip solely for single company and discover that all you have in common with your fellow travelers is your marital status, the trip will be a washout.

The first question to ask yourself, then, is what you want from your vacation. Here are some points to consider:

- Do you need to relax and wind down or do you want a pick-me-up, a totally new adventure to spice up your life?
- What kind of physical shape are you in—and how much physical challenge do you want on your trip?
- Do you want to expand your present hobbies or interests or develop a new one?
- Is there some particular area you want to visit? If so, do you prefer seeing a little bit of a lot of places or spending time getting to know one destination in depth?
- Are you seeking a warm climate?
- How important is the quality of the food and lodging?
- Will you be happier making arrangements on your own and moving at your own pace, or would you be more secure as  part of a group with all the planning done for you?

The more carefully you analyze what you are hoping for, the more likely you are to find it. Suppose, for example, that you want to visit the south of France. Your goals are to see the countryside, get some exercise, meet other people ages 30 to 40, and sample gourmet food. Many luxury tours could supply the gourmet part of the formula, but they would provide little exercise and probably attract an older clientele. An upscale biking or hiking trip might fill all of the requirements. What remains then is to research who offers such trips in this area and contact each with the right questions.

If you have the same destination in mind, but want a less strenuous trip, you might look into a learning vacation—one that stresses cooking, learning a foreign language, architecture, photography, or art. For a younger scene, consider tours geared to those under 35.

When your sights are set on sunshine, beware. A Caribbean island or the Mexican Riviera can hold perils for single travelers. Romantic resorts naturally attract loving couples, and there is nothing more depressing than feeling like odd man out in a lovers' hideaway. Look for other possibilities instead. Depending on your tastes, a trip to the Yucatan ruins in Mexico, a tennis camp in Florida, or painting lessons in the Caribbean are warm-weather options that should offer companions whose enthusiasms match your own. Windjammer sailing cruises attract lots of active, sociable people in the Caribbean, or you could check into a sunny spa resort that tends to draw many solo participants, married and single alike.

Should you join a tour or take off on your own? A lot depends on your travel experience and disposition. Do you dislike regimentation and prefer setting your own pace? Are you content to amuse yourself at home on occasion with solo walks, shopping expeditions, or museum visits? Are you able to talk to strangers? Are you willing to spend time and effort researching and planning your trip? Most of all, are you an optimist, ready to make the most of what you have rather than pining about what is missing? If the answers are yes, don't hesitate to try a trip by yourself; often going solo is the most rewarding way to go.

A good way to test the waters is to join a group or a tour, then afterward spend extra time in a city on your own. Or you might break up a solo city visit with short group tours to nearby attractions, providing a chance for a day or two of companionship.

Browse through all of the categories of vacations included in this book, including suggestions for travel on your own. You should find enough ideas to get you happily to almost any part of the world that intrigues you, and inspiration to try some new travel experiences as well. The key to traveling happily on your own is simply to do it in the way that will be most comfortable and enjoyable for *you.*

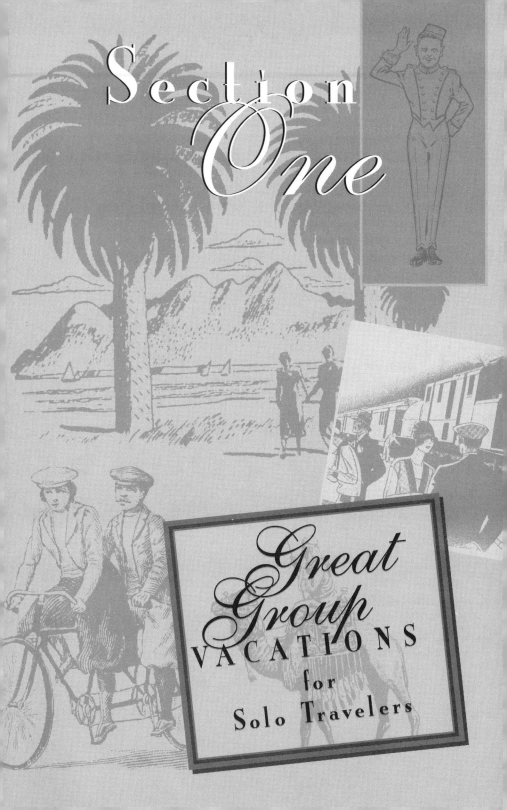

Section
One

Great
Group
VACATIONS
for
Solo Travelers

# Learn A Sport

**S**PORTS ARE THE PERFECT VACATION ICEBREAKER WHEN YOU are alone. It is easy to get to know others when you are learning new techniques together. Whether you improve your old game or pick up a new one, you'll also be adding a valuable dimension to your life when you get home. On a sports vacation, everyone is a winner.

Which sports are offered? Almost any you can name. From tennis and golf to scuba diving or mountain climbing, if you want to learn it, you can find someone to teach you on your vacation. You can learn to cross-country ski, canoe, ride a horse—or even live out your fantasy of being a major leaguer at a spring training baseball camp.

### Tips for Enjoying Sports Camps
- Try to avoid blisters. If you buy new shoes for the trip, leave plenty of time to break them in at home before you go.
- Be prepared for hours out-of-doors with proper protection—sunscreen, sunglasses or a visor, and a protective hat.
- Start an exercise routine at home, stressing aerobics, for about a month before you go. Beginner or expert, you'll get more out of sports instruction if you build up your stamina in advance.

### Here's a survey of the sporting vacation world.

## Tennis

Tennis camp is one of the most popular sports vacations. Since there is a wide variation in facilities and rates, your first decision in choosing a tennis camp should be based on its ambience—resort versus campus dormitory-style living. This is often a matter of budget as well as preference, since resorts are obviously more expensive. Locations with group dining are often more sociable for single participants, but tennis instruction at resorts can provide a way to meet people on a resort vacation that might otherwise be lonely.

Your next decision depends on how intensive an instructional program you prefer. Finally, the season will make a difference. Decide whether you want to head for the mountains or the sunshine—or maybe let tennis camp solve the problem of planning a Caribbean vacation on your own.

While the lodgings and atmosphere may vary, the essential teaching programs all are much like the program I experienced at the Topnotch resort in Stowe, Vermont.

The instruction began with an orientation session and a few minutes of individual play with  instructors who graded and divided us by ability into groups of four. Then we spent about an hour learning the right way to volley at the net.

During the next few days, we moved on to forehand, backhand, serve, overhead, and short strokes, with special drills devised to work on each stroke. Each day began with about fifteen minutes of warm-up exercises. One morning we were videotaped and got to see firsthand what we were doing right and wrong. Another day we got a private half-hour lesson to work on individual problems. On the last day we received an honest but upbeat evaluation sheet, with tips as to what to watch out for at home. The pros were excellent—outgoing, encouraging, and fun as well as fine teachers.

Will tennis camp work miracles on a mediocre tennis game? Unfortunately, you can't radically change your game in a few days, and most camps don't try. Instead they work on improving your existing strokes. With such concentrated practice, you do see encouraging improvement—and at the same time meet many people who share your interest in the sport.

### Following is a listing of a variety of tennis camps.

The most spartan—those on school campuses—attract the most singles because everyone dines together.

# Tennis Tips

Before you sign up for any tennis program, you should know the answers to the following questions:

- What is the instructor/student ratio? It should be no higher than one instructor per four students.
- How long has the program been running?
- What are the qualifications of the pros—are they certified by the U.S. Tennis Association and /or the U.S. Professional Tennis Association?
- Are there ample indoor courts so your vacation won't be washed out if it rains?

## TOTAL TENNIS

Box 1106, Wall Street Station, New York, NY 10268; (800) 221-6496; (718) 636-6141. (I)

| | |
|---|---|
| YEARS IN BUSINESS: | 17 |
| AGE RANGE: | 20–60 |
| MOST COMMON AGE: | 30–45 |
| PERCENT ALONE: | 50 |
| NUMBER OF PARTICIPANTS: | 60 |
| MALE/FEMALE RATIO: | 50/50 |

JUNE TO AUGUST; ROOM SHARES ARRANGED ON REQUEST, BUT THE SINGLE SUPPLEMENT, WHEN ROOMS ARE AVAILABLE, IS MODEST.

This program is conducted on the campus of the Williston-Northampton School in Easthampton, Massachusetts. Guests are housed in brick-walled dormitory rooms, share the bath facilities, and eat together in the cafeteria, where meals are served buffet style. Evenings offer volleyball and swim parties, a Monte Carlo night, a barbecue, and tennis movies. Groups are divided into foursomes by ability and assigned to one instructor for the entire stay. Teachers are given freedom to use their own particular method. Reports here are enthusiastic; half the guests are repeat-customers.

COMMENTS *Male, 30s: You have to work to get the most from this, but being serious about a game is an escape. Though hours of instruction seems like hard work, the atmosphere is friendly, and everyone has fun. Evenings can be social but are usually laid-back and quiet. There is a wide range of ages, with most people in their 20s and 30s and others up to the 60s. There are always many singles, a good mix of men and women, and no one has to worry about finding people at compatible levels of play.*

*Female, 30s: Low-key, friendly, and open. Good instruction. I felt perfectly comfortable alone.*

## TENNIS CAMPS LTD.

444 EAST 82ND STREET, NEW YORK, NY 10028;
(212) 879–0225 OR (800) 223–2442. (I-M)

| | |
|---|---|
| YEARS IN BUSINESS: | 16 |
| AGE RANGE: | 30–65 |
| MOST COMMON AGE: | 35–45 |
| PERCENT ALONE: | 80 |
| NUMBER OF PARTICIPANTS: | 24 PER WEEK |
| MALE/FEMALE RATIO: | 40/60 |
| LATE JUNE TO MID-AUGUST; NO SINGLE SUPPLEMENT IN DORM LODGING; SINGLES WEEKS OFFERED | |

Held on the manicured acres of Swarthmore College, 12 miles from Philadelphia, this summer program attracts many singles. Six-day clinics include five hours of instruction (with a 4:1 student-to-instructor ratio) and three half-hour private lessons. There is a choice of accommodations. Dorms, where everyone dines together, are recommended for meeting people. Strathaven, with modern hotel accommodations, and Ashton House, a Victorian mansion on campus, are more comfortable alternatives with a modest supplement. Both of the latter serve breakfast and lunch only; you are on your own for dinner. Campers have use of the school swimming pool and Nautilus equipment.

COMMENTS   *Female, 50s: I've gone for four successive summers and plan to go back. I choose the singles weeks since more people come alone. It is very relaxed, and there's a variety of people, from early 20s to 70s, about evenly divided male and female, and backgrounds from a housewife to an ex-marine. You can be alone if you want, but someone is always looking for company for dinner or a movie. The staff really goes out of its way to make everyone comfortable, and they are good about getting people together. They suggest places to eat and often go along.*
*Male, 30s: The instruction is terrific, and you get a lot of tennis—six hours a day. I don't play regularly, and I liked this because there was enough playing time to reinforce what we were learning. My game improved a lot. I chose the dorm accommodations, spartan and simple, with a shower down the hall. There was a wide mix in ages, 20s to 60s, a good mix of men and women. Most of the other people were either couples or*

*friends who came together, but it was very easy being alone because every day had a focus. The instructors were enthusiastic and helpful and very sociable. On Saturday night a whole group, including the instructors, went into Philadelphia for dinner. It was a very good experience.*

---

## TOPNOTCH AT STOWE RESORT AND SPA

4000 MOUNTAIN ROAD, P.O. BOX 1458, STOWE, VT 05672; (802) 253-8585 OR (800) 451-8686; TWO-HOUR PROGRAM, M; FOUR-HOUR PROGRAM, E (NO MEALS).

| | |
|---|---|
| YEARS IN BUSINESS: | 24 |
| AGE RANGE: | 35–65 |
| MOST COMMON AGE FOR TENNIS: | 35–65 |
| PERCENT ALONE: | VARIES |
| NUMBER OF PARTICIPANTS: | VARIES |
| MALE/FEMALE RATIO: | VARIES |
| YEAR-ROUND | |

Topnotch is exactly that: a beautiful setting in the Green Mountains and a first-class resort offering horseback riding, and mountain biking, and a lovely spa as well as tennis. A tennis-spa package is available. The tennis program has been rated number one in the Northeast by *Tennis* magazine. Singles weeks are held in mid-June and early September. Ten outdoor courts are supplemented with four indoor courts in case of rain.

Topnotch no longer holds an organized tennis week like the one I attended. Though there is a minimum stay of three days, you can begin on any day, and the participants will vary from day to day, even during singles weeks. There is a choice of two- or four-hour programs, and everyone gets a half-hour private lesson for every three-day stay.

---

COMMENTS *E.B.: Topnotch has been doing this for a long time, and they do it very well. Be prepared for a lot of tennis, even if you choose just two hours of instruction. What with playing with fellow campers in the afternoon, practicing my serve, working on strokes with the ball machine, and taking part in friendly tournaments, four hours of tennis was the average every day.*

*But our group was on its own after the day's lessons ended, and many couples chose to eat at area restaurants rather than in the dining room. It was harder getting to know people well than if one were in a group that shares meals. A singles week might be a better choice. During those weeks, everyone gathers for cocktails late in the day and almost naturally stays together for dinner. There is no predicting male/female ratio. Some groups have even had the unusual problem of too many men!*

*Female, 20s: The singles week was very social, with an equal number of men and women. Ages were from early 20s to late 40s. We all went out to dinner and the bars together. The program was very well run. The people were interesting, from all over the U.S. and Canada. The accommodations were wonderful.*

*Male, 30s: The tennis program is staffed by pros of exceptional ability in tennis and also in dealing with people. To a man, they are polite, supportive, and lots of fun to be with. Their acute observations of my strokes and personalized attention was much appreciated. What is so nice is that after a very short time at Topnotch, you feel you really know the pros and other players.*

## JOHN NEWCOMBE TENNIS RANCH

P.O. Box 310469, New Braunfels, TX 78131; (210) 625–9105 or (800) 444–6204. (E)

Australian John Newcombe, former U.S. Open and Wimbledon champion, believes that tennis should be fun. When "Newk" and his partners converted this former one-time dude ranch, the program they created reflected his philosophy of good tennis and good times.

| | |
|---|---|
| YEARS IN BUSINESS: | 28 |
| AGE RANGE: | 30–60s |
| MOST COMMON AGE: | VARIES EACH WEEK |
| PERCENT ALONE: | 20 |
| NUMBER OF PARTICIPANTS: | MAXIMUM OF 80 |
| MALE/FEMALE RATIO: | 30/70 |
| YEAR-ROUND WEEKLY AND WEEKEND PROGRAMS | |

The program begins with tips from the various pros. Then come two and a half hours of drill work on the courts, developing shot techniques, reflexes, concentration, and conditioning. Video replays and a roving coach reinforce the teaching. Each group of four moves from court to court and from pro to pro.

If you choose the intensive program, afternoon brings more drills, strategy sessions, and supervised match play. Otherwise you can relax at the pool or in the Jacuzzi.

Good food and lots of it is one of the big attractions here. Accommodations are in courtside condominiums; unfortunately, there is no matching program, so there is no way around a single supplement—possibly the reason why singles are in the minority. Given the Texas climate, the best times to come are spring and fall. Avoid school vacation weeks, when the resort fills up with families.

## NICK BOLLETTIERI TENNIS ACADEMY

5500 34TH STREET WEST, BRADENTON, FL 34210; (941) 755-1000 OR (800) USA-NICK. (I-M)

| | |
|---|---|
| YEARS IN BUSINESS: | 20+ |
| AGE RANGE: | 19–80 |
| MOST COMMON AGE: | 27–40 |
| PERCENT ALONE: | 40 |
| NUMBER OF PARTICIPANTS: | VARIES |
| MALE/FEMALE RATIO: | 3/1 |
| YEAR-ROUND; WILL TRY TO ARRANGE SHARES | |
| ADDITIONAL LOCATIONS AT SOME RESORTS AND ON | |
| SEVERAL SCHOOL CAMPUSES IN SUMMER. | |

Bollettieri, whose school has produced the likes of André Agassi, Monica Seles, and Jim Courier, runs one of the largest tennis-training operations in the world. The Bradenton headquarters boasts more than seventy-one courts. Five and a half hours of tennis instruction are the focus of each day, including work on strokes, plus the academy's "mental toughness" program, taught by a sports psychology expert. Groups change pros every half hour.

Guests are housed four per two-bedroom townhouse overlooking the courts. Meals are served buffet style in the recreation center. Swimming and Jacuzzi are also available, and Longboat Key's beaches and Sarasota shopping are not far away. During the summer camps also are held at satellite school campuses; check current offerings.

## RAMEY SPORTS AND FITNESS CENTER

5931 HIGHWAY 56, OWENSBORO, KY 42301; (501) 771-4723. TWO-, THREE-, AND FIVE-DAY PROGRAMS (I)

| | |
|---|---|
| YEARS IN BUSINESS: | 34 |
| AGE RANGE: | 19–70 |
| MOST COMMON AGE: | 35–55 |
| PERCENT ALONE: | 75 |
| NUMBER OF PARTICIPANTS: | 21 |
| MALE/FEMALE RATIO: | VARIES |
| YEAR-ROUND, WEEK-LONG, AND WEEKEND | |
| PROGRAMS; WILL TRY TO ARRANGE SHARES | |

This "total immersion" program, located in a pleasant country setting among farms and orchards, is geared to high achievers, with the day planned from 8:00 A.M. to 9:00 P.M. Tennis takes up to five hours daily or can be extended for diehards. Strategy sessions, stroke presentations, tennis videos, and a tennis psychology program are on the full agenda. Four campers work with one pro and also get to work individually with director Joan Ramey, a U.S. Professional Tennis Association Master Professional. Campers are housed in cottages with cooking facilities or in nearby motels. Facilities include three indoor and three outdoor tennis courts, an outdoor pool, a Nautilus fitness room, sauna, racquetball courts, and a lighted sand volleyball court. A masseuse can be arranged to ease tired muscles. Food is home cooked and farm fresh. Horseback instruction is available at the riding stables, and campers have the option of combining tennis and riding programs.

COMMENTS  *Male, 40s: The ages varied from teens to 50s; people were mainly from the Midwest. You naturally get to know people, especially those in your tennis group, but we all ate meals as a group, making it even easier. Food was excellent, the accommodations fine, the program well run. It was a great experience.*
*Male, 40s: There were some singles, but mostly couples or two friends who came together. But I was alone, and I didn't feel lonely. It was easy to meet people, even though I stayed at a motel in town, because we all ate together. The food was the high point of the trip. I was very impressed also by the structure of the lessons. We worked for eight hours a day, but it was spaced so that you didn't get worn out.*

## VIC BRADEN TENNIS COLLEGE

2335 Avenida La Caza, Coto de Caza, CA 92679 (inland from Newport Beach); (714) 581–2990 or (800) CALL VIC in CA; (800) 42–COURT outside CA. Program also offered at Vic Braden Tennis College, Green Valley Spa, 1515 West Canyon View Drive, Saint George, UT 84770; (801) 628–8060 or (800) 237–1068. (M)

| | |
|---|---|
| Years in business: | 23 |
| Age range: | All ages |
| Most common age: | 30s, 40s |
| Percent alone: | 20 |
| Number of participants: | 30–40 per week |
| Male/female ratio: | almost 50/50 |
| Year-round weekly programs | |

Vic Braden, a fifty-year coaching veteran and winner of dozens of awards, is part teacher, part psychologist. His dual method aims to guide you in breaking bad habits that spoil your technique and help you get over the mental hurdles that hurt your game. Braden's approach is part lighthearted humor, part sophisticated high tech, such as instant-replay videotape analysis. The student-to-pro ratio can reach 6 to 1, but you're on the courts with your pro for a minimum of six hours a day. The extensive facilities include seventeen hitting lanes with ball machines for practice. Courts are painted with targets so you can practice drills without an instructor. Guests stay on the premises in guest lodges with a choice of hotel rooms or suites with kitchens. The courts, two swimming pools, and a whirlpool are within walking distance, and there is a restaurant on site.

Though he is not present in person, Braden's technique is also used at the facility in St. George, Utah. Attendees here stay in condominiums at the tennis center and eat at the restaurants at the facility. The restaurant features spa and vegetarian cuisine.

## VAN DER MEER TENNIS CENTER

P.O. Box 5902, Hilton Head Island, SC 29938; (800) 845–6138. (I—NO MEALS)

| | |
|---|---|
| YEARS IN BUSINESS: | 17 |
| AGE RANGE: | 29+ |
| MOST COMMON AGE: | 40 |
| PERCENT ALONE: | 40 |
| NUMBER OF PARTICIPANTS: | 7,500 ANNUALLY |
| MALE/FEMALE RATIO: | 1/3 |
| YEAR-ROUND; WILL TRY TO ARRANGE SHARES. | |

Veteran pro Dennis van der Meer personally conducts many of the adult clinics at his twenty-four-court tennis center on Hilton Head Island. The program includes stroke clinics, drill sessions, round-robins, and private and group lessons. Special clinics are offered for seniors. There are also junior clinics, making this a good choice for single parents. Accommodations are at the oceanfront Hilton Head Inn or the Beach Arbor Villas located across from the tennis center and one block from the beach. Villa rates include membership at the Players Club Health Club, a fitness center with indoor and outdoor pools, Nautilus, Jacuzzis, and sauna. Van der Meer also offers clinics at some of the resort complexes on Hilton Head and at other resorts from the Ozarks to Canada, as well as on the Sweet Briar College campus in Virginia in the summer. Call the Tennis Center to check the current offerings.

COMMENTS  *Male, 30s: I have been to Hilton Head and to Sweet Briar alone. Both are comfortable, but most of the socializing goes on during the day, so you only meet people in your own group. At night everyone goes their own way. The people are mostly in their 30s and 40s. The adult clinic is half male, half female; the advanced group is 70 percent male. The instruction is good and the program well run, but it is for tennis, not socializing.*

*Male, 30s: I go with a Parents Without Partners group that returns every Thanksgiving. Other than our people, there seem to be few sin-*

gles there. *The food and accommodations are excellent and the instructors are great, but I recommend it for single people only if they really want to improve their game.*

## JOHN GARDINER'S TENNIS RANCH

P.O. Box 228, Carmel Valley, CA 93924;
(408) 659–2207. (EE)

## JOHN GARDINER'S RESORT ON CAMELBACK

5700 East McDonald Drive, Scottsdale, AZ 85253;
(602) 948–2100 or (800) 245–2051. (EE)

The number of single participants is very small, but these two facilities deserve mention as the ultimate luxury in tennis camps. The intimate California ranch, a pioneer in tennis instruction now past its thirtieth year in business, provides court space for twenty-eight players. Guests are requested to wear tennis whites; for dinner, men wear jackets and ties and women dress up. Dinner is served buffet style and there are no tables for two, so guests do get to know each other. They may range from Texas ranchers to feminist lawyers, but all tend to be interesting and well-heeled people. The program includes five hours of instruction daily and all meals. The camp operates March to November.

The Scottsdale facility, bigger and more luxurious, is set in the beautiful Arizona desert and offers lodging in spacious casitas on the grounds. It upholds the high instructional standards of the original ranch, but the program is less intense, with three and a half hours of instruction daily. The fee for the seven-day program includes two half-hour massages; three-day packages offer one massage. Meals are served both indoors and out to take advantage of the scenery. Both tennis clinics are kicked off with a champagne reception on the night of arrival.

**There are many more tennis camp options on campuses around the country in summer. Here are a few possibilities:**

## NIKE TENNIS CAMPS

- Amherst College, Box 2203, Amherst College, P.O. Box 500, Amherst, MA 01002; (800) 526–NETT.

- OBERLIN COLLEGE, C/O DR. BOB PIRON, RICE HALL, OBERLIN COLLEGE, OBERLIN, OHIO 44074; (216) 775-8763 OR (800) 433-6060.
- UNIVERSITY OF CALIFORNIA, IRVINE AND UNIVERSITY OF CALIFORNIA, SANTA CRUZ, BOTH C/O U.S. SPORTS, 919 SIR FRANCIS DRAKE BOULEVARD, KENTFIELD, CA 94904; (800) 645-3226.

## DUKE TENNIS CAMP

- DUKE UNIVERSITY, P.O. BOX 2553, DURHAM, NC 27715; (919) 479-0854.

*Resorts with large tennis instructional programs include:*

## ARTHUR ASHE TENNIS CENTER

DORAL RESORT, 4400 NW 87TH AVENUE, MIAMI, FL 33178; (305) 591-6454.

## NAPLES BATH AND TENNIS CLUB 4995 AIRPORT ROAD NORTH,

NAPLES, FL 33942; (813) 261-5777 OR (800) 225-9692.

## HARRY HOPMAN TENNIS ACADEMY, SADDLEBROOK RESORT,

5700 SADDLEBROOK WAY, WESLEY CHAPEL, FL 33543 (NEAR TAMPA); (813) 973-1111.

## COLONY BEACH AND TENNIS RESORT

1620 GULF OF MEXICO DRIVE, LONGBOAT KEY, FL 34228; (813) 383-6464.

## BOCA RATON TENNIS CENTER, BOCA RATON RESORT AND CLUB,

P.O. BOX 5025, BOCA RATON, FL 33431; (407) 395-3000 OR (800) 327-0101.

## THE POINTE ON SOUTH MOUNTAIN TENNIS CLUB

THE POINTE-HILTON RESORT, 777 SOUTH POINTE PARKWAY, PHOENIX, AZ 85044; (602) 432-6453 OR (800) 876-4683.

*For further listings of tennis schools, consult the following resources:*

## PETERSON'S TENNIS CAMPS & CLINICS,

1995, PETERSON'S PUBLISHING, PRINCETON, NJ.

## FODOR'S GREAT AMERICAN SPORTS AND ADVENTURE VACATIONS, 1996, FODORS PUBLISHING, NEW YORK.

## TENNIS MAGAZINE, 5520 PARK AVENUE, BOX 395, TRUMBULL, CT

06611; (203) 373-7000. PRINTS AN ANNUAL LISTING OF TENNIS CAMPS AND CLINICS IN ITS FEBRUARY ISSUE.

....................................................................

# Golf

Golf schools based at top resorts give single vacationers a focus to the day and a way to meet people, as well as the chance to improve their game. With locations from coast to coast, they provide opportunities for a comfortable resort vacation year-round.

## THE GOLF SCHOOL

MOUNT SNOW RESORT, MOUNT SNOW, VT 05356;
(802) 464-3333 OR (800) 240-2555. (E)

| | |
|---|---|
| YEARS IN BUSINESS: | SINCE 1978 |
| AGE RANGE: | 12–75 |
| MOST COMMON AGE: | 50s |
| PERCENT ALONE: | 25–30 |
| NUMBER OF PARTICIPANTS: | 50–80 |
| MALE/FEMALE RATIO: | MORE MALES |
| OFFERED YEAR-ROUND; SUITABLE FOR BEGINNERS | |

This popular school has winter headquarters in Crystal River, Florida, and warm-weather bases at Ocean City, Maryland, and two scenic New England ski resorts—Mt. Snow in Vermont and Sugarloaf/USA in Maine. It offers a low teaching ratio—four students per instructor—and instruction that ranges from fundamentals for beginners to fine nuances for the experts. Videotape plus other training aids and classroom instruction are part of the two-, three-, four-, and five-day programs offered. Special offerings include clinics for women and juniors and a parent–child program. Balls and clubs are provided, so beginners don't have to worry about equipment.

COMMENTS *Female, 40s: A special effort is made to make single people feel comfortable. There is a get-together party and buffet dinner the first night, a banquet the last night, and a "captain's table" so that you can always find company for dinner. There were many more single males than females! The small teaching groups mean you get to know people well. A good learning experience, a lot of golf, and a lot of fun.*

## GOLF DIGEST SCHOOLS

5520 PARK AVENUE, BOX 395, TRUMBULL, CT 06611; (800) 243-6121 OR
(203) 373-7130. (EE)

Schools at nearly twenty resorts around the country operate under the auspices of this golfing magazine. Many top pros are teachers, and instruction is geared to every level from beginner to advanced. Classes are held at the practice tee, the practice bunker, and the putting green, as well as on the golf

| | |
|---|---|
| YEARS IN BUSINESS: | 26 |
| AGE RANGE: | 25–65 |
| MOST COMMON AGE: | OVER 35 |
| PERCENT ALONE: | HIGH |
| NUMBER OF PARTICIPANTS: | 4–28 |
| MALE/FEMALE RATIO: | VARIES, BUT MORE MEN |
| OFFERED YEAR-ROUND. SUITABLE FOR BEGINNERS; SINGLE SUPPLEMENT CHARGED | |

course. Videotapes are also used. The welcoming cocktail reception and dinner with instructors is a good chance to meet other participants; programs close with another reception and special dinner. Among the resorts and golf clubs participating are Innisbrook Resort and Golf Club, Tarpon Springs, Florida; Carmel Valley Golf and Country Club, California; Sea Island Golf Club, St. Simons Island, Georgia; Sun Valley Golf Club, Sun Valley, Idaho; Pine Meadow Golf Club, Mundelein, Illinois; the Golf Club at Chateau Elan, Brazelton, Georgia; the Williamsburg Inn in Virginia, and the Sonnenalp Resort at Vail, Colorado.

COMMENTS *Female, 40s: I've attended two schools, with very different lodgings—villas at one, a lodge at another, but both were quite comfortable. Generally there are couples and men alone; women are in the minority. You all start as strangers, then quickly become friendly. Many people get together for dinner. I never ate alone. Ages were from 20s to 70s; the larger group is divided into smaller sections, and you get to know your own group very well.*

## CRAFT-ZAVICHAS GOLF SCHOOL
600 DITTMER, PUEBLO, CO 81005;
(719) 564-2616 OR (800) 858-9633. (E)

The second-oldest golf school in the country (and the only one operated by a woman) holds clinics that range from two and a half to five days at a variety of resort locations. Groups are divided into classes of four or less, with

| | |
|---|---|
| YEARS IN BUSINESS: | 25 |
| AGE RANGE: | 30 AND UP |
| MOST COMMON AGE: | 55 |
| PERCENT ALONE: | 30 |
| NUMBER OF PARTICIPANTS: | 24–30 |
| MALE/FEMALE RATIO: | 30/70 |
| YEAR-ROUND. SUITABLE FOR BEGINNERS; WILL TRY TO ARRANGE SHARES | |

male instructors for the men, and female instructors for the women. In addition to the personal instruction, split-screen, slow-motion video analysis is given to each student to take home. The atmosphere is friendly, with many meals planned with students and instructors in attendance.

---

COMMENTS   *Male, 60s: I went alone, and it was fine, though there were hardly any other singles. There are many couples where only one plays golf, so it works out. The people were from all over the U.S. and about evenly divided male and female. The program was well organized with good instruction. Classes are small: five students to one instructor. The days are full, and I was too tired to worry about doing anything at night. They do a great job.*

*Female, 40s: I've been there twice, first alone and I came back with my sister. About one-third of the people come by themselves. The food was only so-so, but the staff was excellent—I dropped my handicap by seven strokes after my first time there. You get lots of individual attention. The staff really concentrates on you and your game. It's pretty easy to meet people. You all wear name tags, and you meet lots of people at meals. Many people return—over half the people there had been before. I highly recommend the women-only classes—especially to women going alone—since there is no distraction so you concentrate on your golf, which is what you're there to do.*

---

## JOHN JACOBS' GOLF SCHOOLS

7825 East Redfield Road, Scottsdale, AZ 85260; (602) 991–8587 or (800) 822–1255. (M–EE: cost varies with the resort chosen)

| | |
|---|---|
| Years in business: | 26 |
| Age range: | 20–70 |
| Most common age: | 40–55 |
| Percent alone: | 20 |
| Number of participants: | Varies |
| Male/female ratio: | 60/40 |
| Offered year-round | |
| Guaranteed shares if requested thirty-one days in advance | |

A long-established program that graduates more than 12,000 students annually, the John Jacobs' Golf Schools are found in a host of locations from Point Clear, Alabama, to Palm Desert, California. Three- and five-day sessions include a comprehensive teaching program and opening and closing dinner parties with instructors and classmates.

*For additional golf school possibilities, see the following:*
**Golf Digest,** 5520 Park Avenue, Box 395, Trumbull, CT 06611;
(203) 373-7000.
**Golf Magazine,** 380 Madison Avenue, New York, NY 10017;
(212) 687-3000.

# Horseback Riding

## Horseback Riding, Western Style

Why don't more single people go to ranches? It's hard to imagine a more informal, relaxing vacation. Everybody is in jeans; nobody puts on airs; "dudes" come from all over the country and are all ages. This is a favorite family vacation, but while solo guests are few, ranches are the best examples I know of why an easy ambience, family-style meals, and a common pursuit are more important for a good vacation than the presence of lots of "singles." I've not met anyone who went to a ranch alone who did not report a wonderful time.

Besides riding, many ranches offer activities such as river-rafting, short pack trips, and hiking. They are the perfect introduction to the panoramas and pleasures of the American West.

Ranches vary in ambience, but the routines at most of them are similar. Guests mount up the first day so that the wranglers can judge their ability. Beginners get instructions in starting, stopping, turning, and getting to know a horse. Your horse is assigned according to your ability to ride. Each day adult rides are offered morning and afternoon for both beginners and advanced riders.

Since many people arrive with little or no riding experience, lessons also are offered every day to help you sit tall in the saddle. Some wind up the week galloping across the meadows; others are content to stay with the "slow ride" each day, a trek into the wilderness that is no less beautiful when the horses move at a reassuring, steady walk.

Evenings bring informal group activities from nature talks and slides to square dancing. Sometimes there is a trip to a nearby rodeo.

If you want to avoid the family scene, come in spring or fall, when school is in session.

I've visited two very different kinds of ranches, both places that I would recommend to anyone who loves the outdoors and wants to learn to ride.

## TANQUE VERDE RANCH
14301 East Speedway, Tucson, AZ 85748;
(520) 296–6275. (E–EE)

In a sublime setting 2,800 feet high in the foothills of three mountain ranges, the ranch sits amidst millions of acres of national forest and adjoins the Saguaro National Monument, a veritable forest of giant cactus. Guests ride over silent, open desert, up rocky canyons, and into towering mountains. The food is plentiful and delicious, especially cookouts over a mesquite fire; almost every belt was out at least a notch by the end of the week. A tradition here is the early morning ride where a chuck-wagon breakfast of eggs and pancakes awaits in the desert, served up against a backdrop of cactus haloed by the glow of the morning sun.

The main building of the ranch is historic, dating to the 1880s, but the fifty-nine air-conditioned rooms in modern casitas are downright luxurious. The ranch has Arizona's largest riding stable, with more than 100 mounts. Five tennis courts, indoor and outdoor pools, and a workout room are available when you are not in the saddle. Nature programs and walks are an added feature for those who are interested.

Despite the comparatively large number of guests here, singles need not feel left out. As the brochure says, "It's easy to be alone, but hard to feel lonely." I met a friendly couple in the van from the airport who invited me to their table at dinner that night, and I never lacked for company the rest of the week. Meals are family style, so each day was an opportunity to meet more people. The other two singles in residence during my stay were a male visitor from Japan, about age 35, and a woman in her 60s.

COMMENTS  *Female, 30s: I've been there ten times, three or four times alone, and I'd tell anyone to come alone. It's very comfortable, the kind of place where you can feel really safe, relax, and have fun. No one is looking at you because you're there by yourself. I made friends quickly each time, and I got to know the staff, too—they were always good for conversation and companionship. There's always something going on, so you can be alone or with people whenever you want. It is evenly split among men and women, but not many men by themselves. The food is great and plentiful. They have a new chef, and the menu is lighter now, more health oriented.*

*Female, 40s: I first went here with my husband and kids, then was divorced, and I've gone alone for the past four years. There are very few singles, but it's very easy to meet people, starting at meals, which are served family style at tables for ten. A separate kids' program for much of the day means you aren't surrounded by children even though many families do come. I love the fact that it is so quiet, that you can be alone or with people as you choose. I'm planning to go back next year!*

## VISTA VERDE RANCH

P.O. Box 465, Steamboat Springs, CO 80477;
(970) 879–3858 or (800) 526–3858. (E–EE)

This is an equally stupendous setting in the high meadows north of Steamboat Springs. At 8,500 feet, surrounded by national forest and wilderness areas and the 12,000-foot peaks of the Rockies, the air was crystal clear and the views glorious. Though food and accommodations are upscale and amenities include a whirlpool and a sauna, this is a working ranch, with cattle, plenty of farm animals, and its own stable of more than sixty horses. With a maximum of thirty-five guests and a friendly staff, making friends was a snap. Besides enjoying riding, eating, and evening entertainment together, guests share adventures such as whitewater rafting trips, hot-air balloon rides, hiking, and rock climbing. If you don't feel at home and don't know everyone well by the time the week is over, it's your own fault. Special weeks featuring cattle drives, pack trips, and fly-fishing are especially recommended for single guests, and the hiking is superb in early June with wildflowers and waterfalls abound.

At both ranches, the guests were well educated, interesting, and went out of their way to include someone who was alone.

COMMENTS  *Female, 30s: I've been there six times total, with someone and on the cattle drive alone. There aren't many singles—on all
my trips I've encountered only two other singles—one male in his 40s
and one woman on the cattle drive with me. But it was nice to go
alone because it seems like they pay more attention to you to make
sure you're having a good time. The staff treated me like family—
they were very welcoming and took care of me. It's a great experience
that I'd recommend to anyone.*

## CASTLE ROCK GUEST RANCH AND ADVENTURE RESORT
412 COUNTY ROAD, 6NS, CODY, WY 82414;
(307) 587–2076. (E)

Castle Rock rates a mention for its varied program, which supplements riding instruction and ranch life with a chance to try out easy
adventures such as llama treks, mountain biking, kayaking, rafting, sailing, windsurfing, and rock climbing. Trips to see the sights of Cody and
Yellowstone National Park are included in the rates.

COMMENTS  *Male, late 30s: I went with my daughter. There were
mostly families, just a few singles with kids and a few couples. Most
adults were in their 30s and 40s. The days were structured, but the atmosphere was very relaxed. They had set riding times each day and
many planned activities like kayaking, climbing, fishing, and llama
packing. They also have a pool, so there is always something to do.
They play games the first day that introduce everyone, and it is very
friendly. The food was wonderful, the accommodations okay—sort of
suburban rustic. The instruction was great, and I had a wonderful
time.
Female, 40s: It was a totally positive experience. Guests were mostly
couples, a few families, and one other single parent with his son, from
all over the U.S. and from Europe. Everyone was easy to get along
with and compatible. You could do as much or as little as you wanted,
with the group or on your own. The food was served buffet style and
was outstanding. The staff was top-notch. I would recommend it to
any single traveler, but especially those with kids.*

# How to Choose a Ranch

There are enough ranches out West to fill a separate book, and because none attract a large number of single guests, the best bet is to get a comprehensive listing, narrow the choices by location, and write for brochures. The first determining factor will be price, since ranches can range from $600 to $2,000 a week, and from five-star to pure rustic. When you have a few possibilities in mind, call them directly. You'll get a good idea of the flavor of the place just from the way you are received on the telephone. Here are a few considerations you should learn from the brochure or the owner:

- Emphasis: Are single adults welcome? How many came last year? Do more come at certain times of year?
- Rates: Many ranches give a break to single adults with only a modest added supplement.
- Location: To experience the true beauty of the West, pick a ranch with mountain views and access to rides in the wilderness. If you are traveling alone, you may prefer a ranch that provides transportation services or that is easy for you to reach from a major airport.
- Size: Outgoing people will do fine almost anywhere, but on the whole, it is easier to meet people at a smaller ranch.
- Ambience: Is this an authentic working ranch or a resort? Are accommodations modern or rustic?
- Amenities: If you are a new rider, chances are you will soon be a "tenderseat." You may welcome facilities such as whirlpools or the ministrations of a masseuse on the premises—services that can be found even on working ranches these days.
- Facilities: Do you care about a pool or tennis courts in addition to riding? If so, check whether they are available.
- Activities: Are there options beyond the ranch itself—trips to the rodeo, rafting expeditions, fishing, etcetera? Is there an evening program?
- Staff: What is the ratio of staff to guests? Who gives the riding instruction? How much teaching experience do they have?
- Horses: Are there more horses than guests? Will you be assigned the same horse each day?
- References: Every ranch should be able to provide you with the names of guests who have visited recently. Call them before you decide where to go.

## LAZY HILLS GUEST RANCH
Box G, Ingram, TX 78025;
(512) 367–5600 or (800) 880–0632. (I)
Will try to arrange shares

In business for more than thirty-five years, this is a family-owned, working ranch in beautiful country, a good choice for those who want to sample Texas-style ranching. Besides riding, the ranch offers swimming, tennis, basketball, volleyball, archery, hiking, fishing, hayrides, and cookouts. Owners say that it is a good choice for singles, even though they are few in number, because they are included when they want to be, yet are not pressured to participate in activities.

COMMENTS *Female, 30s: I've gone a number of times, alone and with my son. It is a working ranch with trail rides, tennis, a pool, a lovely environment. Meals are served family style, so you get to know everyone. Guests come from all over the world and range in age from 20s to 90s. There have been a number of single people on my visits, more women than men.*

*Female, 40s: There were few other singles, but I had a wonderful time. It was easy to be there solo because the owners made sure I was never by myself if I didn't want to be. The area is very beautiful and peaceful. The hayrides were absolutely wonderful. I would recommend this place to anyone.*

*Here are sources that can supply ranch listings; some can also offer advice on selection:*

### COLORADO DUDE AND GUEST RANCH ASSOCIATION
P.O. Box 300, Tabernash, CO 80478; (970) 887–3128.
Publishes annual state directory and offers guidance.

### THE DUDE RANCHERS ASSOCIATION
P.O. Box 471, Laporte, CO 80535; (970) 223–8440.
Publishes annual directory including ranches in Arizona, Arkansas, California, Colorado, Montana, Nevada, New Mexico, Oregon, South Dakota, Texas, and Wyoming. The association will give advice on choosing a ranch.

## OLD WEST DUDE RANCH VACATIONS, AMERICAN WILDERNESS EXPERIENCES, INC.

P.O. Box 1486, Boulder, CO 80306; (800) 444–DUDE, (303) 444–2622. Handles sixty-seven ranches in Arizona, Colorado, Idaho, Montana, New Mexico, Wyoming, and British Columbia, and offers a central reservation service with guidance in selecting the best place for your needs.

## ARIZONA OFFICE OF TOURISM

West Washington, Phoenix, AZ 85007; (602) 543–8687.

## TRAVEL MONTANA

1424 Ninth Avenue, Helena, MT 59620; (800) 541–1447.

## WYOMING TRAVEL COMMISSION

I–25 at College Drive, Cheyenne, WY 82002–0660; (800) 225–5996; in state, (307) 777–7777. Publishes state listing.

*For more information on individual western ranches, consult Gene Kilgore's Ranch Vacations, John Muir Press, (800) 474–6247.*

### Horseback Riding, Eastern Style

For easterners who can't make the trip out West, here are a few places that teach riding in rustic, informal, and scenic surroundings:

## JORDAN HOLLOW FARM

Route 2, Box 375, Stanley, VA 22851; (703) 778–2285.

## WEST RIVER LODGE

RR 1, Box 693, Newfane, VT 05345; (802) 365–7745.

## KEDRON VALLEY INN

Route 106, South Woodstock, VT 05071; (802) 457–1473 or (800) 836–1193.

## ROCKING HORSE RANCH

Highland, NY 12528; (800) 43–RANCH or (914) 681–2927.

## PINE GROVE RANCH

Cherrytown Road, Kerhonkson, NY 12448; (914) 626–7365 or (800) 346–4626.

## ROARING BROOK RANCH & TENNIS RESORT

Lake George, NY 12845; (518) 668–5767.

......................................................................

# Baseball

Every guy—or gal—who has ever fantasized about being a major lea-guer can make the dream come true at one-week spring training camps where guests become the rookies and former greats of the sport turn coach. Said one participant, "You walk into the clubhouse, grab a cup of coffee, head for your locker, and get your freshly laundered uni-form, with your name stitched on the shirt above your number. You look around and you see baseball stars, telling stories about the old days, and you're one of them . . . for one week, you're on the team." This partici-pant, one of three women in the camp, not only got to play but actually got a hit in the final game, a thrill she will never forget.

Baseball camps, aptly named "Dream Weeks" by one promoter, attract as many nonathletes as aces. Nobody under age 30 is allowed. Campers are coached in every phase of the game by former greats. They get drafted for teams, play each other, and sometimes play the pros. Talk is centered on baseball—past, present, and future. Most participants haven't played ball for years—but they have a ball! Who comes to baseball camp? One recent roster included surgeons, lawyers, a dentist, a comic-book distribu-tor, a real estate broker, a bartender, two mailmen, a plumber, and a con-gressional analyst.

The programs are basically alike, and most will try to arrange shares. All are in the EE category, but participants find them a once-in-a-lifetime fantasy come true.

---

COMMENTS   *Male, 40s: I've attended the Randy Hundley Cubs camp twice. I went alone and was placed with a roommate. You can't help meeting people. Most of the men were over 40, married but traveling on their own, and Cub fans from the Midwest. It is well run.*
*Male, 30s: I've been to baseball camp three times and I am going again. It is so easy to meet people—there is instant "team spirit." The men are mostly married, from 30 to 50; there were very few women. I had a great time each time and am looking forward to returning.*

---

## Baseball camps for adults include:

### DREAM WEEK, INC.

P.O. Box 115, Huntingdon Valley, PA 19006;
(215) 938–1200 or (800) 888–4376.
Weeks and weekends offered feature the Phillies,
the St. Louis Cardinals, and Major League All-Stars.

### RANDY HUNDLEY'S FANTASY BASEBALL CAMPS, INC.

130 South Northwest Highway, Palatine, IL 60067;
(847) 991–9595.
Nirvana for Chicago Cubs fans.

### LOS ANGELES DODGERS ADULT BASEBALL CAMP

Box 2887, Vero Beach, FL 32961;
(561) 569–4900 or (800) 334–7529.
Former stars from both Brooklyn and L.A. Dodgers take part.

# Sailing

Attending sailing school is a wonderful combination of learning a skill and experiencing the exhilaration of being at sea. In a week you learn the ropes from port to starboard. You start on land, learning what to expect, then head on board with instructors. Pretty soon the crew mates are working as a team, beginning to speak the language of sailing, and getting to know their boat. Friendships come easy working in such close quarters toward a common goal. By the time the week is over, the crew is usually able to chart a course and set out on its own.

Sailing schools are a wonderful way for singles to visit the Caribbean, as well as scenic ports in the United States.

## STEVE COLGATE'S OFFSHORE SAILING SCHOOL

16731–110 McGREGOR BOULEVARD, FORT MYERS, FL 33908;
(800) 221–4326 OR (941) 454–1700. THREE- TO SEVEN-DAY PROGRAMS, SPECIAL WEEK
FOR WOMEN. (E)

School locations: Jersey City, New Jersey; Stamford, Connecticut; Newport, Rhode Island; Captiva Island, Florida; St. Petersburg, Florida; Chicago, Illinois; Tortola and St. Lucia in the Caribbean. Will try to arrange shares—two to five per villa at Captiva Island, two per room in Tortola.

| | |
|---|---|
| YEARS IN BUSINESS: | 32 |
| AGE RANGE: | 12–75 |
| MOST COMMON AGE: | 30S |
| PERCENT ALONE: | 45 |
| NUMBER OF PARTICIPANTS: | 60,000 GRADUATES |
| MALE/FEMALE RATIO: | 70/30 |
| YEAR-ROUND | |

Captiva Island offers a special singles unit; single supplement on live-aboard cruises is very small. Meals are included only while cruising.

The seven-day "Learn to Sail" program for beginners is based at a resort and kicks off with a sociable get-acquainted party. Days are divided into morning classes and afternoons on the water. No more than four students are assigned with an instructor to each Olympic-class 27-foot Soling sailboat, and a real bond develops among them. Once the basics are mastered, students can increase their knowledge with more advanced sailing and cruising weeks. A special live-aboard cruising course combines curriculum with a thrilling one-week sail on a 40- to 50-foot boat in some of the world's ultimate sailing destinations—Tortola in the British Virgin Islands and St. Lucia in the Grenadines, depending on the time of year. Graduates can become members of the Offshore Cruising Club, eligible to enjoy cruising vacations in more beautiful locales, and the Sail Away Club, sailing regularly on club-owned boats at offshore branches.

------

COMMENTS  *Female, 40s: My St. Lucia classmates, numbering just two, were also female—one slightly younger and one slightly older than me, one married and one divorced, all of us from different walks of life and enrolled for vastly different reasons. By the end of the week we enjoyed a very special breed of friendship based on a combination of shared apprehension, excitement, embarrassment, fear, joy, panic, and amazing mutual support.*
*Male, 30s: On the last day, like kids, you stay out past the allotted*

*time until, finally, the instructor arrives in his launch to see you home. You wish you could spend a month of sailing days like these.*

## ANNAPOLIS SAILING SCHOOL

601 Sixth Street, P.O. Box 3334, Annapolis, MD 21403; (800) 638–9192 or (410) 267–7205. (M–EE, depending on location; meals included only aboard ship)

| | |
|---|---|
| Years in business: | 38 |
| Age range: | 16 and up |
| Most common age: | 25–35 |
| Percent alone: | Varies |
| Number of participants: | 3,000 annually |
| Male/female ratio: | Varies |
| Year-round; branches in St. Petersburg, Florida, and St. Croix, U.S. Virgin Islands; seasonal locations in Annapolis, Maryland, and the Florida Keys; suitable for beginners; will try to arrange shares | |

The nation's largest sailing school boasts 80,000 graduate sailors. The New Sailors Vacation Course includes two days of classroom and on-board instruction and three days of supervised sailing to reinforce new skills in a variety of sailing conditions. Having mastered the basics, you can elect to continue with a five-day Flotilla Cruising Course, a cruise vacation at sea that continues your instruction. Sail Away weekends are also offered.

Package arrangements with nearby inns and hotels are made by the school at each location.

COMMENTS *Female, 20s: I went alone on a two-day program, liked it so much I decided to work there. The age range is about 25 to 50, but most people are in their 20s and 30s, and from the Northeast. There are a few couples and many singles, though many are groups of friends who come together.*
*Male, 50s: It was a very good experience. The instruction was excellent, and there was no problem being alone. I learned a lot and had fun, though I stayed in a hotel and there was no real socializing at night. Of nineteen people, there was one couple and all the rest were single. They were quite a diverse group of people, but mostly from the Northeast.*

# Scuba Diving

More Americans every year are descending to discover the eerie beauty at the bottom of the sea. Recent statistics show that around 12 million people now have their diving certification, and with it a kinship that makes it easy to find friends on any diving vacation. If you want to join their numbers, the easiest way is to head for Club Med locations in the Bahamas, Sonora Bay, Mexico, or the Turks and Caicos Islands, each with a dedicated dive center where you can learn and be certified. Many other Club Meds also offer lessons.

Or you can choose one of the great diving spots—Bonaire in the Dutch West Indies or the Cayman Islands—to gain your certification. For the most current list of courses available, as well as a selection of hotel brochures, contact the island tourist offices at the following addresses/telephones.

## BONAIRE GOVERNMENT TOURIST OFFICE

10 ROCKEFELLER PLAZA, NEW YORK, NY 10020;
(212) 956-5911.

Diving is what Bonaire is all about, and all major hotels have learning programs. The most luxurious accommodations are at the Divi Flamingo Beach, where Peter Hughes' Dive Bonaire is located, and at the villas of the Harbour Village Beach Resort, where there is a full-service health spa as well as Great Adventures Bonaire with a variety of diving courses. The most knowledgeable divers head for the no-frills Habitat, run by Cap'n Don Stewart, an island legend. Ask the tourist office for dive package information and the color booklet *Diving Bonaire, The Official Dive Vacation Guide*.

## CAYMAN ISLANDS DEPARTMENT OF TOURISM

420 LEXINGTON AVENUE, SUITE 2312, NEW YORK, NY 10017;
(212) 682-5582. (OFFICES ARE ALSO IN ATLANTA, CHICAGO,
CORAL GABLES, DALLAS, HOUSTON, LOS ANGELES, TAMPA, AND TORONTO.)

Information packets from the Caymans include a long list of dive packages, many based at resorts and almost all including a certification course for beginners.

...........................................................

# Fly-Fishing

Fly-fishing is a sport rapidly gaining fans for the challenge of learning to select and tie the right flies as bait and for the enjoyment of the serene beauty of fishing in remote trout streams.

## ORVIS FLY-FISHING SCHOOLS

10 River Road, Manchester, VT 05254; (802) 362-3622. (I; DOES NOT INCLUDE LODGING)

| | |
|---|---|
| YEARS IN BUSINESS: | 30 |
| AGE RANGE: | 10–92 |
| MOST COMMON AGE: | 20s, 50–65 |
| PERCENT ALONE: | 30–50 |
| NUMBER OF PARTICPANTS: | VARIES |
| MALE/FEMALE RATIO: | 3/1 |

YEAR-ROUND. LOCATIONS ALSO IN EVERGREEN, COLORADO, CAPE COD, THE FLORIDA KEYS, AND MILLBROOK, NEW YORK. SOME CLASSES ARE FOR PARENT-CHILD AND FOR WOMEN ONLY. LODGINGS ARE SUGGESTED, BUT PARTICIPANTS DO THE BOOKING ON THEIR OWN.

This longtime sports outfitter offered the first organized fly-fishing school in the United States and still sets the standard as the sport grows in popularity. The instructors at the two and a half-day course are professionals who give a solid foundation that includes lessons on how to cast, how to make essential knots for tying on flies, how to select the right flies for the right fish, how to read a trout stream, how to wade a stream safely, how to manipulate the lines in tricky currents, and how to play, land, and release a fish. Classes are taught on casting ponds, in an indoor classroom, and on beautiful trout streams.

Orvis also runs classes in a variety of locations in conjunction with its stores in Philadelphia, Pennsylvania; Roanoke, Virginia; Jackson Hole, Wyoming; Short Hills, New Jersey; Chicago, Illinois; Dallas and Houston, Texas; and San Francisco, California. As more stores open, more offerings will be added.

# Kayaking, Canoeing, and White-Water Rafting

Among the many appeals of these water sports is the opportunity to be outdoors on a river in some of America's most beautiful wilderness country. You can learn some of the necessary skills on a regular rafting trip, but these programs focus on instruction.

## NANTAHALA OUTDOOR CENTER

U.S. 19 WEST, BOX 41, BRYSON CITY, NC 28713; (704) 488–2175. (I–M)

| | |
|---|---|
| YEARS IN BUSINESS: | 25 |
| AGE RANGE: | 10–70 |
| MOST COMMON AGE: | 20–55 |
| PERCENT ALONE: | MAJORITY |
| NUMBER OF PARTICIPANTS: | 3,200 YEARLY |
| MALE/FEMALE RATIO: | MORE MALES |
| MID-MARCH TO OCTOBER | |

Located on a mountainside along the Nantahala River near Great Smoky Mountains National Park, this employee-owned center boasts many paddling champions and is a terrific place to learn water skills. *Esquire* magazine called the center "the Oxford of white-water canoe schools." Courses in canoeing and kayaking run the gamut from beginner to expert, one day to one week. Participants in longer courses try several rivers. The student/teacher ratio is never more than 5:1.

Lodgings range from vacation cabins to motel rooms to a modern, comfortable dorm-style lodge. Reasonable packages include instruction, room, and meals. Three restaurants include the newly remodeled River's End on the river and Relia's Garden up the hill, where the tasty, fresh-picked vegetables and herbs come from their own garden. Courses are also offered in rock climbing and mountain biking.

COMMENTS  *Female, 30s: I've gone half a dozen times alone, and it was great every time. The program is terrific, the instructors world-class—and it's cheap! There are plenty of singles—in my last group, in fact, there was only one couple out of ten people. There are always more men, usually in their 30s and 40s. There is no social pressure;*

*you eat as a group, and it's easy to get to know people. Cabins are lovely, with wooded views from the balcony. The food is very good, all natural and with homemade bread. I definitely recommend it.*

*Male, 40s: I've been on lots of kayaking trips, and I think this is the best instruction in the country. I've gone several times, alone and with a friend. You feel at home as soon as you get there. Most people come alone; the majority are from the East Coast, but more seem to be coming from all over. The age range is from 20s to 50s, about 2:1 male. The lodges have beautiful views; the food is so good they put out their own cookbook. And the instruction is great—five students to one instructor, and very patient, understanding teachers.*

---

## DVORAK'S WHITEWATER PADDLING SCHOOL

17921 U.S. 285 NATHROP, CO 81236;
(800) 824-3795 OR (719) 539-6851. (I)

The first licensed outfitter in Colorado, this experienced company offers instructional seminars where students begin on flatwater to learn the basic strokes necessary to control a raft, canoe, or kayak, then move down the river to practice their skills in moving water. As skills sharpen, so does the challenge. All of their river trips offer this instruction option. More Dvorak information and participants' comments are on page 113.

# Downhill Skiing

Downhill skiing attracts everyone—singles, couples, families—because this is one sport everyone can enjoy. Each ski area has special ski runs reserved for beginners, intermediates, and experts. A lodge at each ski area provides a place for everyone to come together at mealtimes and at day's end. Learning the sport is easier than ever with the new "shaped" skis that make carving turns a snap. Once you learn to ski, you'll actually look forward to winter.

Of all the many types of sports schools available, ski schools are the easiest to find. Almost every slope has midweek five-day learn-to-ski packages at substantial savings over their weekend rates. The most com-

# Singles' Favorites

In its 1996 reader's survey Snow Country magazine reported the following resorts as singles' favorites: In Canada and the western U.S.: Aspen, Colorado; Whistler/Blackcomb, British Columbia; Vail, Colorado; Beaver Creek, Colorado and Snowmass, Colorado; in the eastern U.S.; Whiteface/Lake Placid, New York; Sugarloaf, Maine; Stowe, Vermont; Mad River Glen, Vermont; and Killington, Vermont.

As a rule, there are more single skiers at the big, better-known resorts, more families at smaller areas. For guaranteed company, there is the Club Med at Copper Mountain, Colorado. Besides having unlimited skiing privileges on the mountain, guests here are graded for ability, then divided into groups of ten for lessons in the morning and afternoon, a total of four hours of instruction. Beginner or advanced, that much instruction is bound to improve skiing skills. Videotaping also helps demonstrate what you are doing wrong.

One recent participant reports that great camaraderie grows within each group, so there is a lot of moral support and encouragement to help overcome your fears. During her week at the club, guests came from England, Australia, and France, as well as the United States. Adults' ages ranged mostly from 25 to 50, and singles were roughly one third of the total of 450. Another third were families with children in tow. The lodge is a five-minute walk from the lifts, so skiers can return for lunch. There is a heated room for donning and removing boots and skis, which veteran skiers will recognize as a nice little luxury. All meals are included in the price, along with ice skating, exercise classes, a sauna and Jacuzzi, and nightly entertainment and dancing.

This is still Club Med—you'll enjoy (or endure) silly songs with hand motions and homemade entertainment, and you'll probably share a room. But you won't lack for learning or companions. Phone (800) CLUB–MED for information.

Most major ski areas have discovered that females-only ski clinics are very popular with women who would rather do their slipping and sliding without a male audience. Squaw Valley, California, was the pioneer. Now you can find women's programs all over the United States.

fortable way to approach this alone is to be part of a package plan where the group will remain together for the five days; if you simply sign up for individual lessons, you may have different classmates and instructors each day and will have little opportunity to become friendly with those in your class. Ask in advance.

The entire ski-week group generally meets at a welcoming party on arrival, then is divided into smaller groups according to ability. There is the opportunity also for evening get-togethers for ski movies or entertainment. Ski lodges are friendly places anyway, albeit crowded, and it is easy to meet people naturally during the day, at lunch, or at the bar after skiing. Singles are also paired up with other singles in the lift line, though that could as likely mean a ten-year-old child as a possible dinner companion. It's all in the luck of the draw.

Lodgings can be informal meeting places as well, with guests gathering in front of the fire for drinks at the end of the day. If you are in your 20s or 30s, dorm-style accommodations are a good place to find other singles. Many ski area lodging offices will steer you to the right places if you ask. Avoid condominium accommodations if you are alone; they limit your sociability.

# Cross-Country Skiing

Cross-country enthusiasts are growing, lured by the time to enjoy the quiet and beauty of the snow-covered countryside and the lack of lift lines. Almost every major area today offers cross-country trails and instruction; a day or two of practice is all it takes to get started. Local chambers of commerce can point you to inns that have cross-country trails outside the door. But lessons won't necessarily guarantee company. If you are looking for a cross-country group, the best bet is to contact outdoor organizations such as the Appalachian Mountain Club or Colorado Mountain School (see below) or check the winter offerings of outdoor trip organizers, beginning on page 40.

# Outdoor Skills

The more comfortable and adept you are at outdoor activities, the more you will enjoy and appreciate the outdoors. This kind of enrichment is the goal of these multifaceted programs.

## APPALACHIAN MOUNTAIN CLUB

5 JOY STREET, BOSTON, MA 02108;
(617) 523-0636. (I)

At Pinkham Notch Visitor Center in Gorham, New Hampshire, in the heart of the White Mountains, this active club offers year-round weekend workshops for both beginners and advanced outdoor enthusiasts with 700,000 acres of national forest as a classroom.

| | |
|---|---|
| YEARS IN BUSINESS: | 121 |
| AGE RANGE: | UP TO 85 |
| MOST COMMON AGE: | 28–55 |
| PERCENT ALONE: | 35 |
| NUMBER OF PARTICIPANTS: | 70,000 MEMBERS; GROUPS ARE SMALL, VARY IN SIZE |
| MALE/FEMALE RATIO: | 50/50 |
| YEAR-ROUND | |

Among the many topics offered are camping, ski touring, snowshoeing, bushwhacking, map and compass reading, nature studies, mushroom hunting, ecology, music, storytelling, drawing, and a host of winter programs from dogsledding to cross-country skiing, from hawk-watching to nature photography. The lodge is sociable, with many individual hikers staying overnight. Meals are family style. Lectures and slides on outdoor topics are often presented on Saturday evening.

Other AMC lodges with varying seasonal programs include Valley View Lodge in Oliverea, in the Catskill Mountains of New York, and the Mohican Outdoor Center in Blairstown, New Jersey, along the Appalachian Trail in the Delaware Water Gap. Seasonal programs are offered also at Bascom Lodge in Adams, in the Berkshire Mountains of Massachusetts.

---

COMMENTS   *E.B.: I'm a longtime AMC member. The lodges are not luxurious, but they are comfortable, the people are outgoing outdoors lovers of all ages, and the club and its program are tops. East coast singles who love the outdoors should consider joining their local chapters for many congenial activities.*

---

## ADIRONDACK MOUNTAIN CLUB

P.O. Box 867, Lake Placid, NY 12946;

(518) 523-3441. (I)

Educational workshops, field trips to see wildflowers or birds, guided hikes, and winter cross-country skiing are among the programs of this venerable club for outdoorsmen and nature lovers. Classes in outdoor skills include wilderness fishing, paddling, map and compass reading, introductory rock climbing, and basic canoeing and kayaking.

| | |
|---|---|
| Years in business: | 120+ |
| Age range: | 20–80 |
| Most common age: | 30–50 |
| Percent alone: | 30 |
| Number of participants: | 46 |
| Male/female ratio: | 50/50 |
| Year-round | |

There are also workshops to learn about nature and creative arts from field sketching to creating a birch-bark picture frame. Lodging is in private rooms or coed bunkhouses; family-style, home-cooked meals are served in the pine-paneled dining room. Also see under Nature, page 119.

COMMENTS *Male, 40s: There's lots of diversity because accommodations vary from a dorm for eighteen to family rooms for four to six to private rooms. People come from all over; about half are single, and men outnumber women. There are classes in kayaking and winter sports. A family atmosphere makes it easy to strike up conversations, and everyone is friendly. The staff is wonderful. This attracts outgoing, well-educated people and is great for singles who are into the outdoors.*

# Mountain Climbing

Are you up for a challenge? Want to prove you can conquer a mountain? Mountain climbing school can teach you the techniques and the right equipment to get to the top!

## COLORADO MOUNTAIN SCHOOL

Box 2062, Estes Park, CO 80517;

(970) 586-5758.

(I—DOES NOT INCLUDE LODGING)

Located in the shadow of Rocky Mountain National Park, this group offers five- and seven-day Beginning Rock Camps, as well as three-day weekends teaching the proper techniques for backpacking, mountaineering, and rock

| | |
|---|---|
| YEARS IN BUSINESS: | 20+ |
| AGE RANGE: | 8–60 |
| MOST COMMON AGE: | LATE 20S–30S |
| PERCENT ALONE: | 40 |
| NUMBER OF PARTICIPANTS: | 3,000 ANNUALLY |
| MALE/FEMALE RATIO: | 4/1 |

climbing. Longer stays have the advantage of time to hone your skills. Once you've learned the basics, there are intermediate and advanced camps as well as many guided climbs and mountain hikes both in the Rockies and abroad. Lodging in Colorado is your choice of nearby motels or the dorm-style, inexpensive Climbers Lodge, where there is plenty of company from other climbers and hikers. Meals are not included. In winter the emphasis shifts to skiing, mountaineering, and ice climbing, and once again there are programs for beginner to advanced.

The owners say: "Many people have met and become good friends through these courses and outings. In mountain travel, there is ample opportunity for a tremendous amount of honest, open discussion, and the mountain atmosphere encourages this. Our participants always exchange addresses, etcetera, at the end of trips and stay in contact with each other afterward."

COMMENTS   *Female, 40s: I've been once, am going again. It was a lot of fun, there was a lot of instruction, and it was very good. All the participants were from Colorado, and most came alone. I signed up for a more difficult workshop, so there were few women. Ages were 25 to 50.*

## Climbing enthusiasts might also consider these other mountaineering schools:

### YOSEMITE MOUNTAINEERING SCHOOL
YOSEMITE NATIONAL PARK, CA 95389; (209) 372–1335.

### JACKSON HOLE MOUNTAIN GUIDES AND CLIMBING SCHOOL
BOX 7477, JACKSON, WY 83001; (307) 733–4979.

**AMERICAN ALPINE INSTITUTE, Ltd.**
1515 12th Street, Bellingham, WA 98225; (206) 671–1505.

**INTERNATIONAL MOUNTAIN
CLIMBING SCHOOL, INC.**
Box 1227, North Conway, NH 03860; (603) 356–5287.

.........................................................

# Wilderness Skills

Programs teaching wilderness skills aim to do more than give you techniques for outdoor activities like backpacking, canoeing, or climbing. They present mentally and physically challenging situations meant to stretch your ability to the limit. Success means enhanced self-confidence that will carry over into the rest of your life.

## OUTWARD BOUND
Route 9D, R2 Box 280, Garrison, NY 10524;
(914) 424–4000 or (800) 243–8520
(I–E, depending on location, includes food and camping)
Year-round; special classes offered for women and for parent and child

Outward Bound courses are in a class by themselves. Those who participate, many of them beginners, come to be stretched mentally and emotionally as well as physically—with the wilderness as a classroom. If you want to learn about backpacking, canoeing, mountaineering, rock climbing, mountain biking, white-water rafting, ski mountaineering, dogsledding, snowshoeing, or almost any other outdoor adventure, their five schools in Colorado, North Carolina, Maine, Oregon, and Minnesota and in several urban centers are ready to teach you these skills—and much more. Several courses combine skills such as backpacking, canoeing, and mountain climbing.

Most courses include solo time for reflection. Renewal courses are outdoor experiences specially intended for adults wanting to examine more closely their personal or career goals and renew their energies in an outdoor setting.

The courses usually have five parts. Phase one is a training and physical conditional period, giving instruction in technical skills, safety, first aid, shelter construction, wilderness cooking, environmental awareness and conservation, map and compass reading, etcetera. Next, in phase two, these skills are applied. Groups of eight to twelve are formed and as participants become more self-reliant, instructors turn the leadership role over to them. The third phase, the solo, is a period of solitude—one to three days in the wilderness alone. Afterward, the group comes together to execute an expedition with a minimum of supervision. Then comes a final event, a last fling with your body that involves running, paddling, cycling, snowshoeing, or skiing—more miles than you may have thought possible. Finally, there is a period of reflection on your experiences, feelings, and personal discoveries during the course.

| | |
|---|---|
| YEARS IN BUSINESS: | 25 |
| AGE RANGE: | 30 AND UP |
| MOST COMMON AGE: | 55 |
| PERCENT ALONE: | 30 |
| NUMBER OF PARTICIPANTS: | 24–30 |
| MALE/FEMALE RATIO: | 30/70 |
| SUITABLE FOR BEGINNERS, WILL TRY TO ARRANGE SHARES. | |

Over 400,000 alumni, from troubled youths to corporate executives to adults in a period of life transition, testify that meeting the challenges of Outward Bound has helped them to go beyond what they believed they could do and to develop new self-confidence as a result.

## NATIONAL OUTDOOR LEADERSHIP SCHOOLS

288 MAIN STREET, LANDER, WY 82520; (307) 332-6973. (I–E, DEPENDING ON COURSE)

| | |
|---|---|
| YEARS IN BUSINESS: | 32 |
| AGE RANGE: | 14–75 |
| MOST COMMON AGE: | EACH COURSE HAS A SUGGESTED AGE RANGE, FROM 17–22 TO OVER 50 |
| PERCENT SINGLE: | HIGH |
| MALE/FEMALE RATIO: | VARIES WITH THE COURSE |
| NUMBER OF PARTICIPANTS: | 8 TO 17 PER GROUP |

Formed by one of the founders of Outward Bound to train wilderness leaders and educators, NOLS still attracts many who are planning a career in wilderness education, but others attend to learn outdoors skills from experts or to learn how to deal with physical and mental challenges. Natural history, horsepacking, white-water rafting, mountaineering, rock climbing, sea kayaking, sailing, and winter skiing are among the wide range of pursuits offered.

Many of these courses run for three weeks or more. A few are for women only.

Special courses are designed for people who have always wanted to acquire outdoor skills but do not have time for a longer course. Eachcourse specifies the recommended ages; some are designated for a minimum of age 50.

NOLS has certified more than 800 outdoor instructors; typically about 300 of them work for the school each year. Their ages range from 19 to 61.

COMMENTS *Female, 20s: I learned that almost all the challenges were fun and that living without the so-called conveniences of everyday life is often more pleasant than living with them.*
*Male, 40s: I was blown away by the beauty; I think heaven must look like the Wind Rivers. I will never forget it. These were the best instructors in the world. They engendered confidence in us all. They were confident, and it rubbed off.*

# Stretch Your Mind

**E**VER WISHED YOU TOOK BETTER VACATION PICTURES . . . OR could paint a picture? Would you like a better understanding of the stock market . . . or a wine list . . . or what an archaeologist actually does on a dig? What about a yen to try your hand at quilting or carving or playing the fiddle?

Whatever your interest—or your fantasy—you can indulge it on a learning vacation that stretches your mind and talents in scenic surroundings.

In a situation where everyone is learning together, there is automatically a common interest, a natural bond, and a lot of mutual support. Many programs are set up so that the group eats together, but even when meals are optional, students who have shared classes naturally tend to get together for dinner.

The choices are enormous, as is the range of settings. You can learn to paint in Italy, to cook in Provence, or to twang a banjo in the West Virginia hills. Here are some of the many wonderful options.

## Learning Vacations

**L**earning vacations come in many forms, from formal campus settings to research in the field. Besides the programs listed here, most universities also have a week of "Alumnae College," and many also welcome non-alums to share the learning.

### CORNELL ADULT UNIVERSITY
626 THURSTON AVENUE, ITHACA, NY 14850–2490;
(607) 227–6260. (I)

"A getaway for nature enthusiasts, armchair philosophers, art and music lovers, romantics and pragmatists of all persuasions," says the brochure, and indeed this largest of all summer university programs offers something for almost every interest. Classes are taught by

| | |
|---|---|
| YEARS IN BUSINESS: | 20+ |
| AGE RANGE: | 30–70 |
| MOST COMMON AGE: | 30S AND 40S |
| PERCENT ALONE: | 35 |
| NUMBER OF PARTICIPANTS: | 150 PER WEEK |
| MALE/FEMALE RATIO: | VARIES |
| JULY TO EARLY AUGUST; FIVE 1-WEEK SESSIONS IN ITHACA; LEARNING SESSIONS ALSO YEAR-ROUND IN VARIOUS OFF-CAMPUS LOCATIONS | |

university faculty; subject matter runs the gamut. Some recent offerings: "The Genie Unleashed: DNA in the Modern World," "What Makes Great Paintings Great? Color, Form and Space in Art," "The Human Mind: Marvels and Mysteries," "Seeing With a Camera; A Photography Workshop," and "Outdoor Skills and Thrills."

This is a "back-to-school" week of dorm living and cafeteria dining with all the many athletic and cultural facilities on campus open to participants. And while there is a large program for young people, which attracts many families, single adults will find plenty of company. The evaluation sheets at the end of each session are enthusiastic: More than 90 percent of the participants say they plan to return.

Cornell also sponsors interesting year-round programs in the United States and abroad. Some examples recently were "Tropical Botany and Coral Reefs" in Tortola, British Virgin Islands; "The Civil War Along the Mississippi River," and "Mountain and Marine Habitats of Costa Rica."

---

COMMENTS  *E.B.: The Cornell campus is magnificent, in the heart of the Finger Lakes, a region of spectacular natural gorges. I chose "Gorgeous Gorges of the Finger Lakes," a course that offered a daily walk of about 3 miles through the gorges, many of them remote locations tourists would ordinarily miss. It didn't feel like class—the instructor was like a knowledgeable friend who could point out a million interesting things you would never have noticed on your own, from bird calls to the marks of the last glacier. There were no assignments, but readings were available if we wanted to learn more.*

*Our group of a dozen ranged in age from 30 to 80, equally divided between men and women. At least half of the group was on its own during class; even couples at the program tend to choose different subjects. Classmates and dorm mates provide a natural base for making friends. The cafeteria food was so-so, but the setting was another congenial place for meeting people. All you have to do is say, "May I join you?" and set down your tray.*

*The evening schedule included a wine tasting at a nearby vineyard, a cookout, and a campus concert. If these didn't appeal, there were plenty of activities around campus as a substitute. The week ended with a banquet followed by a "graduation" party. Going to college for a week proved to be a congenial and relaxing vacation. The cost was nominal, and, as a bonus, I learned a lot.*

*Male, age 39: The combination of camaraderie and intellectual stimulation brought me back twenty years to my days as a student.*

*Female, 40s: I had a splendid time. Although I came by myself, the program is so well organized, the people so friendly, and your time so full, I never felt at loose ends for a moment.*

---

## VACATION COLLEGE

PROGRAM IN THE HUMANITIES AND HUMAN VALUES, COLLEGE OF ARTS AND SCIENCES, CB#3425, 3 BOLIN HEIGHTS,
UNIVERSITY OF NORTH CAROLINA, CHAPEL HILL, NC 27599; (919) 962-1544.

(I—DOES NOT INCLUDE LODGING OR MOST MEALS)

| | |
|---|---|
| YEARS IN BUSINESS: | 18 |
| AGE RANGE: | 15 TO 92 |
| MOST COMMON AGE: | 60s |
| PERCENT ALONE: | 50 |
| NUMBER OF PARTICIPANTS: | 60–120 PER WEEK |
| MALE/FEMALE RATIO: | VARIES WITH TOPIC |
| FROM LATE JUNE TO EARLY AUGUST | |

Each summer this lovely campus in Chapel Hill offers a changing series of three- and four-day seminars led by university faculty. A new theme each week means a choice of topics that have recently included "Politics and Health in America," "The Age of Reason," "Jane Austen," "East Asia" and "The Swing Era: Jazz of the Big Bands."

In addition to alumni, these programs attract many adults looking for a stimulating change of pace, exploring important cultural and social topics. Lodging can be in residence halls or in local motels. An opening dinner gives a chance to get acquainted; after that, classmates often get together to try the many good restaurants in Chapel Hill. Some seminars include a film or two (with popcorn) in the evening.

## SUMMER CLASSICS IN SANTA FE

ST. JOHN'S COLLEGE,
1160 CAMINO CRUZ BLANCA, SANTA FE, NM 87501;
(505) 984–610. (M)

| | |
|---|---|
| YEARS IN BUSINESS: | 7 |
| AGE RANGE: | 20 TO 80 |
| MOST COMMON AGE: | 40S |
| PERCENT ALONE: | 75 |
| NUMBER OF PARTICIPANTS: | MAXIMUM OF 20 PER SEMINAR |
| MALE/FEMALE RATIO: | 40/60 |
| SUMMER; NO SINGLE SUPPLEMENT | |

Remember those "great books" you were always going to read someday—Shakespeare, Dostoyevsky, or Plato? Each summer, participants in these week-long seminars read and discuss world classics in literature and philosophy. The changing reading list may include such works as the *Bhagavad Gita,* Greek dramas, Plato's *Republic,* or Rousseau's *On the Origin of Inequality.* They also discuss the text of great operas, followed by attending an actual performance by the highly regarded Santa Fe Opera. Participants choose one seminar of the three offered each week and can stay for one or more weeks. Afternoons are left free so that students can explore the historic buildings, archaeological sites, and the many art galleries of Santa Fe. Accommodations are in recently built campus dormitories. Rooms are suite-style, with five individual bedrooms sharing a common living room and a large bathroom, which is partitioned for privacy. The beautiful setting of the college, the lures of Santa Fe, and the unique content combine to give this one of the highest return rates among learning programs.

COMMENTS  *Male, 40s: I can't put into words how this program nurtures me and calls all of my intellect into play. It's magic. There are no lectures—tutors begin with a question about the text, and stimulating discussion follows with fascinating people from every walk of life. We develop together and learn from each other. The attractions of Santa Fe greatly add to the experience. I've hiked at Bandolier National Monument and gone to the Chamber Museum Festival and the Santa Fe Opera. It is a total change from my work and home life and has been so rewarding that I've returned three times and this year took a sabbatical to enroll in the college's graduate program.*
*Female, 50s: This is a wonderful place because it combines so many*

*things. The classes provoke exciting discussion that one normally does not get at home, important interesting topics, but never stuffy. The people are very bright, the discussion is lively, and you combine one week of reading, another of opera. There's so much available in Santa Fe, and the location of the college in the hills is simply beautiful. It is a marvelous experience.*

---

## CHAUTAUQUA INSTITUTION

CHAUTAUQUA, NY 14722;

(716) 357–6200. (I–M)

This is where the idea of learning vacations began. Chautauqua was founded as a training camp for Sunday school teachers and evolved into a nine-week summer feast of arts and education, served up in a period Victorian village. The religious element, while still present, is optional.

| | |
|---|---|
| YEARS IN BUSINESS: | 120+ |
| AGE RANGE: | 2–102 |
| MOST COMMON AGE: | 50s |
| PERCENT ALONE: | 40–50 |
| NUMBER OF PARTICIPANTS: | 140,000 PER SEASON |
| MALE/FEMALE RATIO: | 40/60 |
| SUMMER | |

The lineup of activities is staggering. Twice-a-day talks by prominent lecturers are on a new theme each week, from arts and humanities to the Americas to sports in American life. The summer school topics include the arts, languages, human relations, public speaking, nutrition, parenting, self-improvement, foreign cultures, and much, much more. Activities like line dancing, t'ai chi, and aerobics keep the program up to date. Evening entertainment may feature the resident symphony and theater companies, opera, ballet, Shakespeare performances, or guest stars ranging from such jazz greats as Pete Fountain or the Preservation Hall Jazz Band to the Russian Male Chamber Choir. And for a sporting change of pace by day, golf, tennis, and sailing are available.

Chautauqua lodging includes hotels, inns, guest houses, condominiums, or private homes. The clientele has tended to be on the older side but is changing somewhat as an active children's program has begun to attract young families. For single participants, Joan Fox, director of public information, says, "Chautauqua is a safe haven where cars and cares are outside, a secure gated community where a single vacationer falls in easily with others attending the same lectures, concerts, or classes."

COMMENTS *Female, 40s: I've been alone and with friends; I keep going back for the intellectual stimulation. The lecturers are great, and the hotels and food are very good. It's a very special place and is great for singles . . . people are friendly, and it's easy to meet them. Female, 50s: Chautauqua has rounded my personality and sharpened my intellect. How I love it!*
*Female, 60s: The program is wonderful. You buy a gate ticket and can participate in any and all activities. You can stay busy all day long. The group is heavily female and there are many widows, but many families also come and the age range is wide—from children to those in their 70s. There is a good number of singles, and it is very suitable for them. You can stay in a hotel and have meals family style. People come from all over, but most from the Northeast. The place started as a religious institution and is still highly religious for some, but it doesn't have to be.*

---

## SMITHSONIAN SEMINARS

c/o Smithsonian National Associates, 1100 Jefferson Drive SW, Washington, D.C. 20560; (202) 357-4700. (E)

| | |
|---|---|
| YEARS IN BUSINESS: | MORE THAN 20 |
| PERCENT ALONE: | 60 |
| MOST COMMON AGE: | 45–50 |
| MALE/FEMALE RATIO: | VARIES WITH TOPICS; USUALLY HEAVILY FEMALE BUT MORE MALES FOR SUBJECTS SUCH AS AVIATION. |
| NUMBER OF PARTICIPANTS: | 20–40 |
| YEAR-ROUND; WILL TRY TO ARRANGE SHARES UNLESS SINGLE IS REQUESTED | |

Three- to five-day programs for museum associate members (membership is $22) in Washington and at many locations around the country. The variety of topics should please all tastes, from current major art shows to the Civil War, Barrier Island ecology to designing a garden. Programs last most of the day. Lodging is in area hotels; seminars may include some meals and a welcome reception.

## THE CLEARING

P.O. Box 65, Ellison Bay, WI 54210; (414) 854-4088. (I)

Inspired by Danish folk schools for adults that stress teaching, learning, and living together in scenic surroundings, this program calls itself "a

unique school of discovery in the arts, nature, and humanities." In a setting meant to
provide a clearing of the mind, it presents
dozens of courses, from watercolors, weaving, and design to ecology, astronomy, writing, and philosophy. Classes are taught
outdoors and in the cathedral-like school-
house designed by Frank Lloyd Wright disci-

| | |
|---|---|
| YEARS IN BUSINESS: | 62 |
| AGE RANGE: | 18–85 |
| MOST COMMON AGE: | 55–65 |
| PERCENT ALONE: | 75 |
| NUMBER OF PARTICIPANTS: | 28 |
| MALE/FEMALE RATIO: | 1/3 |
| SPRING THROUGH FALL; WILL TRY TO ARRANGE SHARES | |

ple Jens Jensen, located in a wooded setting overlooking the water in
Wisconsin's scenic Door County. Participants live in dorms or in charming log-and-stone cabins and enjoy family-style meals at hand-carved
wood-plank tables. Inexpensive rates, no bar, hassle-free atmosphere,
healthful food, time to meet interesting people, plus quiet, contemplative
time in unspoiled natural surroundings are part of the experience.

COMMENTS *Female, 60s: I have been at least twenty times. The
Clearing is quiet, serene, a true retreat with time to think and exchange ideas with new people. It's inspiring. Most people are middle-
aged and from the Midwest. Accommodations are simple but
adequate; meals are not gourmet but good and very social, with lots of
lively conversation. The scenery is just beautiful, and you really get to
know everyone.*

*Male, 60s: I've been with and without my wife. It is easy to be there
alone. The group is mostly professionals, many single people, and
many women. There is a rule that you can't sit down at the same
place twice at meals, so you're almost forced to meet everyone. It is
quiet and informal, but with a purpose. I recommend it to anyone,
single or not.*

## STAR ISLAND CONFERENCE CENTER

P.O. BOX 178, PORTSMOUTH, NH, 03802
SUMMERS; 110 ARLINGTON STREET, BOSTON, MA 02116;
(617) 426–7988. (I)

The Star Island Corporation, comprised of Unitarian Universalist and
Unitarian Universalist Church constituencies, owns and operates this

seasonal religious and educational conference center. Open to all denominations, the center offers discussion/instruction in a variety of weekly themes, such as natural history, art, and international affairs. Outdoor recreation includes swimming, boating, tennis, volleyball, and games. A marine laboratory provides near-natural habitats for native biota, and naturalists

| | |
|---|---|
| YEARS IN BUSINESS: | 82 |
| AGE RANGE: | WIDE |
| MOST COMMON AGE: | VARIES WITH WEEK'S PROGRAM |
| PERCENT ALONE: | 50 |
| MALE/FEMALE RATIO: | MORE FEMALES |
| NUMBER OF PARTICIPANTS: | 180–260 |
| WILL TRY TO ARRANGE SHARES | |
| SEPTEMBER TO JUNE | |

lead narrated ecology walks. Evening candlelight services are held in the historic chapel. Living quarters are in a century-old "grand hotel" and a few cottages. Family-style meals and the small size of the island are conducive to meeting other people. A list of the coming year's programs is available by sending a stamped, self-addressed envelope to the Boston office.

---

COMMENTS *Female, 50s: This is a place to get in touch with your spiritual side. There are more single people than married, more women than men. It is very comfortable to be alone. The programs are very well organized, and I would recommend this to anyone. When you get there, you're not a stranger.*

*Male, 40s: I've gone for seven years, sometimes alone, sometimes with a friend. It's an easy group to get to know—meals are family style, everyone wears a name tag, about a quarter are single, but many married people come without their spouses. All activities are optional. Over half choose to go to morning chapel, even more to evening chapel. Workshops are in photography, painting, dance, music, drama, and writing—no experience necessary. Afternoons are free for trips to nearby islands. At night there are guest artists and folk dancing.*

---

### Similar Unitarian-sponsored retreats are:

## MOUNTAIN HIGHLANDS CAMP AND CONFERENCE CENTER

841 HIGHWAY 1067, HIGHLANDS, NC 28741; (704) 526–5838.

## ROWE CAMP AND CONFERENCE CENTER

KINGS HIGHWAY ROAD, ROWE, MA 01367; (413) 339–4954.

# Study Vacations Abroad

A number of short-term study and educational tour programs are available abroad, sponsored by U.S. universities in association with colleges in other countries. These offer memorable stays in the ivied surroundings of schools such as Oxford and Cambridge, as well as the chance to meet interesting people. Some use dorm facilities on campus; others utilize hotels. The offerings vary from year to year, so it is best to call for current information.

## HUMANITIES INSTITUTE

533A Putnam Avenue, Cambridge, MA 02139;
(617) 497-8665 or (800) 754-9991,
No single supplement on most programs; will try to
arrange shares; small single supplement in Florence.
(I plus air)

| | |
|---|---|
| Years in business: | 22 |
| Age range: | 25–70 |
| Most common age: | 40–50 |
| Percent alone: | 80 |
| Number of participants: | 25 |
| Male/female ratio: | 1/3 |

E ducation and culture are the focus of this varied program for those who want to learn more about the countries they visit. Some classes are based at such institutions as Cambridge and Dublin's Trinity College, where mornings are devoted to lectures and discussion and afternoons are free for exploring the area. These two- to three-week in-depth seminars are equivalent to a short university course and may actually be taken for academic credit. Other noncredit trips are less rigorous, but still education-oriented, concentrating on such topics as the gardens of England or the art and architecture of Italy. Florentine Renaissance takes in art, architecture, and literature. Each program offers some sight-seeing and evening lectures. About 80 percent of the participants are teachers.

COMMENTS *Female, 50s: I went alone and was very comfortable. There was a diverse group, ages 30 to 65, heavily female. Mornings were spent in class; in the afternoons there were tours of museums or lectures. There was always something to do. The accommodations were not great, but the trip was inexpensive.*

*Female, 70s: I've been on several trips alone. It is wonderful, and I always make friends. There is a nice mix of people from all over the U.S., ages 35 to 70, most in their 40s. Many are married but travel-ing alone. Meals are as a group and there is lots of discussion, making it easy to get to know people. There is always something to do during the week; weekends are free to do whatever you want.*

---

## More options:

### TRAVEL WITH SCHOLARS, UNIVERSITY OF CALIFORNIA, BERKELEY EXTENSION

MARKETING DEPARTMENT,
1995 UNIVERSITY AVENUE, BERKELEY, CA 94720;
(415) 252-5229. (EE)

The University of California at Berkeley offers two- and three-week travel-study programs in Paris, the south of France, Venice, Sicily, Turkey, and Oxford University in England. A special program in London with distinguished drama critics gives an in-depth look at the London theater scene.

### CAMBRIDGE UNIVERSITY INTERNATIONAL SUMMER SCHOOL

C/O NEW YORK UNIVERSITY SCHOOL OF CONTINUING EDUCATION,
INTERNATIONAL PROGRAMS,
331 SHIMKIN HALL, 50 WEST FOURTH STREET, NEW YORK, NY 10012;
(212) 998-7133. (EE—INCLUDES AIRFARE)

The ivied halls of Cambridge, England, host this two-week annual summer program with a choice of more than twenty courses, from English architecture and art to the history of medicine or twentieth-cen-tury British political history. Students select two morning courses; after-noons are free for exploring. The program also includes field trips, evening events, and a visit to London.

## INTERHOSTEL

UNIVERSITY OF NEW HAMPSHIRE DIVISION OF CONTINUING EDUCATION,
6 GARRISON AVENUE, DURHAM, NH 03824;
(603) 862-1147 OR (800) 773-9753. (E-EE)

Study tours for adults over age 50 are held in fifteen countries, in conjunction with local sponsoring host universities and educational institutions abroad.

## UNIVERSITY VACATIONS

10461 NW 26TH STREET, MIAMI, FL 33172;
(800) 792-0100. (E-EE)

This organization sponsors a series of one- and two-week cultural vacations at Oxford and Cambridge universities, with lodging in dorm rooms on campus.

## UNIVERSITY OF LONDON

BIRKBECK COLLEGE, CENTER FOR EXTRA MURAL STUDIES,
26 RUSSELL SQUARE, LONDON, ENGLAND;
01-71-631-6682; FAX, 01-71-631-6688. (I)

This reasonably priced program offers one-week theater study groups for adults, who read three current plays, attend theater productions, and then discuss them. Directors and actors from plays in the series participate in the seminars. Participants live in the college dorms; they are an interesting mix of ages and cultures from many parts of the world. The school also offers many other courses in its summer catalog.

*More information on study opportunities for adults abroad can be obtained from:*

### Institute of International Education

809 UNITED NATIONS PLAZA, NEW YORK, NY 10017
(212) 984-5413; AND FROM

### Transitions Abroad, The Complete Guide to Work, Study & Travel Overseas

TRANSITIONS ABROAD PUBLISHING, INC., P.O. BOX 1300, AMHERST, MA 01004;
(800) 293-0373.

.......................................................................

# Field Research
# Volunteer
# Programs

A ssisting scientists and archaeologists in their work is a wonderful way to widen your horizons and get a new perspective on an area. As a side benefit, many of these trips are tax deductible. The cost is considered a donation to underwrite the research.

## EARTHWATCH

680 MOUNT AUBURN STREET, BOX 403N,
WATERTOWN, MA 02272;
(617) 926–8200. (I-EE)

| | |
|---|---|
| YEARS IN BUSINESS: | 26 |
| AGE RANGE: | 16–85 |
| MOST COMMON AGE: | 35–55 |
| PERCENT ALONE: | 50 |
| NUMBER OF PARTICIPANTS: | 4,000 PER YEAR, DIVIDED INTO 600+ INDIVIDUAL PROJECTS |
| MALE/FEMALE RATIO: | 40/60 |

M ore than 40,000 volunteers, known as the EarthCorps, have gone out on nearly 2,000 Earthwatch vacation-learning experiences in 118 countries and thirty-six states, helping scientists and researchers in field projects ranging from anthropology to zoology. Most participants have college degrees and are a well-traveled lot: professionals, scientists, managers, students, retirees, and teachers.

Would-be volunteers read about the projects by becoming members of Earthwatch and receiving the bimonthly *Earthwatch* magazine. They can send for a more detailed briefing of the projects that interest them. Among the hundreds of possibilities are archaeological excavations; surveys of plants, birds, or animals; underwater and environmental impact studies; and research in agriculture, public health, and art history. Some recent projects: tracking snow leopards in the Himalayas, uncovering aboriginal prehistory in Australia, monitoring wild dolphins in Florida, excavating sites of prehistoric civilizations in Mallorca, capturing and studying hawks in Michigan, collecting stories and songs of Dominica, documenting maternal healthcare in Zimbabwe, and helping to census and monitor elephants in Botswana. Costs vary widely, depending on distance and living conditions.

COMMENTS *Female, 50s: For two weeks we lived in splendid isolation studying honey eaters on Australia's Kangaroo Island. I shared a bunkroom with four other women. Just outside my door were kangaroos, koalas, emus, and other creatures people seldom encounter outside a zoo. We did simple but necessary jobs such as hand-pollinating blooms and marking and bagging clusters of flowers for breeding studies. We also observed honey eaters and bees as they collected nectar and pollinated—or failed to pollinate—the plants. We got two days off for sight-seeing. In the evenings, we played games, sang folk songs, talked a lot. The group, ages 25 to 60, had a wide range of occupations. We were a motley and congenial crew.*

*Male, 40s: I've gone on six trips, each time alone. It was hard the first time, then became easy. There was about an equal mix of men and women, single and married, from varied backgrounds. How well the program runs depends on the "Principal Investigator," the person in charge. One of my trips was not so well run. I would recommend this type of vacation to other singles, but I would also say that you have to really want to do it. This is not a leisure vacation. There is work involved.*

## UNIVERSITY RESEARCH EXPEDITIONS PROGRAM (UREP)

UNIVERSITY OF CALIFORNIA,
BERKELEY, 94720;
(510) 642-6586. (I-EE)

| | |
|---|---|
| YEARS IN BUSINESS: | 21 |
| AGE RANGE: | 16–75 |
| MOST COMMON AGE: | 30–50 |
| PERCENT ALONE: | HIGH |
| NUMBER OF PARTICIPANTS: | 5–10 PER PROJECT |
| MALE/FEMALE RATIO: | VARIES |

Like Earthwatch, UREP programs provide the opportunity to be part of a team doing actual research in the field (this time assisting University of California scholars), while gaining new knowledge, new friends, and insights into another culture. Tax-deductible contributions pay project costs and participants' expenses.

Animal-related projects have included studying the birds of the Mayan forest and the monkeys of Costa Rica. The prehistoric villages of Peru, the castles of County Clare, Ireland, the medieval churches of the Aran Islands, rock art in Baja California and Mexico, and the geology of the Andes are among other recent topics. The only requirements for participation are curiosity about the world and a willingness to invest in learning. For interested participants, UREP holds slide presentations with the chance to talk with past participants in their projects throughout California and in Seattle and New York City; prospective volunteers should phone for upcoming dates.

COMMENTS  *Female, 50s: It was a positive and interesting experience that enabled me to see places and have experiences that I probably would not have had traveling with a tour group or alone. It was eye-opening, energy-expending, socially cooperating, native-appreciating, and thoroughly enjoyable—the most highly concentrated two weeks of learning and cultural immersion that I've experienced in many years of travel. The experience exceeded my expectations. It was one of new understanding of another people and of personal growth.*

*Male, 40s: I've been on four trips with them, to Easter Island, to the High Sierras twice, and to the Sierra Nevadas—all really great programs because you see things that a tourist would never see. Most people do come alone—couples are rare. The leaders help to get the group to bond together. You have to work together and get along because the trips tend to be in isolated places without bathrooms or other comforts. You get to know one another really well. Everyone has a sincere interest in the project and that brings them together right off the bat. I've met a lot of interesting people, everyone from a physicist to a cop to grad students. It's a great program if you're into learning and being outside in interesting places. But it is work, not for the weak!*

# Archaeology

Ever fantasized about being an archaeologist and going on a dig? Here's your chance!

## CROW CANYON ARCHAEOLOGICAL CENTER

23390 County Road K, Cortex, CO 81321; (800) 422–8975. (I)

| | |
|---|---|
| YEARS IN BUSINESS: | 13 |
| AGE RANGE: | 18–75 |
| MOST COMMON AGE: | 35–55 |
| PERCENT ALONE: | 85 |
| NUMBER OF PARTICIPANTS: | 420 PER YEAR |
| MALE/FEMALE: | 30/70 |

Here in the rugged terrain of the "four corners" where Arizona, New Mexico, Utah, and Colorado meet, adults join archaeologists searching for remains of the ancestral Pueblo culture in the Mesa Verde region of southwestern Colorado. They learn the process of excavation, artifact identification, and interpretation by working on a dig, at the same time gaining firsthand understanding of the environment in which these people thrived. Participants live in round log cabins that resemble Navajo hogans and share hot meals at the lodge and sandwiches in the field. Most stay for one week.

COMMENTS *Female, 40s: I went alone for the first time, have gone back five times, and know a lot of people now. This is the best program I've ever found. The group is warm, with amazing backgrounds and levels of intelligence. The ages range from 18 to 80, about evenly divided between male and female, and last time there were only three couples out of twenty-four people. You have classes in the morning, go to the dig site in the afternoon and early evening, and have lectures after dinner. The food was family style and excellent. This program has caused several people to decide to go back to school for a master's degree.*

*Male, 30s: I've been going alone for five years. This is not Club Med, not a summer camp or play time—you are actually contributing to the archaeological work in progress. Accommodations and food are great. It's wonderful for anyone who is into archaeology or southwestern art.*

## ANDOVER FOUNDATION FOR ARCHAEOLOGICAL RESEARCH (AFAR)

Box 83, Andover, MA 01810;
(508) 470–0840. (I–E)

| | |
|---|---|
| Years in business: | 13 |
| Age range: | 15–90 |
| Most common age: | 55–75 |
| Percent alone: | 50 |
| Number of participants: | 10–20 |
| Male/female ratio: | 50/50 |

The archaeological expeditions sponsored by this nonprofit scientific organization have studied the origins of agriculture in New Mexico, dived for the fabled "Little Spanish Armada" in Belize, and uncovered an ancient Iroquois village near the St. Lawrence River in upstate New York. Other recent projects have been in Belize, the Marquesas, and China. There is, as they put it, "a dig for all seasons." Volunteer "Friends of the Foundation" get basic training in archaeological techniques and typically stay two or four weeks. All work is done on weekdays, leaving Saturday and Sunday free to explore the area.

COMMENTS  *Male, 50s: I've been on four trips alone. It is a diversified group, mostly from the Northeast but representing all the U.S., with an equal number of men and women, mostly traveling alone. None of the other men were married. The group is very congenial, always a group situation so you never feel alone; food ranges from fair to superb, depending on the trip.*

*Female, 60s: The group is mostly singles or married people traveling alone. The program is well organized. I've stayed in tents, huts, and a rented house, depending on the trip. There is lots of physical labor, so everyone is pretty tired at night. The group gets along well, and I recommend it for single travelers—I have been on eight of their trips.*

## CENTER FOR AMERICAN ARCHAEOLOGY

Dept. B, Kampsville Archaeological Center,
Kampsville, IL 62053;
(618) 653–4316. (I)

| | |
|---|---|
| Years in business: | 40+ |
| Age range: | Teen to 65+ |
| Most common age: | 20–30 |
| Percent alone: | 80 |
| Number of participants: | 30 weekly |
| Male/female ratio: | 50/50 |

This educational institution offers one-week adult field schools, providing on-site training in archaeological techniques through helping to excavate 1,000-year-old Native American sites in the lower Illinois River valley. Meals are served cafeteria style in an open-air pavilion, an easy place to make friends. Evenings are occupied with lectures, night hikes, and informal outings in local restaurants. Some field school programs enroll many young students; be sure to choose the adult weeks. Adult programs in the summer attract many teachers.

COMMENTS *Female, 30s: This is mostly doing, not classes. It's an intense, very involving program, working all day with planned activities at night. Accommodations are comfortable though not luxurious; the food was substantial and good.*

## PASSPORT IN TIME CLEARINGHOUSE
P.O. Box 31315, Tucson, AZ 85751;
(520) 298–7044 or (800) 281–9176.
No set fees; volunteers pay only their own expenses.

No experience is necessary to join this program, which places volunteers as assistants to Forest Service archaeologists and historians in their research on natural forest lands across the nation. Participants have helped to stabilize ancient cliff dwellings in New Mexico, excavate a 10,000-year-old village site in Minnesota, restore a historic lookout tower in Oregon, and clean vandalized rock art in Colorado. Projects vary in length from a weekend to a month, and facilities vary widely. Some projects involve back-country camping where volunteers are responsible for their own food and gear; others offer meals prepared by a camp cook, often for a small fee. Sometimes volunteers can stay in local hotels and travel to the site each day. There are dozens of interesting opportunities. To learn about current projects and how to enroll, write for the free newsletter published each March and September.

*A good source of information on other archaeology vacation opportunities:*

## Archeology Fieldwork Opportunities Bulletin
Archaeological Institute of America,
675 Commonwealth Avenue, Boston, MA 02215; (617) 353–9361. Call (800) 228–0810 to order book. $11 for nonmembers.

### Nature Volunteer Opportunities

The Sierra Club (see page 90) conducts week-long service trips for volunteers who help maintain trails and preserve the beauty of wilderness locales. The Nature Conservancy (see page 121) holds volunteer programs assisting conservation biologists with bird and wildflower inventories or riparian restoration at the Tensleep Conservation Project site in Wyoming.

Sources for additional volunteer suggestions are *Volunteer Vacations,* Chicago Review Press, (800) 888–4741; *Volunteer! The Comprehensive Guide to Voluntary Service in the U.S. and Abroad,* Council on International Educational Exchange, (800) 349–2433; *Environmental Vacations: Volunteer Projects to Save the Planet,* John Muir Publications, (800) 888–7504.

........................................................................

# Foreign Language Workshops

Learning a new language will allow you to travel abroad with more confidence and may widen your horizons at home as well.

## THE FOREIGN LANGUAGE IMMERSION PROGRAMS

STATE UNIVERSITY OF NEW YORK AT NEW PALTZ,
75 SOUTH MANHEIM BOULEVARD, NEW PALTZ, NY 12561;
(914) 257-3500. (I, PROGRAM ONLY)

| | |
|---|---|
| YEARS IN BUSINESS: | 16 |
| AGE RANGE: | 15 TO 80 |
| MOST COMMON AGE: | 45 |
| PERCENT ALONE: | 75 |
| NUMBER OF PARTICIPANTS: | 6–15 PER WORKSHOP GROUP |
| MALE/FEMALE RATIO: | 40/60 |

This innovative language department sponsors year-round weekend "total immersion" workshops at the New Paltz campus, in New York City, and in Westchester County, plus weekends and a one-week session at the beautiful Mohonk Mountain House resort outside New Paltz. Two-week intensive programs are held in summer at the New Paltz campus.

The approach here is to speak only the new language from day one, perfect for travelers who want to increase their vocabularies and learn conversation quickly. Only enough grammar is taught to give a needed foundation. One hundred to 200 people may enroll for weekend seminars; they are divided into small groups according to ability. The two-week summer classes include fifty hours of instruction and leave plenty of time for recreation. Students arrange their own lodging in area motels or inns.

Winter learning vacations are held in Mexico, and year-round, two-week overseas language-learning vacations are available in Costa Rica, Spain, and France in conjunction with language schools in these countries. Additional programs in Italy and Mexico are in the works. Overseas students can choose homestay, hotel, or apartment accommodations.

COMMENTS *E.B.: My weekend at SUNY was a delight. Teachers are chosen for their outgoing personalities as well as language fluency, and they conduct classes with flair and a sense of fun. A typical assignment: "Pick a French character and describe yourself so that the class can guess who you are." Everybody gets into the spirit, and there's lots of laughter as well as learning. The class stayed together at lunch, still speaking French. Most of us chose to have dinner together as well, though we did give ourselves an English break. The approach dredged up every word of my forgotten college French—I was amazed. It left me in much better shape to tackle a trip to France.*

*Male, 50s: It's easy to come to this program alone. Everyone is learning, and we all make mistakes—alone or with a friend, you'd still have to get up in front of everyone and speak a foreign language. Most people do come alone, but everyone bonds quickly in the class. I've also gone on several trips to Costa Rica. I love the homestay program. I've spent an hour at the dinner table with my homestay family after the dishes were cleared, just talking about life in our different countries, family structure, politics—anything. No class can give you that.*

## NATIONAL REGISTRATION CENTER FOR STUDY ABROAD (NRCSA)

823 NORTH SECOND STREET, MILWAUKEE, WI 53201; (414) 278–0631. (I–E)

The NRCSA is a consortium of 125 universities, language institutes, and specialized schools in thirty countries of Latin America, Europe, and Asia that welcome North Americans as well as participants from around the world. They offer hundreds of programs from a week to a year abroad with lodging options from hotels and pensions to family stays. Through this organization, you can learn French in France, Switzerland, or Canada, study Spanish in Mexico, Spain, Costa Rica, Guatemala, or South America, and improve your Italian in Rome, Florence, or Siena. Programs are also available in Japan, Taiwan, Greece, Sweden, and Russia. Contact NRCSA for details on these opportunities.

*Annual listings of language vacations abroad also appear in* **Transitions Abroad Magazine**
P.O. Box 1300, Amherst, MA 01004; (413) 256–3415.

## Cooking Schools

The opportunity to master the authentic cuisine of France or Italy with instruction from top regional chefs and teachers gives a special dimension to a foreign location and a view of the country most tourists miss. Cooking schools are also a rewarding option for solo travelers in scenic regions of the U.S., giving focus to a trip and a chance to learn more about the area. All of these programs include time for sight-seeing and opportunities to visit local markets and sample fine cuisine—including some that you will produce yourself. Some cooking programs are quite expensive, but participants say they are wonderful experiences worth saving for!

### U.S. Cooking Schools

### GOING SOLO IN THE KITCHEN
P.O. Box 123, Apalachicola, FL 32329; (904) 653–8848. (M)

Jane Doerfer, a veteran cooking instructor and author of the book *Going Solo in the Kitchen,* has designed this delightful six-day sojourn explicitly for single cooks. Classes offered periodically from June to

October emphasize easy-to-prepare recipes for one and easy meals for entertaining. Sessions are held at Doerfer's home in an idyllic fishing village on Florida's Gulf Coast. Guests stay at a nearby inn, gather for morning instruction and lunch, and have afternoons free for beaching,

| | |
|---|---|
| YEARS IN BUSINESS: | 3 |
| AGE RANGE: | 20–70 |
| MOST COMMON AGE: | 40s |
| PERCENT ALONE: | 90 |
| NUMBER OF PARTICIPANTS: | 12 MAXIMUM |
| MALE/FEMALE RATIO: | 1/2 |

boating, sailing, or otherwise relaxing. They regroup in the evening to prepare and enjoy dinner parties together. (Doerfer is also the author/publisher of the *Going Solo* newsletter; see page 194).

COMMENTS *Female, 70s: I'm not a serious cook, but I had the best time and I learned a lot. Jane is a delightful person, and she made it so much fun. There were just four of us, three women and one man, ranging in age from 20s to 70s, from Chicago, New York, Atlanta, and Durham. Everyone came alone. We had very diverse backgrounds, but all were interesting people, and we all got along well. Jane also invited different local people in every night for dinner and that made it livelier than if it had been just the five of us night after night. There was plenty of free time in the afternoon, and I enjoyed Apalachicola because it is off the beaten path, still out of the past and very unspoiled.*

## JANE BUTEL'S SOUTHWESTERN COOKING SCHOOL

800 RIO GRANDE BOULEVARD, N.W., SUITE 14,
ALBUQUERQUE, NM 87104;
(800) 473-TACO. (EE)

| | |
|---|---|
| YEARS IN BUSINESS: | 14 |
| AGE RANGE: | 35–65 |
| MOST COMMON AGE: | 45–55 |
| PERCENT ALONE: | 50 |
| NUMBER OF PARTICIPANTS: | MAXIMUM OF 15 |
| MALE/FEMALE RATIO: | 40/60 |

For chefs who like their menus hot, Jane Butel, the queen of Tex-Mex cuisine and author of fourteen books on Southwestern cookery, shares her secrets in state-of-the-art kitchens with ample room for hands-on learning.

Recipes include regional favorites like fajitas, tortillas, enchiladas, tacos, and tostados, as well as chili stews, tamales, black bean soup, quesadillas, empanadas, and the classic dessert, flan. Students get a taste of Southwest history and lore along with cooking tips.

Three-hour morning sessions are followed by the lunch that has been prepared in class. Continental breakfast and two dinners in local restaurants are included in the weekly rates. Accommodations are in a hotel in nearby Old Town Albuquerque, and afternoons are free to explore the many shops, galleries, and museums of the city. Five-day and weekend sessions are held March through early December.

COMMENTS   *Male, 50s: I loved it. I went to the weekend course and enjoyed it so much, I went back for a week. There were sixteen in my week-long group, from late 20s to 50s, from all over the country and the world. Four of us were alone, and there was no problem at all. We stayed in the same bed-and-breakfast; I'm still in touch with one lady from the Netherlands by e-mail. The day starts with Jane explaining things like different types of chiles. Then we paired off to make the dishes of the day, with Jane and her assistants supervising, and we shared the food over lunch. Afternoons were free to explore Albuquerque, which is a beautiful city with lots to do. Old Town is fun just to wander through, and there are great museums nearby. Some nights we got together for dinner. I had a ball and would definitely recommend this to anyone.*

## LA VARENNE AT THE GREENBRIER

THE GREENBRIER, WHITE SULPHUR SPRINGS, WV 24986;
(800) 624–6070 OR (202) 337–0073. (EE)

| | |
|---|---|
| YEARS IN BUSINESS: | 27 |
| AGE RANGE: | 20–80 |
| MOST COMMON AGE: | 46 |
| PERCENT ALONE: | 75 |
| NUMBER OF PARTICIPANTS: | 60 |
| MALE/FEMALE RATIO: | 1/3 |

Anne Willan, the noted founder of Ecole de Cuisine La Varenne in Paris, presides over an annual spring cooking series at this luxurious resort. Willan does the three-hour demonstrations featuring French specialties on Monday, Wednesday, and Friday. Celebrity guest chefs take over the other two days. All the classes include tastings with specially selected wines. In addition, Greenbrier chefs lead afternoon classes in contemporary American cuisine and offer some hands-on evening sessions. The final night features a champagne reception and the Greenbrier's Gold Service Dinner (black tie optional).

## THE NEW ENGLAND CULINARY INSTITUTE

250 MAIN STREET, MONTPELIER, VT 05602;
(802) 223-6324.

Holds culinary weekends periodically at the Inn at Essex outside Burlington, Vermont. Phone for current offerings.

### *Cooking Schools Abroad*

## COOKING WITH FRIENDS IN FRANCE

c/o JACKSON & COMPANY,
29 COMMONWEALTH AVENUE, BOSTON, MA 02116;
(617) 247-1055. (EE)

| | |
|---|---|
| YEARS IN BUSINESS: | 5 |
| AGE RANGE: | 21–85 |
| MOST COMMON AGE: | 35–55 |
| PERCENT ALONE: | VARIES |
| NUMBER OF PARTICIPANTS: | 8 |
| MALE/FEMALE RATIO: | 1/6 |
| GUARANTEED SHARES | |

The tile-roofed classic Provencal houses once occupied by Simone Beck and her coauthor Julia Child are shared by students at this six-day program in Provence taught by Kathie Alex, who studied with Beck and other French greats. Up to eight students take part in the program, which offers three morning lessons that culminate in lunch and two days of guided excursions exploring local culture and cuisine.

COMMENTS  *Female, late 30s: It was excellent, interesting, fulfilling. There were two couples, two friends, and two single women in our group. Basically you travel and take meals with these people for six days straight—you can't help but get involved. The day is structured until 3: 00 P.M. After that, everyone in the group was very inclusive—always invited everyone to go sight-seeing or share a car to the beach. I was very nervous to get up in front of everyone and try a technique, but the staff made it extremely comfortable, and I felt I had support from the group. The teacher is wonderful, her recipes are great, and her teaching method makes it very easy to learn.*

## ITALIAN COUNTRY COOKING

POSITANO, ITALY, c/o E & M ASSOCIATES,
211 EAST 43D STREET, NEW YORK, NY 10017;
(800) 223-9832 OR (212) 599-8280. (E)

Diana Folonari, of a noted Italian wine family, conducts this nine-day program at her home in Positano, a magnificent setting in the cliffs on the Amalfi Drive. The program begins with a reception and a talk on Italian food and wine. Five mornings are

| | |
|---|---|
| YEARS IN BUSINESS: | 11 |
| AGE RANGE: | 20–60 |
| MOST COMMON AGE: | 25–45 |
| PERCENT ALONE: | 60 |
| NUMBER OF PARTICIPANTS: | 12 |
| MALE/FEMALE RATIO: | 60/40 |

spent in class, with students preparing lunches they share. One late-afternoon session features homemade pizza and country dishes. Special sessions on Italian wines are held as well. Participants stay in a local hotel, have one full day and most afternoons and evenings free for sight-seeing in nearby Amalfi, Ravello, Sorrento, Pompeii, and the Isle of Capri. A final, farewell dinner is held at a fine local hotel.

COMMENTS  *Male, 40s: This is fantastic, one of the best trips I've ever made. I happened to be the only student who enrolled, and Diana and I became great friends. You stay at the best hotel in Positano, with wonderful accommodations. The area is beautiful, the wines delicious, the instruction fantastic. It's expensive but worth it.*

## MARCELLA AND VICTOR HAZAN'S MASTER CLASS IN VENICE

c/o SUSAN COX,
P.O. BOX 285, CIRCLEVILLE, NY 10919;
(914) 692-7104. (EE)

| | |
|---|---|
| YEARS IN BUSINESS: | 12 |
| AGE RANGE: | 30–50 |
| MOST COMMON AGE: | 35 |
| PERCENT ALONE: | 33 |
| NUMBER OF PARTICIPANTS: | 6 |
| MALE/FEMALE RATIO: | 50/50 |

A few times each year, these noted culinary authorities open their sixteenth-century palazzo to a select group of students interested in Italian cooking and wine. Classes are loosely structured and intimate, with a chance to experience at close range the Hazans' approach to cooking. The week opens with an overview of the course over espresso, an escorted tour of the historic produce and fish market at Rialto, and a midday banquet at one of the hosts' favorite Venice restaurants. Classes begin the morning of day two and continue for the next five days, running for five hours. Afterward, students share the dishes they've made at a leisurely luncheon. During each meal, Victor

Hazan presents and discusses rare wines from his private cellar. Despite the high cost, the demand for this course is great—reservations are accepted two years in advance.

## LA VARENNE IN BURGUNDY

C/O ECOLE DE CUISINE LA VARENNE,
P.O. BOX 25574, WASHINGTON, D.C. 20007;
(202) 337-0073.
(EE, INCLUDES TRANSPORTATION FROM PARIS)

| | |
|---|---|
| YEARS IN BUSINESS: | 20 |
| AGE RANGE: | 35–60 |
| MOST COMMON AGE: | 35–60 |
| PERCENT ALONE: | 50 |
| NUMBER OF PARTICIPANTS: | 10 |
| MALE/FEMALE RATIO: | VARIES |

One-week programs designed by Anne Willan combine cooking instruction with good living at the lovely seventeenth-century Chateau du Fey in northern Burgundy. Weekly topics vary from fundamentals of French cooking to French pastry, from traditional French regional cooking to contemporary French cuisine and menus for entertaining. Each program is conducted by a talented French chef, with full translation by trained assistants. The goal is to sharpen kitchen skills and convey the gastronomic heritage of France. Each week includes five practical classes, three demonstrations, and a wine tasting. There are excursions to vineyard areas such as Joigny and Chablis, and the week concludes with dinner at a fine country restaurant. The chateau offers a pool, tennis courts, woodlands, and garden paths.

COMMENTS *Male, 40s: This was the most relaxing vacation I've ever had. I left my wife at home and went to enhance my cooking skills. In my group of ten, there was only one couple—everyone else came alone. The instruction was excellent. We had classes in the morning, preparing a lunch. Then we went to local cheese makers or vineyards or had free time to sight-see or relax. Dinner either was prepared by our chef or in a three-star restaurant. We all had a wonderful time.*

*Male, 30s: The people were interesting; most were alone and from diverse backgrounds. The trip was special because there was nothing touristy about it. . . cooking was the main focus, and because there were few in the group, you really got to know people. I would highly recommend this to anyone who likes to cook. . . or eat!*

## COOKING SCHOOL AT L'ABBAYE DE SAINTE CROIX

ROUTE VAL-DE CUECH, 13300 SALON-DE-PROVENCE, FRANCE;
C/O B & V ASSOCIATES,
140 EAST 56TH STREET, SUITE 4C, NEW YORK, NY 10022;
(212) 688-9538. (EE)

| | |
|---|---|
| YEARS IN BUSINESS: | 10 |
| AGE RANGE: | 20–82 |
| MOST COMMON AGE: | 30–60 |
| PERCENT ALONE: | 15 |
| NUMBER OF PARTICIPANTS: | 6–12 |
| MALE/FEMALE RATIO: | VARIES |

This small three- or four-day cooking course in the heart of Provence gives students the opportunity to prepare elegant four-course dinners with professional instruction, then enjoy the results together with their chef, Pascal Morel, the Michelin-starred chef de cuisine. Though the chef speaks French, translators are on hand to make sure you get every detail right. The setting is a restored twelfth-century monastery, which is now a luxurious four-star Relais et Chateau hotel, set high above the plain with an unobstructed view of the Mediterranean. Besides cooking instruction, the week includes excursions to the colorful market of Aix en Provence and vineyard visits and wine tastings, including the noted cellars of Chateauneuf du Pape. Rates include breakfast and lunch.

## LE CORDON BLEU, PARIS AND LONDON

C/O 404 IRVINGTON STREET, PLEASANTVILLE, NY 10570;
(914) 741-0606 OR (800) 457-CHEF.

While there is no residential program, this world-renowned school offers Paris visitors "Gourmet Sessions," demonstrations, and hands-on classes from a half-day to a month in length, as well as a morning tour of Paris markets with their chefs. A Saturday spent at a soufflé workshop or learning traditional cooking for friends will add a tasty dimension to a Paris visit. All demonstrations are translated into English. Gourmet sessions are also offered in English at the London Le Cordon Bleu school, lasting from three days to one month.

*For a comprehensive list of cooking schools around the world, order*
**THE GUIDE TO COOKING SCHOOLS**
FROM SHAWGUIDES, P.O. BOX 1295, NEW YORK, NY 10023;
(212) 799-6464.

# Learn About Wine

## GERMAN WINE ACADEMY

C/O GERMAN WINE INFORMATION BUREAU,
79 MADISON AVENUE, NEW YORK, NY 10016;
(212) 213–7036. (E)

Six days of learning about German wines include lectures in English by local experts, travel to grape-growing regions for visits to wine estates and cellars, tastings with winemakers, seminars on wine, and a wide spectrum of tastings of some of the world's classic white wines. Several activities are based at the academy headquarters, a twelfth-century monastery called Kloster Eberbach. Among the activities are the festive last night dinner, which includes a blind wine tasting and the presentation of "diplomas." Students are lodged for five nights at the charming Hotel Schwan in Oestrich/Rheingau and spend one day on a Rhine cruise with an overnight stop at the Alte Thorschenke at Cochem, one of Germany's oldest hotels. Areas usually visited include the Mosel Valley, Rheingau, Pfalz, Mittelrhein, and Rheinhessen regions, and the itinerary takes in many picturesque villages.

| | |
|---|---|
| YEARS IN BUSINESS: | 23 |
| AGE RANGE: | 21–70 |
| MOST COMMON AGE: | 35–50 |
| PERCENT ALONE: | NO RECORDS |
| NUMBER OF PARTICIPANTS: | MAXIMUM OF 25 |
| MALE/FEMALE RATIO: | 60/40 |
| NO SHARES ARRANGED; SMALL SINGLE SUPPLEMENT | |

COMMENTS *Female, 30s: Some come for business, some for personal interest, but everyone shares the basic interest in wines; several people came alone. Because groups are small and you travel and eat together every day, it's very congenial and you get to know everyone.*

*Male, 40s: I came first with a companion, came back alone, returned a third time with my 21-year-old daughter, and always had a ball. About half are couples, the rest come alone, and there was plenty of company even for those in their 20s or 30s. I think this is one of the great bargains of the world—the food is great, and you taste more than 250 wines. As the wine flows, so does the fun. Even on the bus we sang songs and told jokes. It was a constant party.*

# Photography

Sharpening your ability with a camera not only makes for a rewarding vacation but gives you skills that will enhance your travel pleasure forever after, guaranteeing wonderful personal souvenirs from any trip.

## MAINE PHOTOGRAPHIC WORKSHOP

P.O. Box 200, 2 Central Street, Rockport, ME 04856; (207) 236–8581. (M)

| | |
|---|---|
| YEARS IN BUSINESS: | 24 |
| AGE RANGE: | 14–70 |
| MOST COMMON AGE: | 30 |
| PERCENT ALONE: | 90 |
| NUMBER OF PARTICIPANTS: | CLASS SIZE, 10 TO 18, TOTAL WEEKLY, 100 TO 200 |
| MALE/FEMALE RATIO: | 40/60 |

With the picture-perfect Maine coast village of Rockport as subject matter and inspiration, one of the nation's leading educational centers for photography offers more than 200 one-week workshops from June to September. The curriculum is designed for serious amateurs as well as professional filmmakers, photographers, storytellers, actors, and writers.

Photography classes range from Photography I and beginning darkroom techniques to master classes in such aspects of the craft as portraits and landscapes, in black-and-white and color. Taught by some of the top people in the field, classes are intensive, all-day experiences aimed to stretch participants to new heights of personal expression, technical excellence, and creative achievement. Workshops also include creative storytelling, feature films, video, and television documentaries.

The home campus in the fishing village of Rockport offers state of the art studios, darkrooms, a theater and gallery, a new digital media center, a production center, dining rooms, housing, and a campus store. The weekly schedule features exhibitions and lectures and screenings by leading photographers and directors. Meals are served in an old New England farmhouse where students dine with the faculty.

Additional workshops are offered in picturesque locations such as Tuscany, Provence, Mexico, Martha's Vineyard, and New York City.

COMMENTS *Letters from past students say:*
> *"There was such an excitement in the air that I jumped out of bed each morning looking forward to being surrounded by such creative, loving, and interesting photographers."*

*"A high-energy, intensely inspirational experience. I have never worked such long hours and had so much fun. Not to mention the fact that I learned in quantum leaps."*

## WILDERNESS PHOTOGRAPHIC WORKSHOPS
P.O. Box 1653, Ross, CA 94957,
(415) 927–4579 (M)

Those who already have a basic knowledge of photography will advance their skills in these workshops offered by photographer Brenda Tharp in scenic locales from the Arizona desert to Olympic National Park to Utah's "canyon country." Workshops range from five to sixteen days. Lodging varies with the site but is included; meals may or may not be included.

| | |
|---|---|
| YEARS IN BUSINESS: | SINCE 1985 |
| AGE RANGE: | 35–70 |
| MOST COMMON AGE: | 45–60 |
| PERCENT ALONE: | 75 |
| NUMBER OF PARTICIPANTS: | 8–12 |
| MALE/FEMALE RATIO: | 50/50 |
| YEAR-ROUND; WILL TRY TO ARRANGE SHARES | |

## FRIENDS OF ARIZONA HIGHWAYS PHOTO WORKSHOPS
2039 West Lewis Avenue, Phoenix, AZ 85009;
(602) 271–5904. (M)

The nonprofit auxiliary of *Arizona Highways,* a magazine known for its quality photography, sponsors more than a dozen three- and four-day workshops in scenic locales around the state, from ghost towns to the Sonoran Desert and Monument Valley, from the Grand Canyon to the Prescott

| | |
|---|---|
| YEARS IN BUSINESS: | 11 |
| AGE RANGE: | 20s–70s |
| MOST COMMON AGE: | VARIES |
| PERCENT ALONE: | MAJORITY |
| NUMBER OF PARTICIPANTS: | 15–20 |
| MALE/FEMALE RATIO: | 60/40 |
| FEBRUARY TO OCTOBER; MODERATE SINGLE SUPPLEMENT | |

Rodeo. Trips have included houseboating on Lake Powell. Participants are "intensely interested" amateur photographers who have basic knowledge of their cameras. Some workshops are activities trips that may include hiking or rafting, and each is graded for easy to strenuous activity levels.

Beginners may also take several Arizona Photo Sampler tours, which offer five days taking in the most famous and fabulous places in the state, accompanied by an *Arizona Highways* photographer who works with the group and with individuals. Many local photography centers in attractive resort communities offer one-day photo workshops as well as longer courses. Enrolling in one of these is an excellent way to give an added dimension to an already-planned vacation and to meet new people. Among the many possibilities are:

## PALM BEACH PHOTOGRAPHIC WORKSHOPS
2310 East Silver Palm Road, Boca Raton, FL 33432; (407) 391–7557.

## CENTER FOR PHOTOGRAPHIC ARTS
P.O. Box 1100, Carmel, CA 93921; (408) 625–5181.

## MENDOCINO ART CENTER
45200 Little Lake Street, P.O. Box 765, Mendocino, CA 95460; (707) 937–5818.

## SUN VALLEY CENTER FOR THE ARTS AND HUMANITIES
418 Knottingham Drive, Twin Falls, ID 83301; (800) 574–2839.

## NANTUCKET ISLAND SCHOOL OF DESIGN AND THE ARTS
Box 958, Nantucket, MA 02554; (508) 228–9248.

## NEW MEXICO ARTISTS' ASSOCIATION
2801 Rodeo Road, Santa Fe, NM 87505; (505) 982–5639.

Photography workshops are also ideal ways to enjoy and fully appreciate national parks and wilderness areas that are sometimes difficult to visit on your own. For national park programs including photography, see nature listings beginning on page 119).

## Art

An art-oriented vacation is more than a chance to develop a lifelong hobby; it means looking at a new locale from a different point of view—with the painter's eye—truly absorbing the details of the landscape and the architecture. The following are among hundreds of art workshops held around this country and abroad each year. For a comprehensive listing, look for the annual directory of art schools and workshops usually published in March in *American Artist* Magazine, 1515 Broadway, New York, NY 10036; (212) 764–7300.

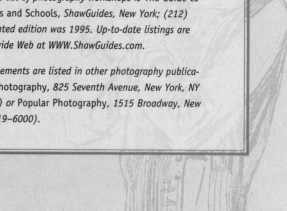

> The most comprehensive list of photography workshops is The Guide to Photography Workshops and Schools, *ShawGuides, New York; (212) 799–6464. The last printed edition was 1995. Up-to-date listings are available on the Worldwide Web at WWW.ShawGuides.com.*
>
> *Many workshop advertisements are listed in other photography publications such as* Modern Photography, *825 Seventh Avenue, New York, NY 10019 (212–265–8360) or* Popular Photography, *1515 Broadway, New York, NY 10036 (212-719–6000).*

## ART WORKSHOP INTERNATIONAL

463 WEST STREET, APARTMENT 1028H, NEW YORK, NY 10014;
(212) 691–1159. (M)

Assisi, Italy, is home base for this three-week program offering painting, drawing, and watercolor instruction. The offerings have expanded to workshops in screenwriting, fiction, poetry, autobiography, and art appreciation.

Work and play at your own pace is the motto, so there is time to enjoy the pool and to explore the countryside. Two days are left completely free for excursions. Breakfast and lunch are included in the tuition.

| | |
|---|---|
| YEARS IN BUSINESS: | 22 |
| AGE RANGE: | 17–80 |
| MOST COMMON AGE: | 40–60 |
| PERCENT ALONE: | 50 |
| NUMBER OF PARTICIPANTS: | 20–30 |
| MALE/FEMALE RATIO: | MAJORITY FEMALE |

ALL ARE ASSIGNED ROOMMATES UNLESS THEY SPECIFY SINGLES; SUITABLE FOR BEGINNERS.

COMMENTS *Female, 40s: This is an excellent program with no pressure. It was very easy to get to know everyone. My group was all women, ages 16 to 72, half of whom were single, and with all levels of art training. The food and the atmosphere were wonderful. We had painting instruction in the morning, afternoons free, and ate all meals together. A few times each week there were lectures and slide presentations. We went to local concerts or went swimming on our own.*

*Female, 50s: A group of very interesting people from all over the U.S. and Europe, mostly women and mostly single, we stayed in a guest house run by nuns with strict rules—you had to dress appropriately for the dining room. But the food was wonderful and the teachers creative. The views were beautiful. Teachers provided a painting theme each day, but you could paint whatever you wanted if you preferred. There was a certain amount of time for peer criticism. We tended to stay together in the afternoon, and the whole group often went out for dinner. It was excellent. I would recommend this to any single person.*

---

## LA ROMITA SCHOOL OF ART

1712 OLD TOWN NW, ALBUQUERQUE, NM 87104;
(505) 243-1924. (M)

| | |
|---|---|
| YEARS IN BUSINESS: | 11 |
| AGE RANGE: | 30–70 |
| MOST COMMON AGE: | 40–55 |
| PERCENT ALONE: | 60 |
| NUMBER OF PARTICIPANTS: | 8–20 |
| MALE/FEMALE RATIO: | 1/8 |
| SHARES USUALLY COMPULSORY; SUITABLE FOR BEGINNERS | |

Two three-week and two two-week summer programs held in the glorious Italian Umbrian hill country between Rome and Florence give participants a chance to tour as well as paint. Studio days are interspersed with visits to such towns as Spoleto, Assisi, Orvieto, and Perugia. The school is housed in a sixteenth-century monastery with modern facilities. The group includes a leader who is bilingual.

---

COMMENTS *Female, 40s: On my three-week trip to Italy, many people came on their own. The group is only twenty people, and we were together all the time. People tended to bond together and pair up, but everyone got along really well. It was a pretty diverse group from all over the U.S, ages 40 to 70s, nineteen women and one guy. It seemed that most people did know at least one other person. It was a lovely location, and the side trips were great—we got to see things other tourists would not. Plus, you don't have to worry about the language. It's a very safe way to travel in a foreign country. It was a fabulous trip.*

*Female, 60s: I've gone three times alone. A lot of people come by themselves, and it is easy to meet people as you all have something in common. There are about sixteen to eighteen people in each group, set up by the type of painting you are working on—watercolor, oils, et cetera. There's a mix of skill levels in each group, from painting teachers to people who are just learning. It's a lovely place—I love the owners and how it is run. But you have to want to be painting—it's not just a vacation—it's all about painting.*

## ART TREK

P.O. Box 807, Bolinas, CA 94924;
(415) 868-9558 or (800) 786-1830. (E)

| | |
|---|---|
| YEARS IN BUSINESS: | 17 |
| AGE RANGE: | 23–60 |
| MOST COMMON AGE: | 30–45 |
| PERCENT ALONE: | 60–70 |
| NUMBER OF PARTICIPANTS: | 12–16 |
| MALE/FEMALE RATIO: | 50/50 |
| SUITABLE FOR BEGINNERS | |

Watercolor painting instruction in beautiful summer locales in France, from Provence to Paris, and studio classes in drawing, painting, and printmaking in a studio in Antibes from October through August are the offerings. Classes are taught in English by well-known contemporary French artists. Summer lodgings vary with the locale; students in Antibes are housed with local families.

COMMENTS *Male, 40s: It was fine to be alone on this trip, doing watercolors in the south of France. It was a great group of people. Most were alone—a few knew each other, but most were there by themselves. There were more women than men, but they were able to find another man as a roommate for me. The ages ran the gamut from 20s to 60s. Some were serious painters, some were on the trip for the scenery and the touring. The staff was wonderful and helped to introduce everyone. The day was structured half for instruction and half free for painting. Some days we did sight-seeing instead of instruction, but we always painted. We stayed in small pensions; the food was excellent. There were traveling artists on staff, but we worked with local artists, too, and that gave it a more local perspective. I'll definitely go again; I would recommend it to any single person—or anyone at all.*

*Female, 50s: I had a great time. I went to France and Greece through UC Santa Cruz, and the quality of the people was excellent, all compatible and all educated about art. Some were teachers and professors—I'm not—but everyone knew a Manet from a Monet. We've gotten together twice since the trip. There were twenty people, eighteen women, and 90 percent came alone. We had a university professor traveling with the group, and we worked with local painting instructors in various towns. The staff knew a lot about art and the region of France where we were; they took us to all sorts of little-known museums, things you wouldn't see on a normal tour. You really get exposed to the culture. The program had an excellent itinerary.*

# Art, Crafts, Music, and More

These multifaceted programs have something for almost everyone.

## CREATIVE WORKSHOPS AT DILLMAN'S SAND LAKE LODGE

Box 98, Lac du Flambeau, WI 54538;
(715) 588-3143. (I)

For the past eighteen years, this family-run resort has offered a weekly roster of workshops under the auspices of the Dillman's Creative Arts Foundation. Running from late May to early October, the courses include more than 100 choices

| | |
|---|---|
| YEARS IN BUSINESS: | 63 |
| AGE RANGE: | 25–80 |
| MOST COMMON AGE: | 50 |
| PERCENT ALONE: | 30 |
| NUMBER OF PARTICIPANTS: | 120 |
| MALE/FEMALE RATIO: | MORE FEMALES |
| SUITABLE FOR BEGINNERS | |

of photography, watercolor and other art courses. The comfortable, rustic lodge is located on a lovely peninsula and offers tennis, lake beaches, canoeing, and miles of hiking and biking trails. This is a family resort, but the workshops draw many guests on their own. Participants are housed in the lodge. Reasonable tuition includes room, but not meals.

## ARROWMONT SCHOOL OF ARTS AND CRAFTS

P.O. Box 567, Gatlinburg, TN 37738;
(615) 436–5860. (I)

| | |
|---|---|
| Years in business: | 52 |
| Age range: | 18–80 |
| Most common age: | 40–65 |
| Percent alone: | 20 |
| Number of participants: | 40–100 per week |
| Male/female ratio: | 1/3 |
| Will try to arrange shares; suitable for beginners | |

Arrowmont is a visual arts complex on seventy wooded acres adjacent to the Great Smoky Mountain National Park. One- and two-week summer workshops draw men and women of all ages and levels of ability who wish to learn both traditional and contemporary crafts. Classes in basketry, quilting, weaving, and enameling as well as painting and drawing and work in clay and fibers are conducted by more than 100 visiting faculty members. Students are housed in simply furnished dormitory rooms in cottage-type buildings. Home-cooked meals are served in a congenial dining room. Having everyone together makes for a warm atmosphere.

COMMENTS  *Male, 40s: This is an intense learning experience, the best school of its type. It is fine to be here by yourself, as about half the students come alone. Most are women. People come from all over the world.*

*Female, 30s: I had a very pleasant experience. My group was mostly women, and many of the men who did come were with their wives, but it was a great mix of people. People here leave their lives behind. It's like summer camp—easy to become close quickly. The instructors are very well qualified. It's a good place to go alone.*

## FLETCHER FARM SCHOOL FOR THE ARTS AND CRAFTS

611 Route 103 South, Ludlow, VT 05149;
(802) 228–8770. (I)

| | |
|---|---|
| Years in business: | 50 |
| Age range: | 20–70 |
| Most common age: | 45–55 |
| Percent alone: | 80 |
| Number of participants: | 40–80 per week |
| Male/female ratio: | 1/10 |
| Late June through August; guaranteed shares; suitable for beginners | |

The lovely setting in Vermont's Green Mountains adds to the enjoyment of students who come to this school to learn a variety of art forms. Sponsored by the Society of Vermont Craftsmen, the courses include painting, basketry, weaving, rug hooking, tinsmithing, wood carving, quilting, and folk arts such as country tin and theorem painting. Single and double rooms are available in two lodges on campus, with shared bathroom facilities. Meals are family style, and students can use the Farmhouse Lounge/Library for visiting and relaxation.

COMMENTS *Female, 20s: I had been quilting for about a year and wanted to learn new techniques. I researched a bunch of schools, and this is where I chose to go. The instructor was great; the accommodations and food were fine. My class of five was all women. It was open seating at meals so you get to meet people—there were always plenty of people to talk to. Many people do come by themselves.*
*Male, 60s: I always travel on my own. I've been going here every year since 1992. I go for wood carving. It's a beautiful spot. I stay in a motel, but I meet people at meals, plus they encourage you to look in on other classes and projects to see what everyone is doing. There are usually eight to ten people in the woodworking class; quite a few come alone. The people are from all over; they range in age from 30s to 80s and there are usually more women than men. The instructors are very competent. There's always a group of nice outgoing people and a lot of camaraderie.*

## HAYSTACK MOUNTAIN SCHOOL OF CRAFTS

DEER ISLE, ME 04627;
(207) 348-2306. (I)

L ocated in a handsome complex in a spectacular setting on the coast of Maine, Haystack attracts many accomplished artisans but also offers a two-week program called "Square One: A Session

| | |
|---|---|
| YEARS IN BUSINESS: | 38 |
| AGE RANGE: | 18–80 |
| MOST COMMON AGE: | MID-30S |
| PERCENT ALONE: | 30 |
| NUMBER OF PARTICIPANTS: | 80 |
| MALE/FEMALE RATIO: | VARIES |

for Beginnings," for artists who want to explore a new medium or individuals who want to begin seriously studying a particular art. Courses in clay, fibers, metals, wood, and glassblowing were offered in a recent session.

COMMENTS *Female, 40s: This is a working vacation ... there's always something to do and you can go from area to area and learn several types of crafts. How structured or loose the course is depends on*

*each instructor. The atmosphere is very warm and people come away
extended creatively. Most students are female—some professional
women, some retired.*

*Female, 30s: There's a cluster of serious art students, and most of the
older people are there for vacation. About half are single or came
alone. There's a nice balance of public and private time. People come
here to have an experience with others who are interested in crafts,
and it's not just surface—they form lasting friendships. The food is
terrific, very healthy and appetizing. There's something to do all day,
and at night there is usually a slide show or a dance or some sort of
program.*

## AUGUSTA HERITAGE CENTER

DAVIS & ELKINS COLLEGE, ELKINS, WV
26241–3996;
(304) 636–1903. (I)

| | |
|---|---|
| YEARS IN BUSINESS: | 25 |
| AGE RANGE: | 10–75 |
| MOST COMMON AGE: | 25–45 |
| PERCENT ALONE: | 30–40 |
| NUMBER OF PARTICIPANTS: | 1,400, DIVIDED INTO SMALL GROUPS |
| MALE/FEMALE RATIO: | VARIES; ABOUT 50/50 |
| SINGLES MATCHED IN DORM ROOMS | |

Appalachian arts—from fiddling, blacksmithing, and basketry to whittling and folk painting—are the focus of this excellent five-week summer program. Dance, storytelling, quilting, songwriting, folk carving, clogging, and music from bluegrass to Cajun are also included in the list of 200 workshops, highlighting folk cultures from around the country and around the world. Most workshops run five days, with classes running from morning until late afternoon. Inexpensive housing is available in twin-bed college dorms or in motels off campus. Rates for those staying on campus include most meals. Evening brings many informal jam sessions and get-togethers. The program ends with a three-day folk festival with home cooking and music and dancing that leaves toes tapping for weeks after.

COMMENTS *Female, 30s: It is very easy to meet people, and a great
number are alone. It's fairly even male and female. I went for the
dancing; the days were strenuous, the instruction very good. The dorm
rooms and food are not good, but that's not why you go. It is creative
time.*

*Female, 40s: There's no way you could feel alone here. A wide vari-
ety of people come from all over the U.S; they are of all ages but most
are in their 20s and 30s. Some of the classes are very structured, running from 8:00 A.M. to 5:00 P.M., then resuming at night. There are
dances at least twice a week, and people who come for the music
classes hold jam sessions in the evening. Most of the people here lead
some type of alternative life-style; they are happy to meet each other,
and many lasting friendships are formed.*

## HORIZONS

THE NEW ENGLAND CRAFT PROGRAM, 5 CLARY ROAD, WILLIAMSBURG, MA:
BUSINESS OFFICE: 108 NORTH MAIN STREET,
SUNDERLAND, MA 01375;
(413) 665-0300.

| | |
|---|---|
| YEARS IN BUSINESS: | 18 |
| AGE RANGE: | 18–80 |
| MOST COMMON AGE: | 28–55 |
| PERCENT ALONE: | MAJORITY |
| NUMBER OF PARTICIPANTS: | 35–65 |
| MALE/FEMALE RATIO: | 30/70 |
| SUITABLE FOR BEGINNERS; PARTICIPANTS PAIRED IN DOUBLE ROOMS. | |

Horizons is a center for the visual arts, located on acres of orchards and rolling countryside. It is minutes from the five-college communities of Amherst and Northampton in western Massachusetts, an area that is a growing center for crafts. The extensive studio and living spaces blend contemporary buildings with historic 1700s farm structures. Workshops include painting, ceramics, metal and jewelry making, hot glass, photography, mosaics, boat building, and much more. Small classes are structured to launch beginners as well as to challenge the more advanced. The center takes pride in its home-cooked natural foods.

COMMENTS *Female, 30s: I've been five or six times. I go mainly for
glass work, but I've done several other programs. The average class has
eight to ten people, a real mix of skill levels from professionals to people who want to learn for fun. The one common factor is that they
are all really creative people with neat ideas. They're all coming to
learn and have fun. I've built some terrific friendships, and now I
schedule my trips with other people I've met there. The ratio was
pretty much sixty/forty women to men, depending on the class. The
age range was 19 to 60s, the average in their 30s and 40s. The staff*

*is excellent—quality instructors and really nice, friendly and helpful*
*people. The rooms are rustic; the food is good. I'd say 80 to 90 percent*
*come alone. I'd recommend it to anyone.*

---

## THE INSTITUTE OF ARTS

Box 5280 NDCBU, Taos, NM 87571;
(505) 758-2793.

| | |
|---|---|
| YEARS IN BUSINESS: | 9 |
| AGE RANGE: | WIDE |
| MOST COMMON AGE: | 30–55 |
| PERCENT ALONE: | 60 |
| NUMBER OF PARTICIPANTS: | 350+ |
| MALE/FEMALE RATIO: | 40/60 |

Intensive workshops in painting, photography, writing and literature, textiles, clay, and jewelry are available in the beautiful setting of Taos, an art colony 7,000 feet high in the Sangre de Cristo Mountains that is deeply influenced by its Pueblo Indian heritage. Classes such as weaving, traditional pottery, mask making, beading, and natural dyeing reflect this Southwestern tradition. Indian culture is also explored in courses with such topics as petroglyphs of northern New Mexico, which offers a chance to take daily hikes to seek out the "rock art" of this region. Tuition for the two- to four-day courses is moderate; students make their own living arrangements, with assistance from the school.

---

## TOUCHSTONE CENTER FOR CRAFTS

R.D. 1, Box 60, Farmington, PA 15437;
(412) 329-1370. (I)

| | |
|---|---|
| YEARS IN BUSINESS: | 25 |
| AGE RANGE: | 35–65 |
| MOST COMMON AGE: | 40–50 |
| PERCENT ALONE: | 20 |
| NUMBER OF PARTICIPANTS: | 35–65 |
| MALE/FEMALE RATIO: | 1/3 |
| GUARANTEED SHARES | |

Painting, drawing, weaving, quilting, basketry, pottery, ironworking, pewter making, stained glass, bead making, and woodworking are all on the agenda in five-day workshops in summer and weekend sessions in May and September. Lodging is in rustic log cabins. The center is located 60 miles southeast of Pittsburgh, a drive of about 3½ hours from Cleveland and 4½ hours from Washington, D.C.

---

COMMENTS *Female, 50s: It's a wonderful place. I've been six times*
*and every time, I never want to go home. Everyone has pretty much*
*the same interests—that's why they are there. They made me feel at*
*home the first time I came and still do.*

# Try Adventure Travel

**"A**dventure travel" is a catchall term for scores of ways to get into uncrowded, unspoiled countryside or untouched wilderness and to be actively involved with the environment and with your fellow travelers. It is an escape from the pressures of urban living, as well as a welcome change from passive travel that shows you the world through the windows of a tour bus or a car. Since groups are small and camaraderie between participants is strong, the percentage of single vacationers who choose this kind of vacation is predictably high.

For years, travel labeled "adventure" was considered exotic, limited to hardy backpackers or thrill-seekers who delighted in climbing Mount Everest or careening over dangerous rapids in a rubber raft. But owing to their explosion in popularity over the last decades, adventure trips have become accessible and safe for almost everyone.

Statistics chronicle this boom. In 1949, eighty years after John Wesley Powell completed the first descent of the Colorado River, only 100 people had ever rafted through the Grand Canyon. By 1972, the National Park Service was forced to limit traffic on the river to 17,000 people a year! By now, millions of people have experienced the thrill of exploring the bottom of the canyon by boat.

With so many people signing on, the number of operators offering adventure outings has zoomed, and the variety of trips is truly amazing. Just a few of the choices include rafting, backpacking, backcountry skiing, horseback trekking, mountain climbing, and gentler pursuits such as sailing, biking, and walking. Tour operators grade their offerings to suit a wide range of abilities, making it easy for travelers to make a wise choice.

Trips are offered on the seven continents and almost every place on earth, from the subarctic ice floes to the jungles of the equator to the placid countryside of Europe or the United States. You can take your choice of camping out or staying in quarters that are positively plush.

The following pages offer a small sampling of the great selection available. The listing represents some of the longer-established operators or the more unusual adventure choices and runs the gamut from rustic to deluxe. Use the additional references given to find more operators in whatever area interests you most.

The majority of these outdoor trips are priced per person, with no single supplement. When necessary, operators try to arrange shares. Where single supplements do exist, they tend to be low. Luxury trips with a substantial supplement are so indicated.

A warning: More than any other type of trip, adventure travel depends for its success and safety on the experience and skill of the operator, so check references carefully before you make your choice.

There are a few sources for information. Groups operating in national parks must have a permit from the superintendent, so you can write or call to verify the credentials and ask park authorities about the reputation of the company. The American Mountain Guides Association (303–271–0984) in Golden, Colorado, offers accreditation for outfitters and certification for individual guides and will provide names of those who have qualified. The Professional Paddle Sports Association (606–472–2205) in Butler, Kentucky, a trade association for white-water rafting outfits, will provide information about choosing a trip, a list of accredited members, and any information on file on a particular company.

..............................................................................

# Operators with Trips in Multiple Categories

## APPALACHIAN MOUNTAIN CLUB

5 JOY STREET, BOSTON, MA 02108;
(617) 523-0636. (I–E FOR SOME FOREIGN EXCURSIONS)

Hiking, biking, backpacking, climbing, cross-country skiing, canoeing, snowshoeing, and rafting are among the pursuits of this vener-

## Choosing an Adventure Trip

There are no standardized requirements for operators of adventure trips or for guides, so choosing a reliable company is important. Here are some questions to ask before you sign on:

- How long has the company been operating? How long have they run this particular trip?
- Can you describe the day-by-day activity and the level of difficulty of this trip? Is there any training or preparation for participants?
- What kind of training is required for guides? How much experience have they had on the route in question?
- Are guides required to know first aid and CPR?
- What kind of insurance does the company carry? (Don't choose any company lacking coverage.)
- On a rafting trip, are life jackets and helmets supplied?.
- What do you do in case of serious injury or illness in the wilderness?
- Can you provide names of recent participants on this trip?

able, conservation-minded club with local chapters throughout the Northeast. In addition to the year-round workshops at its permanent lodges (see page 40) AMC sponsors dozens of major excursions throughout North America and abroad. Organized and supervised by

| | |
|---|---|
| YEARS IN BUSINESS: | 120+ |
| AGE RANGE: | 5–85 |
| MOST COMMON AGE: | 28–55 |
| PERCENT ALONE: | 35 |
| NUMBER OF PARTICIPANTS: | 70,000 MEMBERS; TRIP GROUPS ARE SMALL |
| MALE/FEMALE RATIO: | 60/40 |

volunteer members, these trips range from trekking the Andes to hiking in Norway, from traversing Scotland's Highlands to sailing Maine waters in a windjammer.

## SIERRA CLUB OUTINGS PROGRAM

730 Polk Street, San Francisco, CA 94109; (415) 923-5522. (I)

| | |
|---|---|
| YEARS IN BUSINESS: | 80+ |
| AGE RANGE: | 10–80 |
| MOST COMMON AGE: | Not given |
| PERCENT ALONE: | 50–75 |
| NUMBER OF PARTICIPANTS: | 10,000 total, 10 to 25 per outing |
| MALE/FEMALE RATIO: | Not given |

Another longtime leader in conserving and appreciating the wilderness, the Sierra Club annually offers about 250 outings to every region of the United States and to foreign countries. Trips range from four days to more than three weeks in length, and include backpacking, hiking trips using a single base camp, biking, rafting, canoeing, sea kayaking, and sailing. All are cooperative ventures with volunteer leaders; on camping trips all pitch in with chores and cooking. The club holds special leadership training outings.

The trips require varying degrees of stamina and experience, but the catalog clearly characterizes each outing. Additional brochures available for each trip spell out the details. Base camp trips tend to be easy to moderate and are a good idea for beginners since they allow for taking the day off if you are weary. Highlight Trips are also moderate; they are designed for people who like to hike or walk with only a daypack. International destinations cover the globe—Africa, Asia, Europe, Latin America, New Zealand, even Siberia.

## AMERICAN WILDERNESS EXPERIENCE (AWE)

P.O. Box 1486, Boulder, CO 80306; (303) 444-2622 or (800) 444-0099. (I–M)

| | |
|---|---|
| YEARS IN BUSINESS: | 26 |
| AGE RANGE: | 25–65 |
| MOST COMMON AGE: | 30–45 |
| PERCENT ALONE: | 35 |
| NUMBER OF PARTICIPANTS: | 2,500 annually |
| MALE/FEMALE RATIO: | 45/55 |
| YEAR-ROUND | |

Horseback treks, fishing trips, llama trekking, walking, hiking and backpacking, ranch vacations, canoeing and whale-watching adventures, cattle drives, covered wagon trips, white-water rafting, Alaskan wildlife safaris, and international trips to Peru, Mexico, Spain, Honduras, and Costa Rica are among this group's many offerings. Combo trips are made up of riding and rafting. In winter the list grows to include dogsledding, snowmobiling, and trips to warm-weather destinations.

AWE also has a roster of sixty-seven dude ranches; it promises to help vacationers select the right one. Requirements for these trips: good physical condition—"old enough to get on a horse and young enough to stay on." But they advertise "The Civilized Way to Rough It" and promise comfort and good food. A third of the participants are repeats.

COMMENTS *Male, 30s: I've taken four trips by myself, found the groups about half singles and even numbers of males and females. Most were in their 20s and 30s, from all walks of life, from all over the country. The program is very well managed. I've recommended it to other single friends.*

*Female, 30s: There were mostly families on my ranch stay, with six singles out of nineteen people. The average age was 30s and 40s, but guests ranged from children to one set of grandparents. The accommodations were fine, and each day there was a choice of activities—riding lessons, trail rides, fishing. At night we sat by the fire in the lodge and talked or sang songs. It was a pleasant experience and one I would recommend to singles, especially those with kids.*

## WILDLAND ADVENTURES

3516 NE 155TH STREET, SEATTLE, WA 98155; (206) 365–0606 OR (800) 345–4453.

| | |
|---|---|
| YEARS IN BUSINESS: | 11 |
| AGE RANGE: | 35–80 |
| MOST COMMON AGE: | 40–60; 35–55 |
| | ON HIKING TRIPS |
| PERCENT ALONE: | 65 |
| NUMBER OF PARTICIPANTS: | SMALL GROUPS |
| MALE/FEMALE RATIO: | 45/55 |
| TRIPS YEAR-ROUND; SHARE RATES GUARANTEED FOR ADVANCE RESERVATIONS | |

"Off the beaten path cross-cultural experiences," says the literature for this company with interesting itineraries in Peru, the Galápagos, Guatemala, Turkey, Costa Rica, Honduras, and the U.S. Pacific Northwest. The trips combine active exploration with intellectual stimulation. You can choose lodge-based odysseys, yacht voyages, rafting, or hiking-camping trips. Guides provide local history and discussion of contemporary social issues to make the visit more meaningful.

COMMENTS *Female, 30s: It was a very busy itinerary, but we learned a lot and the guides were very knowledgeable. We went to remote places and saw things no tourist would ever see, like a village that can only be accessed by boat or plane. There were about fifteen in the group, only three singles. It was about 50/50 male/female and ages from 30 to 70. The people were pretty outgoing, and most were bird-watchers, so we all had something in common. Also most were world travelers, so they shared a lot of interests. The accommodations and food were wonderful. My only criticism was that the people were too old for me. It was great, and I'd recommend it, but to someone a little older.*

*Male, 60s: I went once by myself to Patagonia. It is hard to find a tour to Patagonia, so when I heard of this one, I signed up. There were only four in the group—one woman and two other men. They all worked at a university together. It was very comfortable being alone. We all got to know each other intimately. Everything worked right with this tour—they're very good at what they do, and the guides are very knowledgeable. I plan to go again, and I'd recommend it to anyone.*

---

## OVERSEAS ADVENTURE TRAVEL

625 MOUNT AUBURN STREET, CAMBRIDGE, MA 02138; (800) 221–0814 OR (617) 876–0533. (M–E)

| | |
|---|---|
| YEARS IN BUSINESS: | 19 |
| AGE RANGE: | 20–70 |
| MOST COMMON AGE: | 30–50 |
| PERCENT ALONE: | 60 |
| NUMBER OF PARTICIPANTS: | TOTAL OF 2,000 PER YEAR; NO MORE THAN 16 PER TRIP |
| MALE FEMALE RATIO: | 46/54 |
| YEAR-ROUND; WILL TRY TO ARRANGE SHARES | |

Among the wide-ranging activities of this large outfitter specializing in "The Road Less Traveled" are camping trips on the plains of Africa and in Australia's outback, trekking through the Himalayas and the Andes, rafting on the Amazon, cruising the Galápagos Islands of Ecuador, hiking and camping in Hawaii, trekking Mount Fuji and visiting the country inns of Japan, and touring Turkey, Costa Rica, and Antarctica. Trips are labeled easy, moderate, or demanding; several trips come under the heading "Real affordable." Camping often means permanent camps with spacious, comfortable tents and good food. Many trips have attractive lodge, hotel, or inn accommodations.

---

COMMENTS *Female, 40s: I've been to Costa Rica and to Jordan with this company, and each time the trip was very well run. There were about twelve people in the group, probably 60/40 women to men on the first trip and 70/30 to Jordan. The trips seem to attract a lot of older women who like to travel both by themselves and with friends. There were a few singles on the trip; they were teamed with room-mates. The trips attract very nice, outgoing people. You're with a small group for a fairly long time, so it is easy to get to know everyone. OAT is a great way to do this kind of trip–the itineraries are fairly compli-cated, and they take care of everything for you.*

*Male, 40s: I've been to the Amazon and Galápagos. The trip was fairly demanding—a certain amount of walking and climbing, but not overly strenuous. We were informed of the type of physical activity before we left. The materials you receive beforehand are excellent—they really tell you what to expect in all aspects. It was an extremely diverse and interesting group—a woman from Alaska, a man who was the Canadian consul to Bolivia. It was mostly couples or friends, just two single women. The staff/tour leaders were top-notch—they really understood the people and culture of Peru. The food was excellent. They caught fresh fish for us each night on the boat. It's a great trip to take by yourself, but you have to be slightly adventurous.*

---

## HIMALAYAN TRAVEL, INC.

110 PROSPECT STREET, STAMFORD, CT 06901;
(800) 225-2380 OR (203) 359-3669. (I–M)

| | |
|---|---|
| YEARS IN BUSINESS: | 25 |
| AGE RANGE: | 25–70 |
| MOST COMMON AGE: | 40 |
| PERCENT ALONE: | 50 |
| NUMBER OF PARTICIPANTS: | 600 |
| MALE/FEMALE RATIO: | 50/50 |
| TRIPS YEAR-ROUND | |

As the name suggests, Nepal is the prime focus of this group, but they also offer trekking, wildlife safaris, river rafting, Galápagos cruises, and overland expeditions to South America, Turkey, Morocco, Greece, the Alps, and throughout Asia, including India, Tibet, Myanmar (Burma), Thailand, Cambodia, Vietnam, and Indonesia. Many of the Nepal trips can be combined with extensions to other Asian countries.

All trips, including Nepal treks, are graded A to E for difficulty. "A" trips are generally sight-seeing with no sustained walking and with hotel or lodge accommodations. "B" trips, which involve four to six hours daily of trekking, are said to be within the ability of any "weekend athlete."

**COMMENTS** *Female, 30s: The program is excellent, the equipment they provide is great—a down jacket, sleeping bag, water bottle, pack—everything. The food was delicious. We were up at dawn and trekked all day. You could go at your own pace and didn't have to keep up with anyone. If we were in a town, we stayed in guest houses; if not, we camped. It's very cold at night in Nepal! After dinner we sat around and really talked.*

*The group got along very well. The age range was 28 to 66; the majority in their 30s to 40s. Two of us were from the U.S.; the rest were from England. Two guys came together; all others were by themselves; 50/50 male/female. I'd recommend this for anyone who is a little adventurous. If you need to take a shower every day, it's not for you.*
*Male, 40s: I've gone to Nepal twice, alone and with a friend. Neither trip had many Americans. Most were Australian and British, ranging in age from 30s to 50s. On the first trip there was one couple; all the rest had come alone. On the second, there were four couples out of fourteen people. The food was terrific on one trip, terrible on the other. In both groups there were interesting, mature people who became close before the trips were over. The only way to see these views is to walk, so people are willing to put up with a certain degree of discomfort to do it. If you like to hike and rough it a bit, and like mountain scenery, it's for you.*

## MOUNTAIN TRAVEL– SOBEK EXPEDITIONS, INC.

6420 FAIRMONT AVENUE, EL CERRITO, CA 94530; (415) 527-8100 OR (800) 227-2384. (M-E)

| | |
|---|---|
| YEARS IN BUSINESS: | 24 |
| AGE RANGE: | 30–50 |
| MOST COMMON AGE: | 35–45 |
| PERCENT ALONE: | 60 |
| NUMBER OF PARTICIPANTS: | 3,000 ANNUALLY; SMALL INDIVIDUAL GROUPS |
| MALE/FEMALE RATIO: | 60/40 |
| YEAR-ROUND | |

The whole world is the territory for these adventure specialists, a merger between two of the oldest and largest outdoor trip operators. Trekking, hiking, rafting, biking, climbing, skiing—they cover all the adventure categories, plus cultural tours to exotic locales for the less athletic and luxury hiking in France and Italy for those who don't like roughing it. Trips are listed in five categories from easy to strenuous and range from climbing Mount Everest to canoeing in New Guinea to taking African safaris by van. In addition to the comment below, this group seems to get uniformly high marks from past participants.

COMMENTS *Female, 30s: I went on a rafting trip alone, but I never felt alone. The people were ages 20 to 60, half single, twice as many men, and a very interesting group. The food was great, and the leaders even brought hot coffee to each tent in the morning. We all got along and had a great time. The scenery was spectacular, and the instruction was also great. You could do as much or as little paddling as you wanted.*

## ALASKA WILDLAND ADVENTURE

P.O. Box 259, Trout Lake, WA 98650; (800) 334–8730 or (509) 395–2611. (E-EE)

June to September; some offerings in March, April, and October and special winter safaris in February and March; will try to arrange shares; very small single supplement.

| | |
|---|---|
| Years in business: | 20 |
| Age range: | 8–80 |
| Most common age: | around 40 |
| Percent alone: | 40 |
| Number of participants: | 16 per trip |
| Male/female ratio: | 35/65 |

This group offers seven- to twelve-day adventures called safaris, including hiking, rafting, camping, boat trips, natural history, cruises, and sportfishing, all in the national parks and refuges of the great Alaskan wilderness. Part of the thrill is close-up views of wildlife such as bald eagles, moose, brown bears, caribou, puffins, and seals. Trips are led by trained guide/naturalists. The operator maintains comfortable backcountry lodges and cabins exclusively for participants on these tours. The itinerary also includes some camping options for the more adventurous. In winter, safaris travel on cross-country skis and snowshoes or via dogsled.

COMMENTS *Female, 60s: Fantastic! I've never been on a better trip. The guides and food were wonderful; there was something new and different to do every day. Most people were in their 40s and 50s, but the range was to 75. There were more women than men, more single than married, brought together by their spirit of adventure. Days were well organized, but there was no regimentation.*

# More Sources for Adventure Travel

- Adventure Center (1311 63rd Street, Suite 200, Emeryville, CA 94608; 510–654–1879 or 800–227–8747) is an agency representing a number of outfitters offering small-group trips in various categories.
- Wilderness Travel (801 Allston Way, Berkeley, CA 04710; 510–548–0420 or 800–368–2794) publishes a big color catalog listing this organization's 100-plus trips on six continents, from wildlife safaris in Africa to sea kayaking in Fiji to cultural journeys through Japan. Specialty trips, varying from year to year, may focus on special events such as an eclipse, visit archaeologists at work, or concentrate on photography.
- An Outfitters Directory and Vacation Guide *is sold by* America Outdoors, P.O. Box 1348, Knoxville, TN 37901; (423) 524–4814. It includes information on more than 350 professional outfitters.

# Bicycle Tours

Bicycle touring offers an in-depth look at beautiful parts of the United States and the rest of the world with congenial company and plenty of time to explore off the beaten path. Tours are available for intermediate as well as for experienced riders, and all tour operators offer rental bikes, helmets, and other necessary equipment. The tour company maps out a choice of detailed bike routes of varying difficulty. Some bicycle tours camp overnight, but most are "inn-to-inn" with a different comfortable lodging destination each night. Depending on the pace and the choice of routes, you can vary your daily mileage. Everyone is together for breakfast and dinner. Many tours also offer the option of a lunch pool with everyone chipping in and sharing picnics assembled en route by the hosts. Or you may choose to try restaurants along the route. A van accompanies the tour, carrying all the luggage, equipment for repairs, and extra bikes for emergencies. Known as the "sag wagon," the van is also readily available if your legs are weary and you want a ride to the inn.

## BACKROADS BICYCLE TOURING

1516 FIFTH STREET, BERKELEY, CA 94710;
(510) 527–1555 OR (800) 462–2848. (I-M)

| | |
|---|---|
| YEARS IN BUSINESS: | 18 |
| AGE RANGE: | 25–65 |
| MOST COMMON AGE: | 30–50 |
| PERCENT ALONE: | 40 |
| NUMBER OF PARTICIPANTS: | 26 MAXIMUM PER TOUR |
| MALE/FEMALE RATIO: | 50/50 |
| YEAR-ROUND; WILL TRY TO ARRANGE SHARES; GUARANTEED SHARE RATES FOR RESERVATIONS SIXTY DAYS IN ADVANCE; TRIPS FOR SINGLES | |

Backroads tours explores both the Canadian and American West, the Canadian Rockies, California wine country, and national parks such as Yellowstone, Bryce Canyon, Zion, the Grand Canyon, and Mesa Verde. A host of other destinations include the Baja peninsula, Hawaii, the Shenandoah Valley of Virginia, Australia, New Zealand, China, Bali, Costa Rica, Turkey, Italy, Switzerland, Germany, the Netherlands, Norway, and the Loire Valley in France. Some are camping trips; some are cycling excursions from inn to inn; and some offer a choice of either. Tours vary greatly in their demands and are clearly labeled in the catalog for their difficulty. Beginners cycle two to five hours daily, advanced tours may cycle five to seven hours daily. Bikers can always choose to take it easy, enjoying the scenery and attractions and picnicking along the way. Trips range from five to seventeen days. Backroads also has a long roster of walking tours, and many trips combine hiking and biking. A number of trips are scheduled for singles. On some trips you can select the group size you prefer—an intimate group of ten to fourteen or as many as twenty to twenty-six.

For those who want to test their legs before setting out on a longer route, weekend inn-to-inn tours are available in California. Backroads also schedules winter cross-country skiing trips and is expanding its offerings to a variety of adventures, including a hike, bike and catamaran vacation in Ecuador and the Galápagos Islands.

COMMENTS *Female, 30s: I've done a number of their programs, sometimes alone, sometimes with friends. It is very easy to be alone as there are often more singles than couples. The people are from all over the world, with equal numbers of men and women from early 20s to 70. I've made many friends that I keep in touch with. The people are*

*highly educated and health-conscious. The best thing about the pro-
gram is the people who run it. They take care of everything, and you
get pampered. The food is amazing, and the hotels are luxury. It's
ideal for women alone because it is nonthreatening.*

*Male, 30s: I've taken eight tours. The average group is half singles. It
is easy to meet people, and you quickly become like a family. About
half the group is from California, the rest from all over the U.S. and
the rest of the world. It is an upscale crowd. There are several routes
to choose from each day, and you can bike as little or as much as you
want. The food is very good, and the accommodations are fine,
though not elegant.*

## BROOKS COUNTRY CYCLING TOURS

140 WEST 83D STREET, NEW YORK, NY 10024;
(212) 874-5151. (M)

| | |
|---|---|
| YEARS IN BUSINESS: | 12 |
| AGE RANGE: | OVER 30 |
| MOST COMMON AGE: | LATE 30S, 40 |
| PERCENT ALONE: | 75 |
| NUMBER OF PARTICIPANTS: | 22 |
| MALE/FEMALE RATIO: | 40/60 |
| SPRING THROUGH FALL; A FEW WINTER TRIPS TO FLORIDA.; WILL TRY TO ARRANGE SHARES | |

Reasonably priced trips from weekends to week-long journeys offers
some very appealing destinations. In
the U.S., you can tour Louisiana plan-
tations or Florida lake country, explore
North Carolina's Outer Banks or
pedal from Cape May to Chesapeake Bay. Weekend trips take in Cape
Cod, Vermont, the Maryland or Rhode Island shores, and Pennsylvania
Dutch country. European itineraries include biking and barging in
Holland, the Loire Valley, Brittany, Normandy, the Dordogne Valley,
and Provence. Comfortable inns are home base, and days are planned with
enough leisure time so that everyone can pedal at his or her own pace and
stop and sightsee along the way. Trips average 35 miles per day.

COMMENTS *Male, 40s: This is a first-class organization. I've taken
three international trips as well as domestic trips. There is a fairly
equal split between couples and singles, male and female. The people
are special, and I've made good friends. I would definitely recommended these trips.*

*Female, 30s: I've taken many trips with this company and highly rec-
ommend it. The accommodations in China were not luxurious, but*

*the trip was very exciting. The group is mostly ages 30 to 45 and is geared to singles who are expected to share rooms, although this is not compulsory. I've also done trips with Butterfield and Robinson of Toronto—more expensive and more couples.*

---

## VERMONT BICYCLE TOURING

Box 711, Bristol, VT 05443;
(802) 453-4811. (M)

| | |
|---|---|
| YEARS IN BUSINESS: | 26 |
| AGE RANGE: | 22–70 |
| MOST COMMON AGE: | 35-55 |
| PERCENT ALONE: | 50 |
| NUMBER OF PARTICIPANTS: | 6,000 ANNUALLY |
| MALE/FEMALE RATIO: | 45/55 |
| APRIL TO OCTOBER, A FEW MARCH AND NOVEMBER DATES; GUARANTEED SHARES | |

This outfitter was the originator of the inn-to-inn idea in Vermont, but they have expanded way beyond their home state to cover the U.S., eight European countries, and New Zealand. Along with the choicest New England sites, some forty trips cover the antebellum South in Mississippi, Virginia horse country, the Southwest, California, and two lovely Midwestern routes: Door County, Wisconsin, and the northern Michigan lake country, including Mackinac Island, where no cars are allowed. One of the most popular tours is through the quaint fishing villages of Nova Scotia in the Canadian Maritimes. European destinations include France, Switzerland, Italy, England, Ireland, Holland, Spain, and Austria. Trips are clearly identified as easy, moderate, or challenging. They range from weekends to seventeen days and can cover anywhere from 25 to 40 miles per day. Lodging is in country inns.

---

COMMENTS *Female, 30s: It was really easy to meet everyone on the trip. The staff tried to make sure everyone would get along and pointed out similar interests. The age range was from mid–20s to 70s, pretty even male/female, and a great group, really interesting. There were a few friends, one couple, and four or five singles on my trip, and everyone had a great time. It is very well run; the staff really made the trip. They helped everyone get to know each other, designed excellent routes, and were very nice people.*
*Female, 20s: I was very comfortable on a trip to New Zealand alone. There were only two or three married couples. The group ranged in age from 27 to late 50s and came from all over the U.S. We stayed in*

*hotels and always had dinner together. You could do what you wanted each day, pick your routes, and go at your own pace. It was a great trip.*

## BIKE VERMONT, INC.

P.O. Box 207, Woodstock, VT 05091;
(802) 457–3553 or (800) 257–2226. (M)

| | |
|---|---|
| YEARS IN BUSINESS: | 21 |
| AGE RANGE: | 18–65 |
| MOST COMMON AGE: | 30–50 |
| PERCENT ALONE: | 25–35 |
| NUMBER OF PARTICIPANTS: | 15–20 |
| MALE/FEMALE RATIO: | 1/2 |
| MAY TO OCTOBER; WILL TRY TO ARRANGE SHARES | |

This operation arranges inn-to-inn bicycle tours in the lovely Vermont countryside with a new destination every night. Vermont is hilly, but this company's weekend trips and five- and six-day tours are within the ability of beginning cyclists, and the support van is available when you need a rest. Average runs are 25 to 35 miles a day. This is "a nonthreatening, relaxing vacation," say the organizers. "We don't bike as a group, so everyone is going at his or her own pace. It is easy to make new friends."

COMMENTS *Male, 40s: I've taken several tours. There is good mix of singles and couples, plus children from about age 12. Backgrounds vary, but generally the adults are highly educated professionals. It is easy to make friends.*
*Female, 20s: I've done this for six years. When you share a sport, there's automatic camaraderie and all ages mix. You have breakfast together, then set out at your own pace, alone or with others. You meet people along the way, stop together for hot chocolate or a cold drink, and you make friends. I always come home with names and addresses, and often you plan to come back on another trip with these people.*

## BICYCLE ADVENTURES

P.O. Box 11219, Olympia, WA 98508;
(360) 786–0989 or (800) 443–6060. (M)

| | |
|---|---|
| YEARS IN BUSINESS: | 13 |
| AGE RANGE: | 20s to 60s |
| MOST COMMON AGE: | 30–40 |
| PERCENT ALONE: | 40–50 |
| NUMBER OF PARTICIPANTS: | 35–55 |
| MALE/FEMALE RATIO: | 40/60 |
| JUNE TO NOVEMBER; WINTER TRIPS TO HAWAII; NO SINGLE SUPPLEMENT | |

The glorious scenery of the Pacific Northwest is the territory for this outfitter. Their signature trip is an eight-day tour of Puget Sound, using ferries to cover five different islands and staying in delightful inns. Two-day stays on Orcas Island and Vancouver Island in Canada allow for extra sight-seeing. In Vancouver, there is the chance to visit world-famous Butchart Gardens and the city of Victoria. A six-day version of this trip is also available. Other popular destinations are the Olympic Peninsula, the Cascade Mountains, the Oregon coast and the Columbia River Gorge, British Columbia, California wine country, the California redwoods, and Hawaii. Beginner trips can range from 15 to 40 miles daily on easier terrain; intermediate trips cover 30 to 70 miles each day.

COMMENTS *Female, 30s: I would encourage anyone going solo to be adventurous and just do it. The weather, people, food, inns and scenery were all super. It was the best money I've ever spent on myself.*

*Male, 30s: This group is superb——the routes were well planned, the food and inns were wonderful, everything was done professionally. The group was small, one couple and the rest singles in their 30s, all successful professionals, more men than women. Everyone got along well. I've been on more expensive bicycle trips that were nowhere near as good. I also like going with a smaller specialized company; the groups are smaller, and they really know this area.*

## BUTTERFIELD & ROBINSON

70 BOND STREET, TORONTO, ONTARIO, CANADA M5B 1X3;
(416) 864–1354; IN U.S., (800) 387–1147.
(EE; INCLUDES AIR FROM U.S.)

| | |
|---|---|
| YEARS IN BUSINESS: | 31 |
| AGE RANGE: | 30–70 |
| MOST COMMON AGE: | 45–55 |
| PERCENT ALONE: | 30 |
| NUMBER OF PARTICIPANTS: | 18–24 PER SMALL GROUP; 5,000 ANNUALLY |
| MALE/FEMALE RATIO: | 40/60 |
| YEAR-ROUND; WILL TRY TO ARRANGE SHARES | |

This long-established company has a full roster of luxury biking tours through France, Italy, England, Ireland, Germany, Denmark, Austria/Hungary, Spain, and Portugal. All feature elegant country accommodations (usually two nights at each stop) and top restaurants, including some Michelin all-stars. There are stops for tasting at regional wineries as well. Routes are rated for difficulty, but cyclists should be able to ride at least three to four hours a day.

COMMENTS  *Female, 40s: This is expensive, but it's the best vacation I ever had and I am going again. About half the group was unattached, equal numbers of men and women, and everyone quickly formed a close-knit group. The couples usually split up at meals and ate with different people. Ages were 25 to 63, interesting folks from the U.S. and Canada. Days were flexible, at your own pace. They take very good care of you, and there are a lot of repeat customers. Female, 30s: I've been several times. There were a lot of people from the East Coast, more couples than singles, usually more women than men. Sometimes we met for activities like wine tasting; sometimes you cycled at your own pace all day. The lodging and food are tops, and most meals are eaten as a group. I'd recommend it to all singles as long as they don't go expecting to meet someone special.*

## INTERNATIONAL BICYCLE TOURS

P.O. Box 754, Essex, CT 06426;
(860) 767-7005. (M)

| | |
|---|---|
| YEARS IN BUSINESS: | 21 |
| AGE RANGE: | 7–85 |
| MOST COMMON AGE: | 50+ |
| PERCENT ALONE: | 50 |
| NUMBER OF PARTICIPANTS: | 23 MAXIMUM |
| MALE/FEMALE RATIO: | 1/2 |
| APRIL TO SEPTEMBER; WILL TRY TO ARRANGE SHARES | |

Older and novice cyclists are attracted to these leisurely excursions through scenic countryside in the U.S. and abroad. Trips begin at a gentle pace, then gradually increase in daily mileage as everyone becomes more comfortable with cycling. There are periodic stops to relax, share snacks, or take pictures. Destinations include Holland, Denmark, Austria, France, Ireland, and Bermuda. Closer to home, shorter trips are available to Cape Cod, Pennsylvania Dutch country, and along the Chesapeake and Ohio Canal.

COMMENTS  *Male, 70s: I've been on six international trips and four domestic. Every trip has been excellent. I always go alone; there are always a number of singles on the trip. They attract an older crowd— about half are over 50. The staff is fabulous; I've been with other companies and they're not even close. The routes and mileage varies by the trip. Unlike other companies that give you a map and you're on your own, you ride as a group so you can't get lost. You have a real sense of security. The trips are paced for someone who doesn't want anything too strenuous. The food is excellent, and the value can't be beat.*

*Female, 60s: I've been on a dozen trips with IBT, and I'm leaving again in a few weeks. I started out going alone, but I met people on the trips and now we plan to go together. There's always a number of people who go alone. The group is always very congenial and friendly—all very outgoing people. It's a well-run program. They have a unique system with a leader, a corner, and a sweep. The corner stops at an intersection and waves everyone along, and the sweep brings up the rear to make sure no one gets lost or left behind. There are usually a few more women than men, but it varies with the trip. The age range is really 30s to 70s, but I'm bringing my thirteen-year-old-granddaughter on the next trip. The mix of young and old makes it really interesting. You get to know everyone because you ride together all day and sit together for meals. These are great trips.*

---

## ROADS LESS TRAVELED

P.O. Box 8187, Longmont, CO 80501;
(303) 678-8750. (I-M)

| | |
|---|---|
| YEARS IN BUSINESS: | 8 |
| AGE RANGE: | 35-50 |
| MOST COMMON AGE: | 40 |
| PERCENT ALONE: | 35 |
| NUMBER OF PARTICIPANTS: | 14 MAXIMUM PER GROUP |
| MALE/FEMALE RATIO: | VARIES |
| MARCH TO OCTOBER; GUARANTEED SHARES | |

This company specializing in the Rockies and the Southwest offers special tours to Rocky Mountain National Park, Arizona, Colorado, Utah's magnificent canyon country, the Grand Canyon, New Mexico, and Wyoming's Grand Tetons, Yellowstone, and stunning glacier country. Many of the trips combine biking and hiking, and some offer rafting and horseback riding, as well. Lodgings alternate between picturesque village inns and remote backcountry cabins or camping. Breakfast and dinner are at inns or nearby restaurants; lunches and snacks are trailside picnics. Hiking trips can range from 6 to 10 miles a day; biking trips are graded for beginners and intermediates, and a shuttle is always available to see you through difficult stretches.

---

COMMENTS *Female, 30s: The leaders did an excellent job in providing me with the most enjoyable, stress-free, hassle-free wilderness/lux-*

# More Sources for Biking

*There are many other tour operators offering biking vacations.* Bicycle USA Tour Finder *(190 Ostend Street, Suite 120, Baltimore, MD 21230; 410–539–3399) is a comprehensive directory of more than 150 bicycle tour operators in the United States and abroad, published by the League of American Bicyclists.*

*ury trip I've ever had. Ten times better value than Club Med!*
*Male, 30s: I've never enjoyed a vacation so much in my life (and I've had some fun vacations!). It was a sort of life-altering experience . . . being in the quiet of the mountains, lying in the cool grass of a mountain meadow, listening to the laughter of friendships newly formed. It was a unique and wonderful experience.*

# Hiking / Walking

Walking trips with comfortable lodgings awaiting each night are a lovely way to linger through some of America's and Europe's most beautiful areas, far from tourist crowds. There are trips for every ability, from rugged mountain hiking to a relaxed pace in the gentle countryside. A van carries all the gear; walkers need only a light daypack for an extra sweater, a slicker, or snacks. These trips are increasingly popular, and many bicycle touring companies have added walking tours to their offerings.

## BUTTERFIELD & ROBINSON
(SEE PAGE 101)

This is a top-of-the-line organization for walking as well as biking tours with luxury accommodations and food. High recommendations are common from past participants. Each person goes at his own pace, and a van is posted at several points so that walks can be shortened if necessary. Areas covered continue to expand. Recent European walking destinations include the Cote d'Azur on the French Riviera, Burgundy, Tuscany, the Italian lakes, Portugal, and the Swiss Alps. Further explorations on foot take in Turkey, Israel and Jordan, Nepal, Kenya, South Africa, Chile, Argentina, Belize, and Bali. A very popular trip combining biking and walking goes into the Atlas mountains of Morocco. Reservationists try to steer solo walkers to trips where they will find company.

COMMENTS *Female, 50s: The Morocco trip was one of the most wonderful experiences I've ever had. They took us to places ordinary tours never get to. We camped out in the desert, rode camels, had fabulous experiences. My group happened to include a group of six married women who had come together, but my most compatible companions were couples. Everyone was friendly, and being alone was perfectly comfortable.*

## BACKROADS
(SEE PAGE 97 FOR ADDRESS AND TELEPHONE NUMBER)

Best known as one of the biggest operators of bicycle tours, Backroads has gone into walking in a big way, with year-round trips for all abilities in scenic locales as varied as the bicycling routes outlined earlier. Beginner routes cover 3 to 5 miles daily, averaging a gentle two to four hours of walking. Advanced hikers may cover 8 to 12 miles in a day, averaging five to six hours. Several itineraries have departures for singles only. Winter options include inn-to-inn cross-country ski excursions.

## THE WAYFARERS
172 BELLEVUE AVENUE, NEWPORT, RI 02840;
(800) 249–4620 OR (401) 849–5087. (E)

This British-based company has expanded their original English itineraries to cover Ireland, Scotland, Italy, France, and Switzerland, always choosing fine country inns as lodgings. Their interesting trips include a gar-den tour of Dorset, the hills of Tuscany, and for

| | |
|---|---|
| YEARS IN BUSINESS: 15 | |
| AGE RANGE: 26–72 | |
| MOST COMMON AGE: 50 | |
| PERCENT ALONE: 20 | |
| NUMBER OF PARTICIPANTS: 15 MAXIMUM | |
| MALE/FEMALE RATIO: 40/60 | |

hardy walkers, a coast-to-coast route across England. They are the only group offering walks in the Aran Islands of Ireland. An average day's walk covers 10 miles with stops for lunch and morning and afternoon coffee or tea breaks. The van is always close by for those who tire or want to take a day off. The group eats all meals together, allowing plenty of time for so-cializing. The company reports a large number of repeat travelers.

COMMENTS *Female, 50s: I've tried other groups, but I keep coming back to this one because the trips are so well put together and you get so much for your money. Everything is excellent—the leaders, the itineraries, the places we stayed. They are very flexible and go out of their way to see that every single person has a good time. There are mostly couples and single women, not very many single men, but very comfortable for all. I've made friends from Australia and England and planned future trips with people I've walked with in the past. It's a very good choice for singles and the very best way to see a country.*

## FRED JACOBSON ALPINE TRAILS, LTD.
C/O CHAPPAQUA TRAVEL, INC.,
1 SOUTH GREELEY AVENUE, CHAPPAQUA, NY 10514;
(800) 666–5161 OR (914) 238–5151. (M–E)

Hiking June to November; cross-country skiing January to March; will try to arrange shares

Fred Jacobson, the pioneer of orga-nized hiking for Americans in the Swiss Alps, personally leads scenic ten- and fif-

| | |
|---|---|
| YEARS IN BUSINESS: | 24 |
| AGE RANGE: | 30–70 |
| MOST COMMON AGE: | 40–60 |
| PERCENT ALONE: | 30–50 |
| NUMBER OF PARTICIPANTS: | MAXIMUM 20 PER GROUP |
| MALE/FEMALE RATIO: | 40/60 |

teen-day hiking trips with accommodations in charming, comfortable vil-lage inns along the way. Two guided hikes are offered each day—one moderate, one fairly strenuous—but these are definitely hikes, not strolls. The trips have been singled out by many publications as superior; more than half of the participants are repeaters and their friends.  In winter, Jacobson offers cross-country skiing and downhill skiing in the Alps. These are highly personalized trips led by real professionals. Registration is limited.

COMMENTS  *Male, 40s: The program is not very structured—you can be with the group or do your own thing. The people are congenial, outdoorsy, mostly good hikers, ages 45 to 60, and reasonably affluent, with a few more females than males. The majority are married, but there are enough singles to make you feel comfortable in the group. The program is tops, the food and accommodations are outstanding, and there's always something to do. Everyone had a good time.*
*Female, 40s: This is not a typical tour. You hike most of the day, have a chance to do your own thing. The ages range from 20 to 60. The people were terrific. Food and accommodations were wonderful.*

## COUNTRY WALKERS

P.O. Box 180, Waterbury, VT 05676;
(800) 464–9255.
(I–M; includes breakfast and dinner)

| | |
|---|---|
| Years in business: | 19 |
| Age range: | 30s–70s |
| Most common age: | 40–60 |
| Percent alone: | 60 |
| Male/female ratio: | 1/2 |
| Number of participants: | average 14 |
| | per group |
| Year-round; will try to arrange shares; share rate guaranteed on bookings made ninety days in advance | |

The coast of Maine, the valleys of Vermont, Nova Scotia, the Arizona desert, beautiful areas in England, Ireland, Italy, and Spain, and exquisite scenery in Chile, Peru, Costa Rica, and Mexico make up the nearly thirty far-flung itineraries this company covers on foot. Tours focus on the natural history and culture of the area and are led by knowledgeable local guides. Lodgings are first class throughout. Hiking options range from 4 to 12 miles a day, and there is always the option to stroll a few miles to a local village, enjoy a cafe lunch, and relax for the afternoon. Everyone gathers for dinner.

COMMENTS  *Male, 50s: I've been to Peru and Chile, alone both times. There were nine people on the last trip—two couples, two sin-*

*gle women traveling together, and three people traveling alone. I was
very impressed with how they ran both programs. The staff that traveled with us and the local guides were excellent and very knowledgeable. They were also there to help if you need a "leg up." We had no
problems because everything was so well planned. The people were
from all over the U.S., and all had traveled fairly extensively so we
had experiences to share and there was never a struggle for conversation. People got along really well and were very helpful to each other.
The room and food was fine. The Peruvian food was interesting—including eating guinea pig! The commonality of interests—liking the
outdoors, traveling, and being active—brought the group together.*

---

## HIKING HOLIDAYS

P.O. Box 711, Bristol, VT 05443;
(802) 453–4816 or (800) 537–3850.
Affiliated with Vermont Bicycle Touring (see page 99)
Year-round; guaranteed shares

Affiliated with Vermont Bicycle Touring, this group offers a variety
of tours from four to eight days. Typical U.S. itineraries include
Vermont, Maine, the Berkshire Mountains of Massachusetts, Virginia's
Shenandoah National Park, the Blue Ridge Mountains in North
Carolina, southeast Arizona, and New Mexico. International tours have
taken in Provence, the Alps, the Cotswolds, and the west coast of Ireland.
Lodging is always deluxe, whether in country inns, ranches, small hotels,
or national park lodges. The average group is fourteen to sixteen people.

# Sailing

Take to the sea for a windswept adventure like no other, with lazy
days of snorkeling and swimming in solitary coves, convivial shipboard fun at night, and stops in picturesque ports where the big ships
can't follow.

## WINDJAMMER BAREFOOT CRUISES

1759 BAY ROAD, MIAMI BEACH, FL 33139;
(800) 327-2601 OR (800) 432-3364 IN FLORIDA. (M)

| | |
|---|---|
| YEARS IN BUSINESS: | 41 |
| AGE RANGE: | 25–55 |
| MOST COMMON AGE: | 30–40 |
| PERCENT ALONE: | 60 |
| NUMBER OF PARTICIPANTS: | 66–122 |
| MALE/FEMALE RATIO: | VARIES; ABOUT EQUAL |
| YEAR-ROUND; WILL TRY TO ARRANGE SHARES | |

"The thought of a tall-ship cruise to a remote island turns people on," says the captain and founder of this Caribbean fleet that offers sailing vacations on five classic sailing ships. The fleet is based in Tortola, St. Martin, Antigua, Grenada, and Cozumel, Mexico, on its various itineraries, and each week it visits more than fifty islands on six- and thirteen-day outings. This is not a luxury cruise but a chance to experience the exhilaration of sailing and to get to small, isolated islands. The cabins are small, but they are air-conditioned and have private toilets and showers. Meals are served buffet style on ship or on picnics ashore. Dress is always informal, and entertainment can be wacky—toga parties, crab races, steel-drum bands on board.

COMMENTS *Female, 30s: I took this trip with my twelve-year-old son—it is great for both singles and single parents. About half the adults were single, ranging in age from 20s to 50s and 60s, a few more women than men. We were from many parts of the country with very different backgrounds, but everyone had a wonderful time. The food was fantastic, the cabins comfortable and air-conditioned. We sailed mostly at night and spent days on the islands. The crew is great and tells you the ins and outs of each new port. At night there was always an activity. I made a lot of friends—and I can't wait to go on another trip. It's the best vacation I've ever had.*

*Male, 40s: I'm getting ready for my third trip. I've gone with friends and once by myself and I always had a fantastic time. You can let your hair down and relax. There's no pretense, you wear a T-shirt and shorts even for dinner. Everyone is friendly and outgoing, so it's easy to find a group of people you enjoy and go off in port together. The ages were from 20 to 70, but most are 30 or 40, and the 70s are very young at heart. Everyone has fun. You can be alone if you want to, but it's hard not to meet people. The food is very good, but not gourmet. There's only a choice of two entrees at dinner—this is not a luxury liner. But the staff is great and the captain is really accessible. One night he gave an impromptu stargazing class on deck. The itinerary is very special—you meet the local people and see places you can't on a big ship.*

## MAINE WINDJAMMER ASSOCIATION

P.O. Box 1144P, Blue Hill, ME 04614;
(207) 374-2955 or (800) 807-WIND. (I)

| | |
|---|---|
| Years in business: | 60 + |
| Age range: | 16–80 |
| Most common age: | 20–40 |
| Percent alone: | 25–30 |
| Number of participants: | 20–37 |
| Male/female ratio: | Varies, fairly equal |
| June to September | |

This fleet of ten nostalgic nineteenth-century two-masted "tall ships" sets sail each summer from Camden, Rockland, or Rockport for Penobscot Bay to explore the evergreen coast and the islands of Maine and to rest in quiet anchorages of unblemished beauty. Ships range from 64 to 112 feet; there are single cabins, or singles may share. The rates are a real bargain. Passengers can help with the halyards and lines, keep a lookout for seals and ospreys, watch the lobstermen setting out traps, or just lie back and soak up the sun. Family-style meals featuring New England chowder, "Down East" lobster bakes, and Maine blueberry pie are not the least of the attractions!

COMMENTS *Male, 30s: I've been twice, and it was great. I was looking for something I could do without pressure to find a partner, and this was it. There were a few other singles, but it hardly mattered because with such a small group sharing meals and bath facilities, it was informal and comfortable for everyone. The sailing was terrific, and the food was fantastic.*
*Female, 40s: I really enjoyed it and am thinking of going again. There were people from age 30 to one man in his 70s, and nine out of twenty-three of us were single. Everyone got along and enjoyed each other's company.*

## ECHO: THE WILDERNESS CO, INC.

6529 Telegraph Avenue, Oakland, CA 94609;
(510) 652-1600 or (800) 652-ECHO. (EE)
Singles are paired in cabins

B est known for rafting trips, (see page 112) ECHO also runs intimate sailing adventures to the Galápagos Islands and to Turkey.

Two two-week Turkish trips are aboard a sailing yacht with only eight to eleven guests plus a Turkish guide. One covers the Turquoise Coast and Anatolia, the other the Aegean Sea; both include exotic historical and archaeological sites and a visit to Istanbul. The Galápagos Adventure is an eleven-day outing that can be extended with an excursion into the Ecuadorian Highlands (see more about the Galápagos on page 130). If you are willing to share a cabin, these are grand excursions.

..................................................................

# Rafting

W hat's so great about running a river? Those who love it call it "River Magic." One longtime operator says he has found that the cooperation required to meet the challenge of the river facilitates relationships, opens lines of communication, enhances personal growth, and helps participants develop lasting friendships more than any other form of outdoor recreation he has ever experienced—which may explain why so many river trips are available and why so many people sign up for them. Maybe Mark Twain said it best "You feel mighty free and easy and comfortable on a raft."

## SHERI GRIFFITH EXPEDITIONS

P.O. Box 1324, 2231 South Highway 191, Moab, UT 84532; (800) 332-2439 or (801) 259-8229. (L-M)

| | |
|---|---|
| YEARS IN BUSINESS: | 21 |
| AGE RANGE: | 23–60 |
| MOST COMMON AGE: | 25–40 |
| PERCENT ALONE: | 50 |
| NUMBER OF PARTICIPANTS: | 25 |
| MALE/FEMALE RATIO: | 50/50 |
| MAY TO SEPTEMBER | |

T his operator boasts of "Outdoor Adventures with a Touch of Class," priding herself on service of top food on five- to seven-day river-running adventures and canoe trips on the Greene, Colorado, and Dolores rivers. There are runs for beginners to experts, plus some interesting specialty trips, such as "Expedition in Luxury," a luxurious outing in Canyonlands National Park. One river trip is combined with mountain biking on land.

**C O M M E N T S**   *Male, 30s: To a man, every person on the trip would have jumped at the chance to go again ... tomorrow, if not sooner. Female, 30s: A well-organized, smooth-running operation with a courteous, knowledgeable, and fun staff. Their ability in the kitchen was unmatched. The trip was a bargain.*

## ECHO: THE WILDERNESS CO, INC.

6529 TELEGRAPH AVENUE, OAKLAND, CA 94609;
(510) 652-1600 OR (800) 652-ECHO. (M)

| | |
|---|---|
| YEARS IN BUSINESS: | 27 |
| AGE RANGE: | 7–70 |
| MOST COMMON AGE: | 30s – 50s |
| PERCENT ALONE: | VARIES |
| NUMBER OF PARTICIPANTS: | 3,000 PER YEAR |
| MALE/FEMALE RATIO: | 50/50 |
| LATE MAY TO MID-SEPTEMBER | |

River-rafting excitement with this group includes special outings with entertainment such as wine tasting, music, and yoga workshops. U.S. rafting trips are held on the Middle Fork and Main Salmon River in Idaho, the Rogue River in Oregon, and the South Fork of the American and Tuolumne rivers in California.

**C O M M E N T S**   *Female, 20s: I've gone alone twice and been very comfortable. I was really impressed because I went with a very large group and they handled it beautifully. They were very sensitive about pairing the guides with the different groups of people and skill levels. The guides are very congenial. They have lots of games and other things in the evening so everyone gets to know each other, and you have to work together in the boats. There is a comfortable mix of men and women (a few more women), and an age range of 15 to 65. The groups are diverse and interesting, and there are plenty of single people. Female, 40s: I've been going on Echo's trips for fifteen years; I think they are the premier rafting company. I admit that if you go alone you have to be more outgoing—a lot of people do come as a group of friends, and you don't want to intrude. But there are usually one or two singles on each trip and the leaders organize group activities like nature walks and soaking in hot tubs so everyone gets involved. I would definitely recommend these trips to solo travelers. It's a great way to meet people, and I've formed lasting friendships. In fact, I'm planning my next trip with some people I met on an Echo trip.*

## OUTDOOR ADVENTURE RIVER SPECIALISTS (O.A.R.S.) INC.

P.O. Box 67, Angels Camp, CA 95222;
(209) 736–4677 or (800) 346–6277.

| | |
|---|---|
| Years in business: | 26 |
| Age range: | 18–54+ |
| Most common age: | 25–45 |
| Percent alone: | 25 |
| Number of participants: | 16–25 |
| Male/female ratio: | 50/50 |
| May to September; will try to arrange shares | |

With this outfitter you can camp under the stars if sleeping bags are your bag or have the thrill of rafting and the comfort of bed-and-breakfast inn lodgings at night. Choose the challenge of Class V rapids or gentler trips with an "oar" option, meaning the guide does all the paddling while guests sit back and enjoy the ride. O.A.R.S. offers a wide variety of two- to twelve-day outings on the American, Salmon, Kern, Klamath, and Tuolumne Rivers in California; the Rogue River in Oregon; the Salmon and Snake Rivers in Idaho; the Green, San Juan, and Yampa Rivers in Utah; and the Snake River in Wyoming. The catalog ranks each trip for the difficulty of the rapids and describes the scenery.

COMMENTS *Female, 30s: I've gone on two trips alone. You can have time to yourself if you want it, but you never have to be alone. My groups ranged from ages 20 to mid-60s; about half were single and two-thirds were male, and they were from all over the country. The people were great, very congenial. You switch boats each day so you get to meet everyone. The food was terrific and we slept under the stars. If you have a spirit of adventure, this is a great experience.*

*Male, 30s: I've gone on five trips, alone and with my wife. Many of the people are married but come alone. We were up at sunrise, did everything from running rapids to hiking. You get to know everyone as you switch boats. You can do as much or as little work as you want. There is good food and lots of it. It's a good introduction to rafting—easy, relaxed, and everyone can do it.*

## DVORAK'S KAYAK & RAFTING EXPEDITIONS

17921-B U.S. 285, Nathrop, CO 81236;
(800) 824–3795 or (719) 539–6851. (I)

Dvorak's was the first licensed operator on the Colorado River. It has grown to offer trips through scenic canyons on ten U.S. rivers and on rivers in Mexico, Australia, and New Zealand. Among the states covered are Arkansas, Colorado, Utah, New Mexico, Wyoming, and Texas, where rivers used include the Salt, Dolores, Colorado, and

| | |
|---|---|
| YEARS IN BUSINESS: | 28 |
| AGE RANGE: | 25–35 |
| MOST COMMON AGE: | 25–35 |
| PERCENT ALONE: | 60 |
| NUMBER OF PARTICIPANTS: | 2,000+ ANNUALLY; |
| | 12 TO 25 PER TRIP |
| MALE/FEMALE RATIO: | 50/50 |
| LATE MAY TO SEPTEMBER | |

Arkansas. One special trip is the Classical Music River Journey where symphony and Philharmonic artists perform with alpine forests and sandstone canyons as a backdrop.

COMMENTS *Female, 30s: A wonderful experience, the finest thing I've ever done. There were seven of us, all single, age 30s to 50s, about equal numbers of men and women. We stayed in tents, had wonderful, healthful food. The instruction was great—but even less-physical people can enjoy this trip, as you don't have to paddle if you don't want to. Female, 30s: This was a great thing to do. I went with my ten-year-old son, and although he was the only child, it was no problem—the guides took care of him and were wonderful helping him fish when we hit calm water. We slept in tents, had great food. There was just one couple—from New Zealand—the rest were future guides on their first trip.*

## NANTAHALA OUTDOOR CENTER ADVENTURE TRAVEL
U.S. 19 WEST, BOX 41, BRYSON CITY, NC 28713;
(704) 488–2175. (I–M)

This top Eastern teaching center (see page 36) also offers a variety of guided white-water and sea kayaking adventures. Rafting locales include not only North Carolina, the southern Appalachians, and Texas but exotic destinations such as Costa Rica, Honduras, Corsica, Chile, Mexico, and Nepal. Offerings include a three-day weekend for singles in North Carolina.

For more outfitters, *Western River Guides Association Outfitters Directory* (7600 East Arapahoe Road, Suite 114, Englewood, CO 80112; 303-771–0389) offers a comprehensive listing of river-raft expeditions in the western United States.

# Nepal: The Supreme Adventure

There are many mighty mountains in the world, but the trip to the Himalayas is unique. Since it remains on my dream list, I asked Ben Wallace, who helps organize trips for Himalayan Travel (see page 00) {x-ref} and who has visited 609 countries and lived in Nepal for three years, to explain why this experience is so remarkable.

The lure of Nepal is the people as much as the mountains, he says. What makes this different from other mountain treks or climbs is that the trails you follow are the only roads in this remote region, the lifeline of the villagers who live here. Every day you pass through two to six villages, seeing intimately a fascinating and totally different way of life. You can linger, visit homes, and observe how people live, cook, farm, and work. Staying in local homes is an option. Most people come to Nepal thinking the thrill is going to be the big mountains and the view, but find instead it is the local life that is the indelible memory, the cultural rather than the physical experience that is the highlight.

Ben says that most people once were drawn to Nepal for the physical challenge, but that a higher percentage today are looking for something else, a total change from their life-style and environment. The least strenuous treks usually mean four to eight days on the trail, walking four to six hours a day, with a maximum ascent of about 1,500 feet—within the ability of anyone who does any exercising at home.

Trekking can be mindless, he says, in that all you need to do is put one foot in front of the other. Everything is taken care of for you. Someone else puts up and takes down the camp, carries all gear, does all the cooking and cleaning up. You are free to simply soak in the experience. Many people today sign up for the shorter one-week treks, then spend another week sight-seeing or rafting. Ben believes, however, that the longer trips deeper into the mountains are the most rewarding. Those who take the shorter trips enjoy the country but seldom come back. People who spend the time to really immerse themselves in the culture are hooked—they almost always return.

How much stamina does the trip take? Ben explains that the degree of difficulty has three components: the duration of time on the trail, how much altitude is gained or lost, and the living conditions. "Someone who is very fit but not used to living in a tent—a jogger for example—may be able to stand up to the physical challenge but not be happy about spending three weeks in a tent.

"Altitude affects people differently—and the same people differently on different days. Above ten or eleven thousand feet, almost everyone feels discomfort, perhaps headaches. A good operator knows this and allows plenty of time for acclimatization. A serious problem is extremely

# More
# Adventuring
# Ideas

- Specialty Travel Index (305 San Anselmo Avenue, San Anselmo, CA 94960; 415–459–4900) is a quarterly listing of ads from more than 400 operators of adventure and specialty trips of all kinds. It is the source used by many travel agents. Sample index listings: Elephant Ride, Environmental Education, Equestrian Tours, Festival Tours, Film History, Fishing, Foliage Tours, Windjamming, Windsurfing, Winery Tours, Women's Tours. An annual subscription is $10.
- Adventure Center (1311 63rd Street, Suite 20, Emeryville, CA 94608; 510–654–1879 or 800–227–8747) is an agency specializing in adventure travel, offering more than 1,000 annual departures to nearly 100 countries.
- All Adventure Vacations (5589 Arapahoe #208, Boulder, CO 80303; 800–537–4025) is another agency advertising more than 1,000 vacations with carefully selected outfitters.

rare. And there is plenty of time. How fast you walk is up to you. The idea definitely is not to get there in the fastest time, but to appreciate both the culture and the scenery around you. Even the faster walkers seldom hurry to camp. They take side trips or just take more time to enjoy their surroundings."

The food on a trek is a pleasant surprise. A sample menu might include onion soup topped with melted yak cheese, sweet and sour chicken over vegetable fried rice, and cake baked over the campfire. As in any third world country, there may be an occasional stomach bug to contend with. All treks include a medical kit and someone who knows how to use it.

When to come? The trekking season is from late September to May.

# Get Back to *Nature*

**Y**ou don't have to hike or raft your way into the wilderness in order to enjoy the outdoors. Nature-oriented workshops are available in beautiful and remote settings, and there are wonderful tours and cruises geared to appreciating places where plant, animal, and bird life are abundant.

Many nature-oriented tour operators also offer "soft adventures," such as expedition cruises and safaris to remote places that require no camping or strenuous activity. The choice is rich, from watching penguins and polar bears in Antarctica to viewing moose and elk in Wyoming, from seeing brilliantly colored birds in the jungle to close encounters with giraffes and lions on the African plains.

Vacations that emphasize nature these days often come with a catchy label—"ecotourism." Ecotourism at its best means simply respecting nature. Many operators talk about ecotourism, but do not practice it. Careless, commercial tour operators can drive animals from their habitats and destroy the natural wonders that have drawn visitors. If you choose a vacation emphasizing nature, by all means chose responsible operators and organizations who practice and promote conservation.

## Nature Workshops

**T**he nicest thing about nature-oriented workshops is their magnificent settings, where recreation is as appealing as the learning opportunities. These programs aim not only to teach about nature but to inspire appreciation that will carry over into support for conservation when you return home. In that endeavor, the operators often include painting, photography, and writing workshops along with bird and nature walks.

## AUDUBON ECOLOGY CAMPS AND WORKSHOP

NATIONAL AUDUBON SOCIETY,
613 RIVERSVILLE ROAD, GREENWICH, CT 06831;
(203) 869-2017. (I)

| | |
|---|---|
| YEARS IN BUSINESS: | 50+ |
| AGE RANGE: | 18–80 |
| MOST COMMON AGE: | 30s–40s |
| PERCENT ALONE: | HIGH |
| NUMBER OF PARTICIPANTS: | 55 MAXIMUM, DIVIDED INTO SMALLER FIELD GROUPS |
| MALE/FEMALE RATIO: | 40/60 |
| JULY AND EARLY AUGUST | |

Adults from across the country come to the one- and two-week summer sessions held in the society's sanctuaries in Connecticut, off the coast of Maine, and in the Wind River Range of Wyoming.

In these beautiful outdoor settings, adults come to learn, relax, and forge new friendships. Special programs focus on field ecology and birding. The aim is to reintroduce you to nature, to show how all wildlife is interdependent, and to teach what you can do to protect it. Rustic lodgings are mostly dorm style; meals are buffet. Participants are all ages and backgrounds, from college students and retired senior citizens to teachers and firefighters.

COMMENTS   *Female, 30s: A typical day means getting up for an early breakfast and then walking from about 8:30 to 11:30 A.M. with a naturalist who is usually a teacher. The leaders are excellent and really know their stuff. There's time to rest or relax before and after lunch, then there is another program from 2:00 to 5:00 P.M. Depending on the weather and the topic, you might go out by boat instead of on foot. The idea is always hands-on learning. If it rains, classroom talks are held. At night there might be a guest lecturer, square dancing, a slide show, or an evening astronomy walk. The big group is divided into four small groups, and you stay with that group every day for programs, so there's plenty of chance to get to know people. Everyone has an interest in nature, and it's really nice to share that with others. There's a lot of bonding within the group.*

## NATIONAL WILDLIFE FEDERATION CONSERVATION SUMMIT PROGRAM

8925 LEESBURG PIKE, VIENNA, VA 22184;
(703) 790-4363. (I)

Conservation Summits offer a week of nature education and recreation in beautiful locations that rotate annually. The cost is moderate, and the program is excellent. Depending on the site, activities might include boat excursions to observe whales and sea lions, mountain hikes, or a

| | |
|---|---|
| YEARS IN BUSINESS: | 27 |
| AGE RANGE: | INFANTS TO 70S |
| MOST COMMON AGE: | 30–50 |
| PERCENT ALONE: | 33 |
| NUMBER OF PARTICIPANTS: | 800 ANNUALLY |
| MALE/FEMALE RATIO: | VARIES |
| JUNE AND JULY; WILL TRY TO ARRANGE SHARES | |

field trip to a glacier. Nature hikes and outdoor photography are usually featured in all programs, and participants may learn about orienteering, bird watching, geology, and astronomy. Activities are planned to suit all levels of fitness. Lodgings options can vary from rustic lodges to apartment-style suites. All programs serve meals in a central location, either cafeteria or family style. The ambience is relaxed and friendly. Recent sites have included Estes Park, Colorado; Seward, Alaska; and the Adirondack Mountains of New York.

COMMENTS *Female, 40s: The age range is literally infants to senior citizens. You're up early. There are lectures and field trips, yet also plenty of free time. The hiking isn't too strenuous, so anyone can do it. After dinner, there are slide presentations, music, stargazing, or evening wildlife viewing field trips. Accommodations and food vary from fair to excellent depending on location, but the lodgings are always clean and adequate.*

*Female, 50s: Summits have been the reason that I've seen most of the United States . . . and also a way to make lasting friendships. I still keep in touch with and visit friends I met at my first Summit fifteen years ago. But most of all, Summits instill in us a love for the earth and each other.*

## THE NATURE CONSERVANCY

1815 NORTH LYNN STREET, ARLINGTON, VA 22209;
(703) 841–5300; PINE BUTTE INFORMATION,
(406) 466–2158. (I)
APRIL TO SEPTEMBER

Another highly respected conservation group, the Nature Conservancy offers weekend and week-long field trips in several scenic locations. Changing activities are set up by local field offices from New York's Adirondack Mountains to the Nebraska sandhills to the coast of Oregon. Other programs take place at permanent Conservancy properties such as Homestead at Hart Prairie in Arizona, where participants are housed in historic cabins beneath the San Francisco Mountains for explorations of peaks and canyons and a chance to work with ecologists on plant surveys or to watch for Arizona's jewel-hued hummingbirds.

Natural History workshops are held at the Pine Butte Guest Ranch in Montana, with lodgings in cozy private cabins at the foot of the Rockies. Home-cooked meals are served in the rustic lodge. There are planned programs for some weeks on topics such as Indians in Life and Legend, Montana Grizzly Bears, Nature Photography, Mammal Tracking, or Naturalist Tours of the Rockies, with daily treks into Montana mountains and prairies. This is also a wonderful spot just for the serenity and the chance to hike mountain trails, observe wildlife, or read a good book beside the heated pool. The Tensleep Preserve also offers weeks of family adventures and birding in the Bighorns.

For international "tours" sponsored by the Nature Conservancy, see pages 129.

## FOUR CORNERS SCHOOL OF OUTDOOR EDUCATION

P.O. Box 1029, Monticello, UT 84535;
(801) 587–2156. (I–M)

This exceptional program offers a variety of backcountry explorations in the beautiful Southwest that includes the chance to learn about archaeology or rock art, to dig for dinosaurs, to track peregrine falcons and bald eagles, to study plants with an herbalist, or to learn

| | |
|---|---|
| YEARS IN BUSINESS: | 13 |
| AGE RANGE: | 30–65 |
| MOST COMMON AGE: | 40–50 |
| PERCENT ALONE: | 50 |
| NUMBER OF PARTICIPANTS: | 375 PER YEAR, DIVIDED INTO SMALL GROUPS |
| MALE/FEMALE RATIO: | 40/60 |
| APRIL TO OCTOBER, PLUS SPECIAL WINTER NATIONAL PARK PROGRAMS FROM MID-JANUARY TO MID-MARCH; GUARANTEED SHARES | |

Navajo weaving. Some programs include moderate hiking, backpacking, or rafting. Special workshops concentrate on photography and writing. Lodging varies with the program; camping, motels, ranch accommodations, and houseboating on Lake Powell are among the possibilities.

COMMENTS *Female, 40s: I've been on seven trips with them by myself. They're actually responsible for my going back to school and getting my masters in anthropology. I've gone in all four seasons. The groups are small, eight to fifteen, so it's easy to hook up with people and you always get lots of personal attention. Besides the leaders there is always an intern or two who can answer questions or provide extra help if you need it. It's usually 50/50 men and women and ages from 20s to 80s. Many people are by themselves—I always feel comfortable. The food on their river trips is marvelous—I don't know how they do it!! The staff are very tuned into the land and the culture of people. They take a very holistic approach to education. I heartily recommend it to anyone and can't wait to go again myself!*

*Female, 50s: I've gone on a number of trips, alone and with friends. There are about fourteen in the group, and you're with them all the time so it's easy to get to know everyone. The age range is 20 to 65, slightly more men than women. Most people are by themselves. The program is very well run. The staff are knowledgeable and very helpful about getting people to open up. The guides are chosen very carefully, and they really know their stuff.*

## OLYMPIC FIELD SEMINARS
## OLYMPIC PARK INSTITUTE

111 BARNES POINT ROAD, PORT ANGELES, WA 98363; (360) 928–3720 OR (800) 775–3720. (I)

| | |
|---|---|
| YEARS IN BUSINESS: | 11 |
| AGE RANGE: | 30–60 |
| MOST COMMON AGE: | 40–50 |
| PERCENT ALONE: | 70 |
| NUMBER OF PARTICIPANTS: | 10-15 PER CLASS |
| MALE/FEMALE RATIO: | 50/50 |
| MAY TO OCTOBER | |

The lovely setting on majestic Lake Crescent in the mountains of Olympic National Park adds to the pleasure of these weekend courses covering many aspects of the nature, art, and culture of the region. Nature classes look at birds, butterflies, plants, and marine life. Cultural offerings include Northwest Native Indian art, traditional plant uses, and hands-on wood carving in the Northwest Coast tradition. Other possibilities explore painting, storytelling, and photography. Participants stay in cabins nestled in a grove of fir trees; each one has a small common area with four adjacent sleeping rooms. Guests are automatically paired. Everyone shares meals at the historic Rosemary Inn, the rustic lodge built by craftsmen at the turn of the century.

COMMENTS *Male, 50s: I've been there many times and I always go alone—it's a very warm and friendly place. Most people are from the Pacific Northwest, but there's always some from all over the country, with diverse backgrounds and a big age range. There are usually eight to twelve in a group, about 25 percent male, and only a third are traveling with someone else, so you never feel like you're the only person there alone. The staff are excellent hosts, making sure everyone feels a part of things. They're also very knowledgeable about the park. The professors who teach the courses are all experts in their fields. I'd definitely recommend this to people traveling alone because you bond with the group almost immediately and become unified. All the people I've encountered are very warm and outgoing.*

*Female, 60s: I've gone there seven times, alone all but once, and I always have an excellent experience. I've done programs that are more seminars, and I've done purely travel trips, too. The instructors are experts and have a real interest in the ecology of the area. I feel very safe with all these instructors. I've been on outdoor trips with other operators, and they're not as well run. You feel at home here immediately. The food is all organic and natural and extremely fresh. Everyone cares about the ecosystem of Olympic Park and wants to study and preserve it. I've formed lasting friendships.*

**Other national parks offer classes similar to the Olympic Park workshops. Among these are:**

## DENALI NATIONAL PARK WILDERNESS CENTERS

P.O. Box 67, Denali National Park, AK 99755;
(907) 683–2290. (E)

Guaranteed shares; singles will be matched with roommates on request. Five-day programs limited to sixteen participants are offered each summer, with lodgings in cabins deep in the heart of the park—the only accommodations from which you can look out at the snow-clad peaks of the Alaska Range and Mount McKinley. Programs include birds, tundra ecology, natural sciences, and nature photography, as well as guided backcountry hikes, canoeing, cycling, or fishing.

## THE YELLOWSTONE INSTITUTE

P.O. Box 232, YELLOWSTONE NATIONAL PARK, WY 82190;
(307) 344–2294. (I)

Workshops emphasizing the wilderness areas of the park are offered year-round. Classes are small (ten to fifteen students) and can run from two to five days. Classrooms are headquartered at the historic Buffalo Ranch in the quiet, unpopulated Lamar Valley in the northeast part of the park, where roaming herds of wildlife are so abundant that the area has been nicknamed the "Serengeti of North America." The Institute has new, heated log sleeping cabins available for students at a nominal fee. There are also a fully equipped central kitchen, bath, and classroom building.

## YOSEMITE FIELD SEMINARS

YOSEMITE ASSOCIATION,
P.O. Box 230, EL PORTAL, CA 95345;
(209) 379–2321. (I)

Some 1,000 participants each year attend these seminars, taking in many aspects of the park's ecology and beauty, from studying the stars to tracking wildlife to photography and painting. Backpacking and hiking are also offered. Besides the superb surroundings, directors say people come to meet people, have fun, and to feel safe in a wilderness environment. They add that many people come alone. High-country programs require camping; some programs include reserved lodging in the park and dining; others require making your own arrangements.

## ROCKY MOUNTAIN SEMINARS

ROCKY MOUNTAIN NATURE ASSOCIATION,
ROCKY MOUNTAIN NATIONAL PARK, ESTES PARK, CO 80517;
(970) 586–1258. (I)

Among sixty-one courses are two-day workshops that include photography, art, geology, tracking mammals, butterflies and moths, Rocky Mountain flora, mushrooms, herbs, grasses, and nature writing. Students make their own lodging and meal arrangements.

## SNAKE RIVER INSTITUTE

P.O. Box 128, Wilson, WY 83014;
(307) 733-2214. (I-M)

A variety of three-day programs are offered in the Wyoming Tetons and Yellowstone National Park. Some courses, such as photography, include lodging and meals; for others, participants make their own arrangements.

........................................................

# Nature  Tours

Nature tours offer advantages you could not enjoy on your own. They go to remote areas where getting around can be difficult and where required arrangements often are not easily made from home. The trips have been researched to take advantage of the seasons and make the best use of limited time. They provide the benefit of a knowledgeable guide to answer questions and enrich your experience. And you will also learn from other members of the group, who tend to be interested in and knowledgeable about the natural world. While these tours come with a high price tag, they are often less expensive than trying to duplicate the trip yourself.

Selecting a nature tour involves some of the same issues that you must consider with any tour—the reliability of the company and good references from past participants. But when you choose a tour operator, also remember the issues of ecotourism. Find an operator who has been working for a long time in the country you will be visiting, who knows and cares about the local culture, and who uses local guides and services whenever possible. Find out how guides are trained. Ask about conservation issues and what the company does to minimize its impact on the environment.  The background material participants receive often provides a good test of the operator's attitude and sense of responsibility. The best operators send information on cultural traditions and the environment as well as clothing tips and reading lists. Companies listed here have shown their commitment to the environment.

## QUESTERS TOURS AND TRAVEL, INC.

257 PARK AVENUE SOUTH,
NEW YORK, NY 10010-7369;
(212) 673-3120. (EE)

This company offers a host of tours accompanied by naturalists whose knowledge of the areas greatly adds to the experience. Culture is part of the focus; at Machu Picchu, for instance, the architecture and the history of the Inca city are studied along with the birds and wildflowers of the area. Other destinations include Hawaii, Alaska, the western United States, Mexico, Panama, Costa Rica, Guatemala, South America, the Caribbean, Norway, Scotland, the Greek Isles, Australia, New Zealand, the Himalayas, and much of Asia.

| | |
|---|---|
| YEARS IN BUSINESS: | 24 |
| AGE RANGE: | 25–80 |
| MOST COMMON AGE: | 55–70 |
| PERCENT ALONE: | 45 |
| NUMBER OF PARTICIPANTS: | VARIES |
| MALE/FEMALE RATIO: | 20/80 |

YEAR-ROUND; WILL TRY TO ARRANGE SHARES; IF CANNOT, WILL ABSORB THE SINGLE SUPPLEMENT

COMMENTS *Female, 40s: I've gone on seven trips alone. About half the participants come by themselves. The age range is 20 to 80, and there are more women than men. They are from all over the world. Most come to get away from it all, to get back to nature. On some trips there has been a lot of free time; on others everything is group oriented, but you are always free to do what you want to and pursue whatever aspect of the area interests you. There is a lot of driving through wonderful scenery, but this is definitely not the usual sightseeing tour.*

*Female, 70s: I've taken many tours, but these are the best. I've returned ten times and find many people who go again and again. There is a good mix of singles and couples; most of the singles are women. The group is always highly intelligent—this kind of trip does not attract duds—and it is easy to make friends. The tour leaders are excellent and informative.*

## VICTOR EMANUEL NATURE TOURS, INC.

2525 WALLINGWOOD DRIVE, SUITE 1003,
P.O. BOX 33008, AUSTIN, TX 78764;
(512) 328–5221 OR (800) 328–8368.

| | |
|---|---|
| YEARS IN BUSINESS: | 24 |
| AGE RANGE: | 40–75 |
| MOST COMMON AGE: | 55–70 |
| PERCENT ALONE: | 40 |
| NUMBER OF PARTICIPANTS: | 10–18 PER GROUP |
| MALE/FEMALE RATIO: | 40/60 |
| YEAR-ROUND; WILL TRY TO ARRANGE SHARES | |

"Some of the best birding experiences of my life have been on Victor Emanuel Nature Tours," said no less an authority than the late Roger Tory Peterson, the author of so many definitive bird and nature guides and a onetime VENT guide. This is the largest company in the world specializing in birding tours, and their trips guarantee compatible company for birders. They cover the globe, from Alaska and Australia to Africa and the Amazon, moving with the seasons to follow the good weather. Though they declined to give out names of past participants, you need not hesitate to sign up with this respected group.

## AMERICAN MUSEUM OF NATURAL HISTORY DISCOVERY TOURS

CENTRAL PARK WEST AT 79TH STREET, NEW YORK, NY
10024–5192;
(800) 462–8687 OR (212) 769–5700. (EE)

| | |
|---|---|
| YEARS IN BUSINESS: | 24 |
| AGE RANGE: | DEPENDS ON PROGRAM |
| MOST COMMON AGE: | 50 AND UP |
| PERCENT ALONE: | 10–15 |
| NUMBER OF PARTICIPANTS: | 12 TO 120 (FOR CRUISES) |
| MALE/FEMALE RATIO: | 40/60 |
| YEAR-ROUND; WILL TRY TO ARRANGE SHARES | |

You need only browse the catalog of this outstanding museum to appreciate the tremendous range of exciting tours available to explore the natural wonders and cultures of the world. Some fifty tours cover the greatest wildlife regions and archaeological sites around the globe, always with the finest teams of scientists, educators, and expedition leaders. The choices range from the Everglades to Indonesia, Vietnam to Trinidad and Tobago. Train trips cover Canada by private train and travel through the national parks of the west aboard the luxurious American Orient Express. Top-quality African safaris are on the extensive list, as well. Many cruises, including the Galápagos Islands, are available in addition to the land tours. Operators are chosen for their commitment to responsible tourism. These tours are expensive, but they are top quality.

# Other Nature Tours

Other responsible, experienced, nature-oriented tour operators include:
- **Nature Conservancy International Trips,** 1815 North Lynn Street, Arlington, VA 22209; (800) 633–4734. (EE)

The Amazon, Belize, Bolivia, Brazil, the Galápagos, Indonesia, Mexico, Panama, and the Sea of Cortez are among their worldwide offerings.
- **Geo Expeditions,** P.O. Box 3656, Sonora, CA 95370; (800) 351–5041. Small groups visit Africa, India, Nepal, Indonesia, South America, or Australia.
- **Quark Expeditions,** 980 Post Road, Darien, CT 06820; (203) 656–0499 or (800) 356–5699. A wide variety of tours but specialists in Arctic travel.
- **The Nature Conservancy** (see page 121). Worldwide trips to exotic destinations.
- **Southwind Adventures,** P.O. Box 621057, Littleton, CO 80162; (303) 972–0701. Specialists in South America.
- **Wild Horizons** Many nature-oriented photography trips.

COMMENTS *Female, 60s: I've been on five trips. I went to Africa and climbed a mountain to see gorillas, took a fabulous trip to Antarctica, cruised in Asia. I went alone on most of these trips. They are wonderful. There are lectures and daily updates on your itinerary and what you're going to see the next day. You always feel well informed. I love their cruises—it's always open seating at meals, and they'll seat you at a table if you're shy about it—everyone gets to know each other before you're through. All are interesting, wonderful people from all over and all sorts of backgrounds. I'd say a quarter to a third are alone, always more women than men, and an age range from 20s to 80s. It's a relaxed, informal, and easy experience—a great way to travel.*

# Darwin's World: Cruising the Enchanted Galápagos Islands

None of the photographs and none of the shipboard briefings can prepare you for the fantastic reality of the Galápagos, an extraordinary configuration of islands formed by the peaks of million-year-old volcanoes. Isolated some 600 miles off the coast of Ecuador, the Galápagos are unusual in their lava-scarred landscapes as well as their tame wildlife. This is an enchanted world where rare birds and animals that have never been hunted by predators accept human visitors as just one more of nature's species—no more to be feared than a passing bird.

Who lives here? Birds like none you've ever seen. Blue-footed boobies stand a foot and a half high, with feet and legs the color of a clear summer sky. Masked boobies, eyes framed in black, cluck over their tall, fuzzy chicks. Flapping albatrosses, graceful oystercatchers, and exotic lava herons all but pose for the photographers who furiously snap camera shutters in their midst.

In the Galápagos, you'll go swimming with sea lions, step around two-foot-long iguanas, examine bright-red sea crabs, and exclaim at the giant turtles that give the islands their name. Still present are the finches that fascinated Charles Darwin—evolved into thirteen distinct species, each with a beak shaped for most efficiently obtaining its food. Forty-five percent of the plants here are found nowhere else in the world, including the amazing Opuntia cactus that has evolved into a strange and sturdy tree. No matter how much film you bring it won't be enough.

To visit the Galápagos, you must travel to Guayaquil, Ecuador, and board a cruise ship or a sailing yacht. For someone traveling alone, the best bet is the *Santa Cruz,* run by Metropolitan Touring, Ecuador's leading tour company. The most comfortable of the ships, it accommodates ninety passengers. Excursions to the islands are in small boats, each holding only about twenty people, so you will soon be friends with your fellow passengers, marveling together at what you have seen.

As noted in a number of write-ups above, many excellent ecotourism companies schedule cruises to the Galápagos Islands, but the largest company handling this destination (and all of Ecuador) is Metropolitan Touring Galápagos Cruises c/o Adventure Associates, 13150 Coit Road, Suite 110, Dallas, TX 75240; (800) 527–2500 or (214) 907–0414.

## Sources for Expedition Cruises

One excellent source for a number of expedition cruises is the DISCOVERY Tours program run by the American Museum of Natural History (see page 128). The Nature Conservancy also includes Caribbean and Amazon nature cruises on its travel agenda (see page 129).

**Other top operators who run some of the cruises described above as well as a host of others from the Arctic to the Amazon include:**

### SOCIETY EXPEDITIONS
3131 Elliott Avenue, Suite 700, Seattle, WA 98121;
(800) 425–7794 or (206) 285–9400.

### OCEANIC SOCIETY EXPEDITIONS
Fort Mason Center, Building E, San Francisco, CA 94123;
(415) 441–1106.

### LINBLAD TRAVEL INC./SPECIAL EXPEDITIONS
P.O. Box 912, Westport, CT 06881;
(800) 243–5657 or (203) 226–8531.

### ABERCROMBIE AND KENT/CONTINENTAL WATERWAYS
1420 Kensington Road, Oak Brook, IL 60521;
(800) 323–7308 or (312) 954–2944.

## SWAN HELLENIC CRUISES, C/O ESPLANADE TOURS
581 BOYLSTON STREET, BOSTON, MA 02116;
(800) 426–5492 OR (617) 266–7465.

..............................................................

# SAFARI!

Joining a safari to see the big game in East Africa was a longtime dream come true for me—but the reality outdid even my fondest fantasies.

Nothing you've read or seen in picture books can prepare you for the deep emotion that wells up on viewing these magnificent creatures at close range, living in their own environment. It is a jolt of joy and wonder that fills the senses and goes straight to the heart.

Strangers soon become close friends on safari because of this shared emotion and the excitement of the trip. It makes no difference whether you are on your own or with a companion. You are all fellow hunters, intent on prowling the national parks and game preserves, ready to aim your binoculars and shoot on sight with your camera.

The targets are ever-changing. Lightning-swift cheetahs stalk graceful gazelles. A pride of lions sleeps in the sun. Hordes of dizzily striped zebras, big and small, graze in the grasses. Giraffes bat their eyelashes and nibble daintily at the treetops. Thousands of wildebeest stand around like a congregation of bearded old men. Herds of elephants trumpet and splash in a water hole. A family of rhinos stares out like giant, nearsighted Mr. Magoo. Every day, every park holds a new discovery.

The trip is easy for a single traveler because every detail is handled for you. From the moment you are met by a tour representative in your arrival city, you are part of a carefully attended group. There seemed no common denominator for the people who chose this trip, except that they all could afford the high price. The majority of those I met at the lodges were over age 50, but there were younger people as well, and even an occasional family who had brought young children to share the adventure.

While no physical exertion or danger is involved, safaris do mean tiring and difficult travel. The distances between parks are great. Rutted roads are often unpaved, sending up dust or mud, depending on the weather.

We were out by 6:30 A.M. many mornings, since the animals are most active just after daybreak, and we often drove for hours searching for the bigger game. No one could stay awake much past 10:00 P.M. The thrill is worth it all.

In Kenya, the best known park is the Masai Mara Game Preserve at the northern tip of the Serengeti Plains, where literally millions of animals graze and hunt. In two days in this park, we spotted more than thirty species of animals and untold numbers of exotic birds.

Other parks have their own specialties. Lake Nakuru is known for huge flocks of pink flamingoes, Amboseli for its large herds of elephants. Samburu Game Reserve, in northern Kenya, has its own species of zebras and giraffes with marking different from those to the south. At Treetops, you stay up late to watch animals congregating outside at a softly lit water hole. At the Mount Kenya Safari Club, the place made famous by the late actor William Holden, you'll have a break—a day spent relaxing in luxury, dining sumptuously, and coming back to find that the logs in the fireplace in your room have been lit for you.

After a fabulous week in Kenya, we were unsure as to what more could possibly be waiting for us in Tanzania. The answer was simply the most spectacular animal watching in the world.

Ngorongoro Crater, an inverted volcano, is one of the wonders of the world, a veritable Noah's ark. In Kenya, we had driven long stretches searching for the elusive big animals. Here, the naturalist guide who drove us down by jeep had only to say, "Now we'll look for the lions," and there they were. Then, "Here's where the rhinos stay"—and there they were.

Serengeti National Park, with its huge numbers of animals, is overwhelming in its beauty and richness. A recent census counted a quarter of a million gazelles, an equal number of zebras, another quarter million of other species including cheetahs, lions, and other predators, and well over a million wildebeests.

Even the smallest of the national parks, Lake Manyara, was rewarding, with its amazing variety of animals owing to the topography that ranges from lush jungle to flat plains. One sight here fills you with amazement—lions that climb the trees in order to nap undisturbed by the park's large herds of elephants.

We were worried about lodging when we crossed the border into Tanzania. Kenya is relatively prosperous and, with over a million visitors a year, has learned how to provide safari guests with creature comforts. Accommodations were not so different from rustic park lodges in the United States. But Tanzania is poor and undeveloped, and we had been warned to expect difficult living conditions.

"Difficult" meant that we lacked hot water at times and the electricity might be turned off from midnight to 6:00 A.M. Still, the beds were comfortable, and every room had a private bath. I've had worse accommodations in Yosemite Park. The striking architecture and scenic locations of the lodges were a wonderful surprise. True, the food left much to be desired, but when the main course did not please, there were plenty of fresh vegetables and rolls to fill in.

For me, the extraordinary animals made a few inconveniences more than worthwhile. In fact, if I could return to only one country, Tanzania is where I would choose to go.

My experiences were in only two countries; safaris are also available in South Africa and several other African nations. Safaris are expensive, but they are a once-in-a-lifetime experience. Start saving.

## Choosing a Safari

There are many operators offering safaris that vary in price, from budget trips via open trucks with nights spent in sleeping bags to trips that include comfortable vans and accommodations and the services of skilled guides. Deluxe tours such as those sponsored by the Smithsonian Institution add the services of a naturalist. Some of most luxurious trips are the tented safaris, where the cooks pride themselves on turning out remarkable fare over the campfire.

Wildlife is abundant and weather is mild year-round in East Africa, but the "long rains" period from late March through May is not a good time for animal viewing. The big herds of the Serengeti are in Tanzania in the winter months and in Kenya from mid-July to September.

To compare trip costs, look at the actual days spent on safari. Tours that spend extra days in Nairobi may sound like more time for your

# Important Questions to Ask Before You Choose a Safari

- How long has the company been in the business?
- Is Africa their main destination or just one of many?
- Are departure dates guaranteed regardless of how many people sign up?
- How large is the total group? (More than twenty-five is unwieldy; less than fifteen is ideal)
- Will you be guaranteed a window seat in your van? Will you have a naturalist along in addition to the driver-guide?
- Does the company employ local people?
- Are its guides and drivers trained by environmental experts?
- What airline will you fly and where will you stop en route? (All airlines make a stop in Europe. Changing planes in Amsterdam is an advantage because Schiphol Airport is easy to navigate and it is a quick and inexpensive train ride into town if you have several hours to spend.)
- Will you have day rooms during the stopover between Europe and Africa, or simply wait around at the airport?
- Where will you stay when you land in Nairobi? (The Norfolk is the great old hotel.)
- Is the operator a member of the U.S. Tour Operators Association?
- Most important—can they furnish firsthand references from travel agents and recent former passengers?

money, but bed-and-breakfast accommodations in a city are not the point of an African trip. The most important consideration is a guaranteed window seat in your van.

## Among the better-known operators specializing in safaris are:

### ABERCROMBIE AND KENT, INTL.

1420 Kensington Road, Suite 111, Oak Brook, IL 60521–2106; (800) 323–7308 or (312) 954–2944.

Years in business: 30+.

A & K maintains its own offices and staff in Kenya and Tanzania. (EE)

### UNITED TOURING INTERNATIONAL, INC.

1 Bala Plaza, Suite 414, Bala Cynwyd, PA 19004; (610) 617–3300 or (800) 223–6486.

Years in business: 50.

This Nairobi-based company is the largest tour operation in Africa, with offices throughout the continent and a wide variety of offerings. (M–EE)

### PARK EAST TOURS

1841 Broadway, New York, NY 10023; (212) 765–4870 or (800) 223–6078. (EE)

Years in business: 29.

This tour company does trips for the ASPCA, an excellent recommendation for their emphasis on conservation. Offerings include moderate and luxury itineraries. Safari participants receive a year's subscription to *Eco-Traveler* Magazine.

### BORN FREE SAFARIS AND TOURS

12504 Riverside Drive, North Hollywood, CA 91607; (800) 372–3274.(E–EE)

Years in business: 20+.

A wide range of prices, a guarantee of no more than six passengers per vehicle, and some unusual options such as a dine-around plan and safaris that include walking make this operator well worth considering.

### HIMALAYAN TRAVEL-WORLD ADVENTURES, INC.

112 Prospect Street, Stamford, CT 06901; (800) 225–2380 or (203) 359–3669;

# Safaris and Ecotours: Read All About It

For further information and sources for safaris, ecotours, and other nature getaways, you can consult the following resources:

Ecotours and Nature Getaways, Alice M. Geffen and Carole Berglie, Clarkson Potter, New York, 1993.

Natural History, the magazine of the American Museum of Natural History, includes a large number of specialized tour ads in its "Market" section.

OFFERS TWO BUDGET SAFARIS THAT DRAW MANY YOUNG, SINGLE TRAVELERS FROM EUROPE AS WELL AS THE U.S. (BOTH I, BUT NEITHER INCLUDES AIRFARE.) THE TWO GROUPS ARE:

**Tracks:** THESE ARE BRITISH-RUN BASIC CAMPING SAFARIS WITH A MAXIMUM OF EIGHTEEN PEOPLE. THEY INCLUDE WALKING AS WELL AS TRAVEL IN OPEN TRUCKS. EVERYONE PITCHES IN TO A FOOD KITTY AND HELPS WITH COOKING. BUDGET PRICES ATTRACT MANY YOUNG PEOPLE.

**Kumaka Expeditions:** ONCE AGAIN A BRITISH-RUN OPERATION, THESE CAMPING EXPEDITIONS ARE ABOARD 18–SEATER TRUCKS. A COOK IS PROVIDED ON MANY TRIPS. THE CATALOG SPECIFIES AGES 18-40 FOR MANY TRIPS AND 18-55 FOR OTHERS; SOME TRIPS ARE OPEN TO ALL AGES.

## VOYAGERS INTERNATIONAL

(SEE PAGE 167)

SCHEDULES PHOTOGRAPHIC SAFARIS AS WELL AS NATURAL HISTORY SAFARIS.

## SAFARICENTRE

3201 NORTH SEPULVEDA BOULEVARD, MANHATTAN BEACH, CA 90266; (310) 546–4411 OR (800) 223–6046 (800-654-5342 IN CALIFORNIA).

THIS AGENCY SPECIALIZES IN SAFARIS ALL OVER THE WORLD. THEY WILL ADVISE YOU ON APPROPRIATE TRIPS FOR YOUR INTERESTS AND BUDGET.

# Get Into Shape: The Spa Vacation

## The Spa Philosophy

**I**MAGINE A VACATION THAT SENDS YOU HOME SLIMMER, trimmer, free of stress, and full of energy. That's just what you can expect from a visit to a spa, a healthy vacation experience that is gaining a growing group of advocates from both sexes. Because spas provide a *you*-centered vacation that is dedicated to making you look and feel better, they are perfect for solo travelers, and a large number of guests choose to come alone.

Forget about the old "fat farms." Today's spas are really health resorts, geared as much to the over-stressed as the overweight. Exercise means hiking or tennis as well as calisthenics, and, until you've tried it, you won't believe that a low-calorie diet that can be so satisfying.

A week at a spa is designed to show how quickly the results of regular exercise and healthy eating can be seen in your measurements and morale. And to make up for the ache of unaccustomed exertion, you get wonderful pampering messages and other rewards to ease away the pain.

Spa vacationers pay premium prices for their daily regimen of 1,000 to 1,200 calories and enough exercise to burn them off. Yet advocates declare it is a worthwhile investment. For along with a week or two of healthy living, a good spa aims to give a lifetime bonus—education and inspiration for a healthier life-style when you return home.

At a good spa, guests can learn, often for the first time, exactly how their bodies function—how they react to stress, inactivity, different types of exercise, and different types of food. One of the most important benefits is finding out how to eat well without gaining weight. For those who have talked about exercising without doing anything about it, a spa can be a motivation center, reinforcing good intentions and generating lasting new attitudes and behaviors.

Good-natured sharing of the agonies of sore muscles and longings for forbidden treats creates a common bond among guests that quickly cements friendships. Many guests who meet at spas plan future visits together.

For men who fear that spas are still mainly for overweight women, a pleasant awakening may be in store, since the opposite is often true today. People who come to spas tend to be those who are fit or want to be. They are usually people who take care of their bodies.

Along with exercise, many spas offer stress-control techniques to keep you calm, collected, and better able to stick with your good intentions back home. Many have a holistic slant, including meditation, t'ai chi, and similar techniques. You can take part or not, as you wish.

Most spas will try to match you with a roommate to help hold down the cost.

## The Spa Routine

A typical spa day begins with a brisk walk before breakfast. There is a choice of exercise classes, which are spaced throughout the day. The exercises include a balanced mix of aerobics, workouts for body conditioning, and stretching and yoga for both strength and relaxation. Aquatic workouts frequently are part of the routine, turning exercise into fun and games in the pool. Many spas have weight machines and special muscle-building and stretching sessions just for men, accommodating the increasing number of male guests.

Between the workouts come the rewards: soothing messages, relaxing whirlpools, saunas, and steam baths that erase tension and aches. A variety of treatments is offered. Facials, hydrotherapy massage (done in a tub using soothing streams of water), and herbal wraps (mummy-like wrappings of scented moist sheets that draw out body impurities, soften the skin, and relax the muscles) are among the choices. Attendants report that many men whose macho upbringing made them reluctant to try these treatments discover they have been missing out on some of life's nicer luxuries and immediately sign up for repeats.

There is also plenty of time for a leisurely lunch—and a dip in the pool or an hour in the sun with a good book.

Though strong alcohol and fattening hors d'oeuvres are definitely not part of the regimen, some spas do allow a glass of wine at dinner, and many have pleasant pre-dinner "mocktail parties" that offer sociability along with sparkling water, carrot sticks, and surprisingly tasty low-calorie dip. All the food, in fact, is a pleasant surprise. The menus are sophisticated and cleverly served so that every meal has an appetizer, salad, main course, and dessert. While portions are small, wily spa nutritionists know that after four courses, most people do not feel deprived.

Evenings include speakers, how-to hints for stress reduction, tips on establishing good health habits at home, or talks and movies just for entertainment. A number of spas now offer workshops in biofeedback and other behavior-modification techniques.

A week's stay is recommended to get the full benefit of a spa. Some warn you when you arrive that day three typically is a day of muscle soreness and doubts for those unaccustomed to exercise. Each day following, however, finds you feeling better—about your body and yourself.

## Choosing a Spa

Although the basic programs at spas are similar, the ambience can vary as much as the price range, which runs the gamut from a few-frills $800 to a luxury $4,000 a week.

At the top of the scale, and the ultimate spa experience, according to many people, is the Golden Door in Escondido, California, with serene Oriental decor and a staff that outnumbers the guests by 3 to 1. Reflecting current trends, the former all-female spa now offers special weeks for men. Cal-a-Vie is another super-luxury retreat limited to twenty-four guests, each lodged in their own villa-style cottage. Weeks for men only are available here as well.

At the other end of the spa spectrum is the coed Ashram, also in California, described by one recent guest as "a boot camp without food." The raw-food diet and rigorous regimen designed to test guests to the limit of their physical endurance may not be everyone's cup of herbal tea, but those who survive declare it almost an existential experience, and many do return.

Some spas are permissive, leaving it to guests to decide how much or how little activity they want to participate in. Others expect you to maintain a schedule, figuring that if you wanted to loll by the pool, you would have chosen a different vacation.

Locations of spas vary. Some are in the middle of a city; others are in the middle of nowhere. Some are part of a larger resort; others are independent operations. And there are still traditional spas that are for women only.

When you compare costs of spas, be sure to note how many massages and beauty treatments are included; some fees sound inexpensive because you must pay extra for these services.

Spa guest references weren't too helpful, since all were raves. After visits to a number of spas, however, I do have recommendations for best bets for single guests.

Choose a destination spa rather than a resort, where many guests are not part of the spa program and you may be eating spa fare in a dining room where others are enjoying steak and lobster.

················································

# Pick-of-the-List Spas

At the top of the list of the best spas for single guests are two coed "fitness resorts"—Rancho la Puerta and Canyon Ranch. Both are well known, and each attracts an active, generally fit, and interesting mix of guests. Here is what each has to offer:

## RANCHO LA PUERTA

TECATE, BAJA CALIFORNIA, MEXICO (ABOUT AN HOUR SOUTH OF SAN DIEGO; GUESTS ARE MET AT NO CHARGE AT SAN DIEGO AIRPORT);
RESERVATIONS (800) 443–7565; IN CALIFORNIA, (800) 422–7565;
COED; 150 GUESTS; 30 PERCENT MALE. (E–EE)

This rates my first-place vote for tranquillity, beauty, and value. The 150-acre complex, filled with flowers and fountains and ringed with

# The Right Spa For You

*Before you decide on a spa, check current magazines for the latest write-ups or browse through a bookstore or library for more comprehensive coverage. Two good book choices are:*

- *SPA FINDER (Spa-Finders Travel Arrangements, Ltd., 91 Fifth Avenue, Suite #301, New York, NY 10003; 212–924–6800). Published by a travel company that specializes in spa vacations, this annual magazine-format catalog of fitness spas has short descriptions of more than 200 spas.*
- *FODOR'S HEALTHY ESCAPES, Fodor's Travel Publications, New York.*

*Pick several spas whose approach, location, and rates seem to meet your needs. Write for brochures, which will tell you a lot about the philosophy of the spa and its facilities, schedules, and accommodations. It should also tell you whether massages and other services are included in the fee or are extra. It should describe the menu, the number of calories served, whether larger portions are available if you want them, and whether the emphasis is on a balanced diet or a vegetarian menu.*

*If you still have questions, phone the spa's fitness director. Ask about the number of single guests or male guests if it is a concern to you. Find out whether someone seats you at meals to be sure you have company when you want it. Spa vacations are expensive, so be sure you make the right choice for your needs.*

boulder-strewn mountains, was born in 1940, long before the fitness boom. It remains a find for any world-weary traveler who wants a rejuvenating getaway in lovely surroundings. Guests stay in Mexican casitas decorated with hand-painted tiles and folk art. Accommodations have no phones or television; many have fireplaces, stacked with wood and ready to be lit each night.

You do as much or as little as you please here and eat as much as you want—not as hedonistic as it sounds, since the diet is vegetarian and you can hardly avoid losing weight. Eighty percent of the vegetables are grown in the ranch's own organic gardens, and you've never tasted fresher or better. Fish is served twice a week; otherwise main dishes are pastas, lasagnas, Mexican tortillas and beans, and other dishes that belie their calorie count.

The guests are professionals from all over the United States and Canada. The age range is 25 to 65, but because the Mexican location makes this spa a better buy than many of its American competitors, the average age tends to be younger than at more costly spas, and many trim 20s and 30s are around. Everyone arrives on Saturday, making for a cohesive group. By the time you have hiked, exercised, and dined together for a couple of days, you all feel like old friends. The relaxed, friendly, and low-key atmosphere extends to the health and beauty services. You come here for renewal, not expert pampering.

There are lots of tennis courts, lit for night play, and five separate pools, some very private. Most of the lodgings also offer private decks for sunbathing or stargazing. This is the one spa I could imagine coming to for sheer enjoyment, even if I never went near an exercise class.

## CANYON RANCH

8600 East Rockcliff Road, Tucson, AZ 85715; (800) 742-9000 or (602) 749-9000. Coed; 250 guests; 35 percent male. (EE)

The ambience at this first-class facility is charged with energy, even though higher rates are reflected in a slightly older (and often celebrity-studded) clientele. The gyms and the health center are state of the art; the staff is crackerjack; the menu is varied and delicious; and the beauty treatments are first rate. Single guests have the daily option of joining a group table or dining alone. People who come here love it, but while they may recharge, they don't really escape from the real world. Dress can be a fashion parade of designer leotards and sweat suits. Televisions and telephones are very much part of the hotel-ish guest rooms, and there is a fax machine in the office that gets a lot of use from guests keeping up with business.

Canyon Ranch is blessed with wonderful desert and mountain surroundings, but you must board a van to reach the starting points of the hikes. Some people prefer this because it allows for more variety and is more challenging. Hiking is a big part of the program, and special weeks are devoted to it for those who want a more rigorous schedule.

A Life Enhancement Center is a self-contained part of the spa that focuses on helping participants overcome such habits as smoking or overeating. The Behavioral Health Department of the Center uses all the latest techniques, including private counseling, biofeedback, and hypnotherapy.

## CANYON RANCH IN THE BERKSHIRE

BELLEFONTAINE, KEMBLE STREET, LENOX, MA 01240; (413) 637–4100 OR (800) 742–9000. COED; 240 GUESTS; 25 PERCENT MALE.

The location of this newer (opened in 1990) outpost is 120-acre Bellefontaine, one of the great old Berkshire estates. Though not much of the original complex remains, one of the three buildings in the U-shaped complex is the old mansion house, which retains the original library but is otherwise completely changed. It now houses the dining room, offices, and medical and behavioral consultation areas. Exercise facilities are in the new, state-of-the-art fitness complex, which includes tennis, squash, and racquetball courts, an indoor running track, indoor pool, all manner of fitness equipment, and exercise rooms as well as treatment and salon facilities. Another pool and other tennis courts are outdoors. Guests stay in the third building. The rooms, like the dining room, are blandly attractive—like what you'd find in an upscale hotel.

Morning walks may be excursions into downtown Lenox, and hikes take advantage of the lovely Berkshire countryside. Summertime guests can take advantage of the wonderful seasonal cultural facilities of the Berkshires, including Boston Symphony concerts at Tanglewood. In winter, cross-country skiing is added to the agenda. The services here are first rate, but given a choice, I still find the Arizona Canyon Ranch and its exquisite desert surroundings a more satisfying experience.

........................................................

# Luxury Spas

When you have the wherewithal ($300 per night and up), you might want to choose these ultimate spa experiences:

## THE GOLDEN DOOR

P.O. Box 2548, Escondido, CA 92025;
(619) 744–5777; THIRTY-NINE GUESTS.

Dating back to 1958, the Golden Door's Oriental ambience and tranquil setting are still considered by many to provide the ultimate serene retreat. A staff of 160 caters to the thirty-nine "treasured guests" with niceties such as a daily one-hour massage in your own room and a nightly before-sleep massage. Most weeks are for women only, but several are scheduled for men and for coed sessions.

## GREEN VALLEY SPA AND TENNIS RESORT

1871 West Canyon View Drive, St. George, UT 84770;
(801) 673–4084 or (800) 237–1068.

A beautifully appointed spa with a holistic bent, Green Valley's special bonus is the surrounding Utah red rock country, where hiking in locales such as Zion National Park is a joy. The spa offers relaxation, meditation, and nutrition education along with exercise. Singles get a private bedroom and bath in a two-bedroom condo. This is also the home of the Vic Braden Tennis College (see page 16).

## CAL–A–VIE

2249 Somerset Road, Vista, CA 92084;
(619) 945–2055; TWENTY-FOUR GUESTS.

Think of a small village in Provence, and you'll have the picture of this retreat shared by two dozen fortunate guests. Located on 125 acres in a secluded valley north of San Diego, the spa houses guests in Mediterranean style tile-roofed cottages filled with hand-carved furniture and pastel floral chintz. Men's, women's, and coed sessions are offered.

························································

# Good-Value Spas

Finding spas is no problem. They are mushrooming all over the country—so much so that several books are devoted to describing them. What is not easy is finding reasonable prices. Here are a few suggestions:

## THE OAKS AT OJAI

122 East Ojai Avenue, Ojai, CA 93023;

(805) 646–5573 or (800) 753–6257. Coed; eighty guests. (I–M)

Fitness and exercise is the forte of director Sheila Cuff, whose California spas in Ojai and Palm Springs represent good value. With plenty of Cuff's vigorous exercise classes and spa cuisine, guests soon feel healthy and relaxed. The spa opened in 1977 in the center of a quaint arts-oriented town about ninety minutes north of Los Angeles. It attracts many young career women, including starlets from the Los Angeles area. About 20 percent of the guests are male. Some 75 percent of the guests come alone.

## THE PALMS AT PALM SPRINGS

572 North Indian Avenue, Palm Springs, CA 92262;

(619) 325–1111. Coed; ninety guests. (I–M)

This sister to the Oaks has a similar program and a similar clientele. It is equally well priced.

## COOLFONT

Berkeley Springs, WV 25411;

(304) 258–4500. Coed; twenty-nine guests. (I)

A five-day "Health Retreat" is the special offering of this rustic health-minded resort in the mountains not far from Washington, D.C. Included in the program are exercise classes, hikes, yoga, massage, health education classes, self-improvement seminars, hot tubs, and nourishing low-calorie foods. The retreat can be extended by combining it with a "Fitness Weekend," a two- or three-day regimen. The wooded setting is beautiful and serene; there are no phones or televisions in the simple chalet-style rooms to break the spell. Evenings offer a range of cultural offerings—musicians, poets, and other artists.

## NEW LIFE FITNESS VACATIONS
P.O. Box 395, Killington, VT 05751;
(802) 422–4302 or (800) 228–4676. Coed; twenty-five guests. (M–E)
Runs mid-May to early November. Very small single supplement.

Set in an attractive hotel, the Inn of the Six Mountains on the slopes of Killington mountain, this active program emphasizes mountain hikes, one of the most pleasant ways to exercise. The program also includes exercise classes, weight training, an indoor pool, and a healthful low-fat, high-fiber, high-carbohydrate diet. Massage is included in the fee. The small size of the group makes for a highly personal program monitored to each guest's needs.

## NEW AGE HEALTH SPA
Route 55, Neversink, NY 12765;
(800) 682–4348. Coed; seventy-five guests. (I–M) Year-round.

There is a definite holistic emphasis at this well-priced spa set on 160 acres of rolling hills and woodland in the Catskill Mountains. Along with hikes and classes, there are sessions devoted to yoga, t'ai chi, and meditations. A unique feature here is the Alpine Tower, a climbing tower designed to provide extra challenge. A range of optional health consultations and beauty treatments are available. Menus offer seafood or poultry, many vegetarian dishes, and an open salad bar; guests can choose plans from 600 to 1,200 calories daily. Many of the vegetables and herbs are organically grown in the spa's own greenhouse. Mini-van service to this spa is available directly from New York City for a fee.

## LAKE AUSTIN SPA RESORT
1705 Quinlan Park Road, Austin, TX 78732: (512) 266–4363 or (800) 847–5637. Coed; eighty guests. (E)

Set on twelve acres bordering a 23-mile lake, the spa has a full range of exercise equipment plus tennis and volleyball courts, indoor and outdoor pools, and a bonus—paddleboats and sculls to take advantage of the lake. Hiking trails wander the surrounding Texas hill country. Besides the usual aerobics, shaping and stretch classes, guests are offered yoga, visualization, and meditation sessions. The dining room has lovely views of the lake and offers many fresh vegetables and fruits from the on-site organic gardens. Nicely decorated guest rooms are in cottages on the grounds.

## FRANKLIN QUEST INSTITUTE OF FITNESS

202 North Snow Canyon Road, P.O. Box 938, Ivins, UT 84738; (800) 470-3002 or (801) 673-4905. Coed; 125 guests. (I-M)

This is one of the best buys around, especially for those who want to take advantage of the extensive hiking program in Utah's majestic red rock country. The hikes are an integral part of the spa's noted weight-loss program. Each guest is tested and assigned to supervised programs according to ability. A low guest-to-staff ratio assures lots of personal attention. Facilities include tennis, racquetball, pool, a fully equipped gym and weight room, and a new spa building offering the full range of beauty treatments. Simple rooms are in modernistic domed buildings; those willing to share quad rooms will enjoy some of the lowest rates of any spa.

# Mexican Spas

Though nowhere near the class of Rancho la Puerta, two additional Mexican spa resorts deserve mention because their rates are so attractive for Americans.

## RIO CALIENTE

Guadalajara, Mexico; c/o Spa Vacations Ltd., P.O. Box 897, Millbrae, CA 94030; (415) 615-9543. Coed; eighty guests; no shares arranged; small single supplement. (I)

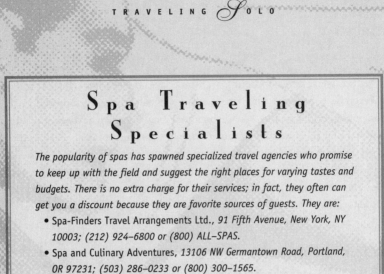

Located in a secluded pine forest 18 miles from Guadalajara, this small, casual, very rustic hot-springs resort is a bargain. The program includes hiking and hot mineral-water baths, along with horseback riding, relaxing yoga, and massage. Beauty treatments are available, but they are not stressed here. Meals are vegetarian; many of the foods are grown in their own garden. In keeping with the away-from-it-all feeling, there are no televisions or telephones on the premises.

## IXTAPAN HOTEL AND SPA,

IXTAPAN DE LA SAL, MEXICO, C/O E & M ASSOCIATES, 211 EAST 43RD STREET, NEW YORK, NY 10017; (800) 223–9832 OR (212) 599–8280. COED; FIFTY SPA GUESTS; NO SHARES ARRANGED. (I–M)

Part of a 600-acre resort complex based around therapeutic warm springs, the spa facilities occupy the fifth floor of a 250-room hotel. The weekly package includes daily massages, three facials, three nail and scalp treatments, and two Roman bath treatments as well as a daily aerobic and aquatic exercise class. Guests can use the spa dining room, where meals equal 800 calories a day, or the regular resort dining room. Everyone dresses up at night. Other diversions are tennis and horseback riding and evening concerts, movies, and nightclub entertainment. Cars meet guests in Mexico City for the two-hour drive to the hotel.

# Join A *Tour*

I F YOU'RE DREAMING OF SEEING THE WORLD, YOU'LL FIND that tour companies are in the dream-fulfillment business. They print up shiny brochures showing the world's wonders, which they will gladly wrap up for you in neat packages.

## The Up Side

Tour packages offer many advantages. On a prepaid tour, you can sit back and let somebody else take care of all the details of travel. A tour relieves you of the chores of getting around on your own in unfamiliar cities, choosing hotels, deciding where to eat, making restaurant reservations, or planning every day's sight-seeing. You'll never have to worry about transporting luggage or finding your way to a hotel. And if your luggage does not arrive, it's the tour manager, not you, whose job it is to follow through.

Tour buses generally offer comfortable seats and big windows that give you the best views as you travel. Not the least of the appeal of a tour is the cost. Because of the economies of group buying, tours almost always save money over trying to duplicate the same trip on your own. In peak season, the clout of a tour company often ensures room reservations that an individual cannot wangle.

Some tours also offer roommate-matching services to avoid the single supplement, allowing a big saving for solo travelers. Single sojourners also enjoy the advantage of companionship, especially important at mealtime. Most often, a block of tables is reserved for tour members, and a single person would naturally join the other members of the group.

Tours are a natural for a first trip to Europe or for travel in the Orient or the South Pacific where getting along and getting around may seem more complicated than in the western world. Tours with a special focus such as art or cuisine may appeal to those who have traveled more widely and done the basic sight-seeing.

........................................................................

# The   Down   Side

Despite the many pros of group travel, however, you should not sign on for a tour without understanding the negative points. In exchange for the advantages, you give up the right to set your own schedule. There's a set time that you must leave your bags outside your hotel room door each morning, as well as a designated hour for breakfast and departure—and those times are likely to be early! The average tour is geared to covering as much ground as possible, so you have little opportunity for browsing or lingering. On a typical "Continental Introduction" grand tour, for example, the highlights in one three-day area might include a canal cruise and a chance to see the Rembrandts at the Rijksmuseum in Amsterdam, Cologne cathedrals, a Rhine cruise, Heidelberg, Nymphenburg Palace in Munich, the Bavarian Alps, and a walking tour of Innsbruck—a lot to take in over a short period of time. You get a sampling, never an in-depth view. And sometimes you get more than you can absorb. You know the old joke—"If this is Tuesday, this must be Belgium ..." It's easy for everything to become a blur on a whirlwind tour.

And while motor coach travel may sound restful, most tours take a lot of stamina. Besides those early departures, there is a lot of walking. Buses are often prohibited from parking in the center of town and are restricted to coach parks. You will get a good bit of exercise just getting to attractions, climbing hills to castles, and following the guides.

Of course, just because you've paid for the full tour doesn't mean that you must climb every hill or see every sight on the itinerary. It's perfectly okay to decline and meet the group afterward. But when the bus is ready to roll, you'd better be on board.

The size of the group also limits your choice of lodgings and restaurants. Intimate inns and cafes cannot accommodate a busload of tourists. So you'll be staying in  larger commercial hotels chosen for their ability to handle a group well, and you will frequently be offered fixed menus in large restaurants, unless you want to pay extra to venture out on your own. Gourmet fare is not the rule, except on deluxe tours. Some hotels and restaurants may be better than you expect; the majority will be quite ordinary. Many tours do not include lunch in order to allow you the chance to visit some local places on your own.

You should also be aware that most motor coach tours tend to attract older travelers. According to the National Tour Association, approximately 70 percent of U.S. motor coach tourists are 50 and older. And the number of travelers by themselves is small, seldom more than four or five per busload. That doesn't mean that couples are not good company, simply that it is not realistic to expect a lot of fellow singles. Budget tours tend to attract more singles as well as a larger number of younger passengers; companies that guarantee shares are also more likely to attract people on their own.

Despite these warnings, the makeup of any one tour is unpredictable, and sometimes you can luck out. One single woman I know reported, "I took a Globus two-week tour of the Orient by myself and to my delight had about eight single people between 30 and 55 for companionship, including a few bachelors and widowers—which the brochure definitely did not guarantee."

What about tours designed exclusively for singles (see pages 192–207)? By all means consider them—many people do. But sign on with the advance knowledge that the greater proportion of the travelers is likely to be female. Not only do single women outnumber single men, but they seem more hesitant about striking out on their own. Choose a singles tour as you would any other—because the destination or itinerary intrigues. And don't be surprised or dismayed at the scarcity of male company.

The one element that makes or breaks a tour is the tour director or escort. It is up to the tour director to see that everyone shows up on time, to appease the inevitable grumblers, and to set a tone of goodwill and fun for the group. Ideally, this person should be all things to all people—friendly, outgoing, humane, intelligent, articulate, witty, well informed, and ever tactful. Directors are usually college educated, and those conducting European tours may speak two to four languages. The better established the tour company, the better the chances that you will have an expert tour director.

# Choosing a Tour

K nowing both the good and not-so-good points of group tours, a little homework in choosing your tour will ensure a more successful trip.

The first consideration is strictly a monetary one. Tours come in three classifications: budget, first class, and deluxe, based on the type of hotels used. Decide on your price range and compare the offerings within it.

You'll also need to choose between general sight-seeing or special-interest tours. Many varieties of specialized tours concentrate on everything from castles to gardens, Mozart to mushroom hunting. These tours most often are deluxe, but if the itinerary is really exciting to you, it may be worth the splurge. A shared interest helps ensure you will find compatible company.

Most group tours are all-inclusive, meaning that they take care of both air and land arrangements, most meals, and an escort. Local guides may be used in each destination, since it is difficult for a tour escort to be an expert on everything. However, the better operators do have one person who stays with the group throughout even if someone else gives the specialized talks. On trips for special-interest groups, particularly those sponsored by museums and universities, the escort is usually also a well-qualified specialist whose knowledge can add a lot to your trip.

Many escorted tours are available also as land packages only, in case you want to combine them with independent travel. Sometimes you can use the group air arrangements from a package and plan your own itinerary.

*There are dozens of tour operators, and since each tour may vary in the number of participants and the expertise of the guides, travel agents who use the companies frequently are your best references. Listed here, as a starting point, are a few reliable, long-established tour operators.*

# Comparing Tours

*To evaluate what makes one general tour more desirable than another, gather a number of brochures covering the areas you want to visit, and do a bit of comparison shopping. A good travel agent can supply you with plenty of material to get you started, and can tell you which companies have pleased their clients in the past.*

*Compare the following areas, then consult your travel agent or the tour operator if you have further questions.*

- **Cost:** *Figure out the cost of each trip on a daily basis by dividing the total price by the number of nights offered. Days are not a safe guide, because many tours start at noon or dinnertime and end with breakfast. Generally, you get what you pay for—higher prices mean better hotels and restaurants.*

- **Food:** *How many meals are offered? Do you have a choice of selections or are you limited to a pre-selected menu? Are there dine-around options?*

- **Accommodations:** *The hotels used by the tour should be noted in the brochure. Look them up in a guidebook to find out how they are rated. If the brochure makes up a name for categories, such as "tourist class," find out what that means. Do all rooms have private baths? Are the hotels centrally located? It's nice to be able to take a walk or visit the shops on your own, not so nice to be stuck miles outside the city.*

- **Airline:** *Will you travel on a regularly scheduled plane or a special charter flight? If a charter, who runs it? Is departure guaranteed or will your flight be canceled if a sufficient number do not sign up?*

- **Pace:** *How hectic is the program? Do you have time to rest up from jet lag when you arrive at your destination? Look for tours that spend more than one night in a location. Time to catch your breath during the day and free time for shopping or a bit of sight-seeing on your own will be welcome.*

- **Group size:** *Will there be one, two, or three buses? How many passengers per bus? When tour groups are too large, there are delays getting into hotels and jams at tourist attractions.*

- **Reputation:** *There are scores of tour operators—a number of whom cancel unfilled trips—or, worse yet, go bankrupt with your money in the till. You should know how long the company has been in business and whether it belongs to the United States Tour Operators Association. That membership means the company has operated for at least three years and has solid refer-*

(continued next page)

ences. The association sets stringent requirements on insurance, liability, and financial responsibility. For a list of their members, write to the address at the end of this chapter.

- **Guaranteed rates:** This can be a big advantage on trips abroad in case of extreme fluctuations in the value of the dollar.
- **Guaranteed departures:** This is the operator's pledge to run the tour as promised regardless of how many sign up.
- **Fine print:** Read carefully both tour descriptions and the page at the back of the brochure—the one without the pretty pictures—to find out exactly what is and is not included. There are many kinds of limitations. The brochure should be explicit as to exactly what your tour price covers. Membership fees needed to qualify for the trip, refund regulations, trip cancellation and trip interruption insurance, departure taxes, travel accident insurance, and medical payments are among the items that may or may not be covered.

# General Tours

## GLOBUS & COSMOS

5301 South Federal Circle, Littleton, CO 80123;

(800) 851-0728, ext. 518. Worldwide.

| | |
|---|---|
| YEARS IN BUSINESS: | 50+ |
| AGE RANGE: | 20s–80s |
| MOST COMMON AGE: | 47–55 |
| PERCENT ALONE: | 30 |
| NUMBER OF PARTICIPANTS: | AVERAGES 36–48 PER TOUR |
| MALE/FEMALE RATIO: | MORE FEMALES |
| GUARANTEED SHARES ON COSMOS | |

This long-established company offers tours on every continent except Antarctica in a choice of price ranges. Globus is first class; Cosmos is more budget-minded and has a slightly younger clientele.

## MAYFLOWER TOURS

1225 Warren Avenue, Downers Grove, IL, 60615;
(800) 323-7604.

Moderately priced tours around the U.S. and Canada, including national parks and hosted holidays in cities such as New York, Washington D.C., and New Orleans.

| | |
|---|---|
| Years in business: | 18 |
| Age range: | 50–65 |
| Most common age: | 50–60 |
| Percent alone: | 20–40 |
| Number of participants: | 35 |
| Male/female ratio: | VARIES |
| Guaranteed shares | |

## MAUPINTOUR

1515 St. Andrews Drive, Lawrence, KS 66047;
(913) 843-1211 or (800) 255-4266.

Luxury tours to Europe, Asia, Africa, South Pacific, and United States/Canada.

| | |
|---|---|
| Years in business: | 46 |
| Age range: | VARIES |
| Most common age: | 50+ |
| Percent alone: | 25–30 |
| Number of participants: | AVERAGES 25 |
| Male/female ratio: | 1:1 |
| Will try to arrange shares | |

## TRAFALGAR TOURS

11 East 26th Street, Suite 1300, New York, NY 10010;
(212) 689-8977 or (800) 854-0103.

Specializing in European travel, first class, and cost-saver tours.

| | |
|---|---|
| Years in business: | 49 |
| Age range: | 45–70 |
| Most common age: | 51 |
| Percent alone: | 10-15 |
| Number of participants: | 35–48 |
| Male/female ratio: | 38/62 |
| Guaranteed room shares | |

## TAUCK TOURS

Box 5027, Westport, CT 06881;
(800) 468-2825 or (203) 226-6911.

A family-owned business, now in its third generation, offering luxury tours in the United States and Canada.

| | |
|---|---|
| Years in business: | 70+ |
| Age range: | 55–70 |
| Most common age: | 55–70 |
| Percent alone: | 15–20 |
| Number of participants: | 40 |
| Male/female ratio: | Entire group, 40/60; among single passengers, 1:9 |
| Will try to arrange shares | |

## ABERCROMBIE & KENT INTERNATIONAL

1420 Kensington Road, Oak Brook, IL 60521;
(708) 954-2944 or (800) 323-7308.

Probably America's best-known operator of luxury tours world-wide, this firm offers top-of-the-line tours including a wide choice of land tours, plus safaris and expedition cruises.

| | |
|---|---|
| YEARS IN BUSINESS: | 35 |
| AGE RANGE: | WIDE |
| MOST COMMON AGE: | 45–60 |
| PERCENT ALONE: | 40 IN U.S., 33 ABROAD |
| NUMBER OF PARTICIPANTS: | 12–20 |
| MALE/FEMALE RATIO: | 48/52 U.S.; |
| | 38/62 ABROAD |

# Special-Interest Tours

There is truly a tour for every interest, whether your love is food, wine, sports, cave art, doll houses, bird-watching, or golfing. Because each of these itineraries is unique, references from past participants are the best way to judge whether you want to sign on. Assume that most special-interest tours will fall into the "very expensive" category, unless otherwise indicated. Here are some of the possibilities:

## INTERNATIONAL STUDY TOURS, LTD. (IST)

225 WEST 34TH STREET, NEW YORK, NY 10122; (212) 563–1202 OR (800) 833–3804. (EE)

| | |
|---|---|
| YEARS IN BUSINESS: | 16 |
| AGE RANGE: | 40–80 |
| MOST COMMON AGE: | 50s |
| PERCENT ALONE: | VARIES |
| NUMBER OF PARTICIPANTS: | 20 |
| MALE/FEMALE RATIO: | 40/60 |

Beginning with itineraries for organizations and special groups, IST has expanded to offer tours to the public, promising to go beyond ordinary sight-seeing to give insight into the culture of destinations in France, Austria, Italy, Greece, Turkey, Egypt, and Israel.

## ARCHAEOLOGICAL TOURS

271 MADISON AVENUE, SUITE 904, NEW YORK, NY 10016; (212) 986–3054. (EE)

| | |
|---|---|
| YEARS IN BUSINESS: | 25 |
| AGE RANGE: | 30–75 |
| MOST COMMON AGE: | 50+ |
| PERCENT ALONE: | AVERAGE 30 |
| NUMBER OF PARTICIPANTS: | 24–30 |
| MALE/FEMALE RATIO: | 40/60 |
| WILL TRY TO ARRANGE SHARES | |

These luxury tour groups are accompanied by expert scholars who stress the anthropological, archaeological, and historical aspects of destinations that include Italy, Greece, Turkey, Israel, Cyprus, Syria, Jordan, Portugal, Chile, Peru, Bolivia, Egypt, Morocco, France, Spain, Yugoslavia, Guatemala, China, Indonesia, Thailand, and India.

COMMENTS *Female, 30s: I've been on trips to Turkey, Sicily and Italy, Cypress, and Crete. There were many people traveling alone on all. Most were in their late 40s and 50s, and there were more women than men. The program is excellent and very structured, with most of the time spent at dig sites. The accommodations and food were the best available considering where we were.*

*Male, 50s: I've been to Sicily, China, and Yugoslavia alone; all were very good experiences. Though the trips are expensive, the group is not just rich people. Many are the people who save up and take a trip every other year. Most were interesting professionals. The destinations are interesting, the itineraries are meticulously planned and the days are active. I highly recommend it.*

## ANNEMARIE VICTORY'S DELUXE GOURMET TOURS

136 EAST 64TH STREET, NEW YORK, NY 10021; (212) 486-0353. (EE)

| | |
|---|---|
| YEARS IN BUSINESS: | 26 |
| AGE RANGE: | 45–70 |
| MOST COMMON AGE: | 55–70 |
| PERCENT ALONE: | 50 |
| NUMBER OF PARTICIPANTS: | 10 |
| MALE/FEMALE RATIO: | 40/60 |
| WILL TRY TO ARRANGE SHARES | |

Food lovers will find that even reading this catalog is a delicious experience. These ultraluxury tours, limited to ten people, include Italy, Austria, Switzerland, Belgium, Luxembourg, Ireland, France, and Spain. All focus on the finest dining in each destination, but there is also generous time for sight-seeing. Recently very upscale biking and hiking trips have been added to the itinerary, along with a gourmet-wine cruise in the Mediterranean and a luxury cruise to the Galápagos Islands.

COMMENTS *Female, 50s: The best of everything—fine small hotels, wonderful food, flowers in your room, the best guides, plenty of free time, never rushed or hectic. On three trips, the average age was 40s to 65; the biggest number of participants was eight. I was often the only person alone, but you eat together and quickly get to know everyone. I can't say enough good things about these trips.*

*Male, 40s: We had just four people, ages 46 to 72. Everything was deluxe, the days were varied, the food was superb. It was a wonderful experience.*

## MOZART'S EUROPE

c/o NEW VOYAGER TOURS, INC.,
DEER LANE, PAWLET, VT 05761;
(802) 325-3656. (EE)

| | |
|---|---|
| YEARS IN BUSINESS: | 13 |
| AGE RANGE: | 32–80 |
| MOST COMMON AGE: | 40–60 |
| PERCENT ALONE: | 50 |
| NUMBER OF PARTICIPANTS: | 26 MAXIMUM |
| MALE/FEMALE RATIO: | 35/65 |
| WILL TRY TO ARRANGE SHARES | |

Mozart lovers, here are your dream trips. There are three variations of this deluxe two-week grand tour of Mozart's Europe, all including Salzburg, Mozart's birthplace. One itinerary visits the state operas in Vienna, Prague, and Budapest; another includes summer festivals in Switzerland. The third combines the Vienna and Budapest state operas with the Wurzburg Mozart Festival and the Schubertiade in Hohenems, Austria. A new offering, the Mozart/Bach/Schubert Grand Tour, includes visits to Eisenach, Weimar, Leipzig, Dresden, and Berlin. Many private concerts and demonstrations are performed on the instruments used by Mozart.

COMMENTS *Female, 50s: This trip exceeded anything I've ever done. My group was older than most —from over 60 to 80—with more women than men and only five or six single people. Still, I made lasting friends, and the tour operators are wonderful people who are always available for companionship. The trip goes to all the pertinent Mozart places, to the opera in Vienna and Salzburg. It is a perfect trip for anyone who loves Mozart.*
*Female, 30s: The trip was a mental adventure, a musical dream come true. Though most of the group was older and married, it was still easy to be there alone. The people were interesting, and I never felt left out. I was sent the name and telephone number of my roommate before the trip, so we had a chance to get to know each other a little bit even before we left. The leader/owners are especially warm and were like parents to me. The hotels and food were tops, and there was plenty of time to do what you wanted. This is for anyone who likes Europe and music.*

## INTERNATIONAL TRAVEL PROGRAM

92ND STREET Y, 1395 LEXINGTON AVENUE,
NEW YORK, NY 10128;
(212) 415-5599. (E–EE)

| | |
|---|---|
| YEARS IN BUSINESS: | 15 |
| AGE RANGE: | 20s–60s |
| MOST COMMON AGE: | 50s |
| PERCENT ALONE: | 80 |
| NUMBER OF PARTICIPANTS: | 25–30 |
| MALE/FEMALE RATIO: | 25/75 |
| WILL TRY TO ARRANGE SHARES | |

This venerable New York cultural institution has an eclectic international travel program of special-interest tours. Some examples: French Impressionist Art in Normandy and Provence; Exotic Papua New Guinea and the Great Sing Sing; The Wonders of India and Nepal; Midnight Sun and the Scandinavian Shores; Exotic Morocco. Domestic trips have included the Spoleto Festival in Charleston and the Aspen Music Festival. These tours have some unique features. Applicants are personally interviewed before being assigned roommates, making for a better chance of congeniality. A meeting is held in New York before the trip to talk about the destination and give everyone a chance to meet. There is a minimum of two nights in each destination. Dinner is not included in the group itinerary to allow participants to try smaller restaurants in each locale. At the end of the day, the group leader suggests possibilities in a variety of price ranges and sets up small groups for each, so that you need never worry about dining alone.

COMMENTS *Female, 30s: Most participants were female and from the New York area, well educated but not necessarily well traveled. The art-oriented program in France was wonderful, the guides in Europe superb, and you were free to leave the group if you wanted. In Paris, for example, I went off on my own. I've always traveled mostly on my own, but I found it so relaxing not to have to worry about details, I will probably do it again—with this group. I learned far more about art than I would ever have done alone.*

## AMERICAN JEWISH CONGRESS INTERNATIONAL TRAVEL

15 EAST 84TH STREET, NEW YORK, NY 10028;
(800) 221-4694 OR (212) 879-4500. (E–EE)

A JC tours go to Israel and thirty other countries on six continents. Nile cruises and Far Eastern odysseys, Western and Eastern Europe, and Costa Rica are among the many choices. Tour members have a heritage and an interest in Jewish affairs in common. They often meet Jewish

| | |
|---|---|
| YEARS IN BUSINESS: | 39 |
| AGE RANGE: | WIDE |
| MOST COMMON AGE: | 50+ |
| PERCENT ALONE: | 20 |
| NUMBER OF PARTICIPANTS: | 25 AVERAGE PER TOUR |
| MALE/FEMALE RATIO: | 1/4 |
| WILL TRY TO ARRANGE SHARES | |

residents in other countries and see sights of special cultural or religious interest.

COMMENTS *Female, late 20s: I've been on two trips alone, to Morocco and on safari in Africa, and to Egypt and Israel. I chose a singles trip, so most people were in their 20s and 30s, though all ages were represented. Women outnumbered men, but everyone seemed to be from similar backgrounds and were fairly successful professionals. Everything was great in Egypt and Israel—guides, food, accommodations. In Africa, the guide left something to be desired and the trip was less structured, meaning you had to do a lot more on your own. I highly recommend the Israel trip but have reservations about Africa*

*Male, 30s: I've been on three trips: singles tours to Israel and to Spain and an "adventure tour" with mostly couples. The singles trips average 130 people, so you can't get to know everybody, but you are divided into tour buses, and you do become very friendly with the people on your bus. Two-thirds of each group was from New York, and women always outnumbered men. I enjoyed the adventure trip because it was less structured than a guided bus tour. These trips aren't like the "love boat"–people are there to travel with others their own ages and with similar interests, not to look for a partner. The group leaders are very good, and I would recommend the tour to anyone.*

**Following is a sampling of other special-interest tours:**

## ARTS SEMINARS ABROAD
## UNIVERSITY OF WISCONSIN–MADISON

610 Langdon Street, Room 716, Madison, WI 53703;
(608) 263–7815. (E)

Offered by UW–Madison Continuing Education in the Arts in coop-eration with UW–Extension, this varied program combines travel abroad with arts-oriented events such as the Edinburgh Festival or Carnival in Trinidad. The prices are more reasonable than many univer-sity-connected programs, but there is a hefty single supplement.

## HISTORY AMERICA TOURS

5920 West Plano Parkway, Suite E5, Plano, TX 75093;
(214) 713–7171 or (800) 628–8542. (I–M)

From the American Revolution to Custer's Last Stand, this group visits the sites of the greatest moments in American history, with a histo-rian guide to provide in-depth background to bring the events to life. Many trips have a low single supplement.

## IN THE ENGLISH MANNER

515 South Figueroa, Suite 1000, Los Angeles, CA 90071;
(213) 629–1811 or (800) 422–0799. (EE)

Six-night programs to England and Ireland for gourmets, garden-lovers, and golfers. Accommodations are with families in private country homes.

## COOPERSMITH'S ENGLAND

P.O. Box 900, Inverness, CA 94937;
(415) 669–1914. (EE)

Tours of Britain and Europe featuring gardens and staying in stately homes, castles, and villas.

## THE ITALIAN CONNECTION

10816 33RD AVENUE, EDMONTON, ALBERTA, T6J 3C1 CANADA;
(403) 438-5712. (EE)

Walking, cultural, and culinary tours including dinners in the homes of Italian friends.

## EXPO GARDEN TOURS

101 SUNRISE HILL ROAD, NORWALK, CT 06851;
(800) 448-2685. (EE)

England's Chelsea Flower Show, Holland at Tulip Time, and the world's largest roses in New Zealand are among the destinations sure to appeal to gardeners and flower lovers.

...................................................................

# Photography Tours

Tours oriented to photography provide plenty of time and opportunity for bringing home great pictures. Inexperienced photographers setting out on a tour that promises instruction and critiques should be sure that other novices are along. It is also well to know the ratio of participants to tour leaders to be sure you will receive personal attention. You should also get references from people who have traveled with your particular leader. Great photographers may or may not be great travel guides.

## CLOSE-UP EXPEDITIONS

858 56TH STREET, OAKLAND, CA 94608;
(510) 654-1548 OR (800) 457-9553. (EE)

| | |
|---|---|
| YEARS IN BUSINESS: | 17 |
| AGE RANGE: | 35–75 |
| MOST COMMON AGE: | 60s |
| PERCENT ALONE: | 65 |
| NUMBER OF PARTICIPANTS: | 5–12 |
| MALE/FEMALE RATIO: | 1:1 |
| WILL TRY TO ARRANGE SHARES; SUITABLE FOR ALL LEVELS | |

These small-group photographic adventures range from seven to twenty-five days and are paced for good photography. Itineraries are planned to take advantage of best light; early morning and late-day shootings sometimes alter mealtimes or call for picnics in a field. Recent foreign destinations have included Costa Rica, New Zealand, Australia, Burma, Turkey, Venezuela, and Indonesia. In the U.S., trips have covered the Southwest, Colorado, Death Valley, Yellowstone, and Yosemite.

COMMENTS *Male, 30s: I found the prices a little high and did not consider the leader a good naturalist. However, this was a relaxed holiday, not rushed like other photographic tours I have taken, and the trip was well organized. The group was about equally male and female, with most traveling by themselves.*
*Male, 30s: The age range of my group to Costa Rica was from 35 to late 60s and 70s, and about half were single. The program is well run and good for a beginner wanting to learn something new on vacation. The food and accommodations were fine. You have the freedom to do what you want, though it is generally a group situation because of the locale—you can't go off by yourself at night in the Coast Rican rain forest!*

## VOYAGERS INTERNATIONAL
P.O. Box 915, Ithaca, NY 14851;
(800) 633-0299. (M)

| | |
|---|---|
| YEARS IN BUSINESS: | 14 |
| AGE RANGE: | 35–70 |
| MOST COMMON AGE: | 55+ |
| PERCENT ALONE: | 50 |
| NUMBER OF PARTICIPANTS: | 11 PER GROUP |
| MALE/FEMALE RATIO: | 50/50 |
| GUARANTEED SHARES | |

"Images of Ireland" is the title of a tour offered eight times annually between April and October to appreciate and capture on film the beauty of western Ireland. The group is led by Ron Rosenstock, who has thirty years of experience as a photography instructor. This group, which plans trips for many universities and museums, also holds photographic and cultural trips to Italy, photographic safaris to Africa, and a variety of other interesting programs, including a sketching trip to Venice and nature-oriented trips to Indonesia, Africa, Costa Rica, and the Galápagos Islands.

## MACRO TOURS AND PHOTO WORKSHOPS
1145 Church Street, San Francisco, CA 94114;
(415) 826-1096. (M)

From two days in California Wine Country to a week in Alaska, Maine, or the Channel Islands National Park, director Bert Banks and his instructors work individually with participants to improve their photo techniques. Their "classrooms" are some of the loveliest

| | |
|---|---|
| YEARS IN BUSINESS: | 14 |
| AGE RANGE: | 35–75 |
| MOST COMMON AGE: | 40–60 |
| PERCENT ALONE: | 90 |
| NUMBER OF PARTICIPANTS: | 10–12 PER WORKSHOP |
| MALE/FEMALE RATIO: | 1/3 |
| GUARANTEED SHARES | |

parts of America at their most photogenic: Yosemite in spring when wildflowers are in bloom, Vermont with foliage in glorious autumn technicolor. Travel is by van; lodging is in motels, inns, or condos. Lunch is often a picnic in the field; everyone joins for dinner at a local restaurant.

COMMENTS *Female, 30s: I've been all over the country with this group, both alone and with friends. All were great trips. They structure the day so that you get to see and photograph things at the peak time for light. The whole trip is a group experience. You eat all your meals together, and you are together all day so you really meet everyone. The groups are about ten to fifteen people, and 90 percent are alone, so it's a very comfortable situation. Ages ranged from 30s to 70s. There are more women than men on most trips, but I've been on one where I was the only woman. It's very safe, and you have the security of the group. Sometimes meals are included, but it is usually just breakfast so the group goes out for lunch and dinner together. Accommodations vary by the trip. The instructors are very good, helpful, and happy to answer all your questions. You get all levels of skill. I'd recommend this to anyone who is interested in seeing and photographing beautiful places at the right time and in the right light!*

**There are many more photo tour advertisements in photography publications such as Modern Photography or Popular Photography.**

# Museum- and University-Sponsored Tours

Some of the best special-interest tours are organized by museums, universities, and college alumni groups. Although generally quite expensive, they are also usually superior and may provide exceptionally knowledgeable escorts. Part of the cost often is considered a tax-deductible contribution.

*To find such trips, start with the groups either in your own city or nearby large cities. You may also want to contact some of the following large institutions:*

## SMITHSONIAN INSTITUTION

c/o Smithsonian National Associates,
1100 Jefferson Drive SW, Washington, D.C. 20560;
(202) 357-4700. (EE)

The Smithsonian has a long roster of both U.S. and foreign tours each year, accompanied by experts on nature, folklore, architecture, gardens, wildlife, theater, and many other special interests.

## AMERICAN MUSEUM OF NATURAL HISTORY DISCOVERY TOURS

Central Park West at 79th Street, New York, NY 10024-5192;
(800) 462-8687 or (212) 769-5700. (EE)

The museum offers tours of the world's greatest wildlife regions and archaeological sites, with expert lecturers. (Also listed under nature, page 128.) The "Market" section and other ads in the museum's publication *Natural History* includes a large number of additional specialized tours.

## NEW YORK BOTANICAL GARDEN, EDUCATION DEPARTMENT

Bronx, NY 10458–5126;
(212) 220–8700. (EE)

Gardens are the focus, but sight-seeing is also included in the tours of this fine organization.

## NATIONAL TRUST FOR HISTORIC PRESERVATION

1785 Massachusetts Avenue N.W.,
Washington, D.C. 20036. (EE)

Tours are to areas known for their well-preserved architecture.

*For more information on tours,*
*consult these two organizations:*

## NATIONAL TOUR ASSOCIATION

546 East Main Street, Lexington, KY 40508;
(606) 253–1036 or (800) 755–TOUR.

This group offers free information on packaged travel and a list of 630+ members in the United States and Canada. They also provide advice on avoiding travel scams, some of which is offered in the box on the facing page.

## UNITED STATES TOUR OPERATORS ASSOCIATION

211 East 51st Street, Suite 12B, New York, NY 10022;
212–750–7371.

This group issues a free list of its member companies, including details of programs and destinations. It also offers pamphlets on how to read a tour brochure and select a package tour.

# Avoiding
# Travel Scams

*The National Tour Association urges travelers to be wary of unreliable or dishonest tour operators. Here are some of the group's tips on playing it safe.*

- *If you work with a tour operator, make sure that the company offers a consumer protection plan.*
- *Use a credit card to purchase tickets, and if cash must be used, always get a receipt—everything must be in writing.*
- *Verify that the tour company has errors and omissions, professional liability insurance—all professional tour companies have this coverage.*
- *Ask for a reference from a client with whom you are familiar.*
- *Avoid high pressure sales with a limited time to evaluate the offer.*
- *Beware of companies sending a courier for a check, requesting a direct bank deposit, or demanding a certified check.*
- *Decline offers requiring a property sales presentation.*
- *Prior to payment, review complete details about any trip in writing.*
- *Request specific hotel and airline names, addresses, and phone numbers—broad terms such as "all major hotels" and "all major airlines" are a warning flag.*
- *Insist on a local phone number if given a toll-free number—this will establish that the tour company or travel agency has a central office from which it operates.*
- *Never use 900 numbers.*
- *If you receive a vacation certificate in the mail, take it to a respectable tour operator or travel agent who can evaluate it.*
- *Call the National Fraud Information Center (800–876–7060), the Federal Trade Commission (202–326–2000), or local and state consumer protection agencies to report all incidences of travel-related fraud.*

# Go To Sea

AYBE YOU DON'T WANT AN ACTIVE VACATION AT ALL. Maybe what you'd really like to do is lie back and soak up some sun. Or maybe you can't decide. You'd like to relax, but you'd also like the excitement of seeing new places.

Cruises offer the best of two worlds—the chance to travel while you enjoy the pleasures of resort life at sea. The new superliners really are floating resorts, with a lineup of activities ranging from exercise classes and trapshooting to lectures, dance lessons, contests, and the chance to strike it rich in the casino. And few resorts can match the menus on a cruise ship, where something is being served almost nonstop from 7:00 A.M. until that fabled midnight buffet.

Best of all, these are resorts where you will never lack for company at dinner.

Ship travel is also safe, easy, and convenient. Accommodations, activities, entertainment, and lavish meals are all part of one package price, often even including transportation to the port of departure. And you can travel to a number of new places on one vacation without the hassles of making plane connections or dealing with luggage. No matter how many ports you visit, once you unpack, you need never face a suitcase again until you head home.

Recent changes in the cruise industry offer more good news for single people. No longer catering only to the wealthy or to older travelers, many cruise lines have updated their facilities and programs, shortened their itineraries, widened their offerings, and whittled their costs to appeal to a much wider audience—including singles. According to a study by the Cruise Lines International Association, the number of single passengers signing on for cruises has doubled since 1986. They represented nearly a quarter of the passengers signing on for cruises between 1989 and 1994, the most recent statistics available.

# A  S i n g u l a r  D i l e m m a

It is only fair to warn, however, that a cruise vacation by yourself does present some special challenges. In spite of the increase in numbers, singles remain a definite minority on most cruises. On a recent sailing aboard one of Carnival Cruise Line's "fun ships," which attract more single passengers than many other lines, the number who showed up for a get-acquainted singles mixer was less than 150 out of about 1,400 people on board—and the women outnumbered the men 10 to 1. Only a few other cruise lines, including Royal Caribbean and Norwegian, make the effort to hold an event for singles on board.

The overabundance of females may be welcome news if you are a male, but therein lies the dilemma for women. After dinner, couples naturally couple up. Evenings on shipboard are romantic, particularly on the nights when everyone dresses up for dinner, and it isn't much fun to be alone. Yet that's exactly what you may be, and you should know it in advance. If you are a female who will feel like a wallflower without a dancing partner, don't go on a cruise by yourself. If, however, you can enjoy the pleasures of days at sea and be content to watch the evening's entertainment and then maybe read a good book at night, cruising is for you.

## Meeting and Mingling

With all those couples around, cruising is a situation where you really want to find compatible single company, even just a good buddy of your own sex. The new cruise liners keep getting bigger and bigger, and it is harder to meet people on an enormous ship. On a large ship, it takes a little luck and a lot of effort because it is easy to feel lost on ships with more than 1,000 passengers.

The only people you see regularly each day are those at your dinner table, your seating assignment is crucial. Ask to be placed at one of the largest tables, which usually seats eight, to increase your chances of meeting people you'll want to spend time with. And request the second, or later, seating. The first seating tends to attract those who are early to bed, and because the dining room must be cleared ahead for the next sitting, there is little time for lingering over conversation.

If you are not happy with your table, ask to have it changed—and do it right away.

Persistence and an outgoing attitude are needed to search out the other unattached passengers on board a big ship. Even on ships that hold a singles mixer, if you don't connect at that early gathering, there are no set places afterward to meet the other single passengers on board. To better your odds of meeting people, sign up for lots of daytime activities. Women should not be afraid to try the bar, which is easy and comfortable to do on a ship. A piano bar is often a particularly pleasant gathering place.

Florence Lemkowitz, a veteran cruise writer, suggests that it is a mistake to go to bed early the first night at sea if you want to meet people, since that's just when other solo travelers are probably checking the scene with the same thought in mind. The first night is the best night to visit the ship's lounges and bars, she says, before people give up on them because nobody seems to be around. She also recommends telling the social director that you want to make friends, putting him or her to work on your behalf.

One veteran cruiser I know makes up little cards with her name and cabin number. These are not meant to serve as invitations to drop in. Ships' cabins have telephones, and, on a large ship a card ensures that the new acquaintances will know where to call if they want to get together. You can't just assume you will run into one another again.

Recognizing the lack of dance partners, several lines have gone out of their way to make things pleasanter for single women at night. Royal Cruises Lines (now part of Norwegian Cruise Lines) was the first to come up with the idea of "gentlemen hosts," but now Crystal, Cunard, Delta Queen, Holland America, Regency, and Orient lines have copied it, and no doubt others will follow suit. They invite congenial single men in their 50s and 60s to come along as hosts to dance with unaccompanied women, attend cocktail parties, act as a fourth for bridge or a partner in dance class, or sometimes just serve as someone to talk to. These men, mostly retired, are carefully screened for both sociability and dancing ability. Forget about romance, however; they receive explicit instructions to mingle, with no favoritism allowed to any one passenger or group.

If you are a male who would like to apply, contact The Gentlemen Host Program c/o Lauretta Blake, 4277 Lake Santa Clara Drive, Santa Clara, CA 95054; (408) 727–9665. Just remember this isn't a restful vacation; dancing every dance takes a lot of energy.

## Boarding the Right Ship

If the lack of romance does not deter you, you can concentrate on the other pleasures of being at sea. And these are plentiful. There's nothing quite like the sense of freedom you feel standing on a breezy deck and gazing at the limitless horizon—or the excitement of watching a new port loom ever closer into view.

Your first decision when planning a cruise should be based on which ports you most want to visit, and that depends a lot on the season. In winter, the Caribbean is by far the most popular destination. The eastern ports of the Bahamas, Puerto Rico, St. Thomas, and St. Martin are the most frequently chosen because they are easily reached on seven-day cruises from Florida. Close seconds are Jamaica, Cozumel, and Grand Cayman. Cruises out of San Juan go farther afield to western Caribbean islands such as Barbados, Guadeloupe, Martinique, St. Lucia, or Antigua. These harbors are less crowded with cruise ships and for that very reason are more appealing to many people. These itineraries are particularly appealing when the fare to San Juan is included in the price.

In summer, Bermuda is a convenient port of call in the east, while Alaska's Inside Passage, with its ice-blue glaciers and some of the continent's greatest scenery, makes for an unforgettable and increasingly popular cruise in the west. Unlike many trips where you see very little from port to port, the views of Alaska from shipboard are often so engrossing that many passengers need no other daytime entertainment than watching the show from their deck chairs.

If you have the time and the fare, there are also wonderful itineraries to South America, the Mediterranean, the Greek Islands and Turkey, the South Seas, and Asia, and a number of exciting and exotic expeditions to remote regions of the world. In fact, there's almost no place on earth you cannot happily explore on a cruise.

One problem you rarely have to consider any longer is seasickness. Today's ships are remarkably stable, and there are plenty of over-the-counter remedies such as Dramamine available as an extra safeguard. Choose a cabin close to midship and near the waterline for the least amount of motion. And relax, knowing that if all else fails, the ship's doctor is ready with an injection that will quickly put you back on an even keel.

## Getting the Best Deal

Once you have decided where you want to go, your next dilemma is choosing among the many companies offering similar itineraries. The makeup of passengers will vary from week to week, but here are a few general guidelines.

Your age may narrow your choices. Generally, longer and more luxurious cruises get older passengers, and many retired people. Three- and four-day cruises to the Bahamas and Freeport from the East Coast and to Baja California from the West Coast tend to attract younger passengers. Seven-day Caribbean trips are perfect winter vacations for all, and they get a good mix of people.

If you are worried about gaining weight from the nonstop meals on a cruise ship, you can choose from many ships with extensive fitness centers and daily exercise classes. Some even offer spa cuisine.

Theme cruises are a boon for single passengers because they have a focus. These are regular sailings with the customary itinerary of ports, but with special guests and entertainment on board to provide a drawing card. The singles percentages on these cruises may be no higher, but the chances of meeting people who share your interests probably will be.

Knowledgeable travel agents and cruise specialists will know about these offerings, which vary each year. Some of the specialty choices in the past have included jazz festivals, guest Cordon Bleu chefs, photography instructors, and themes from natural history to soap operas to sports. There are now cruises aimed at golfers, bridge players, wine and art connoisseurs, opera and film lovers, and Civil War buffs.

The nationality of the crew can affect the ambience of the ship. Greek cruise line operators such as Royal Olympic are known for warmth, for example. Individual ships in a company's fleet may differ in size as well as personality. Read a comprehensive guidebook to cruises to learn more about specific vessels you are considering.

The best guide I've seen is Kay Showker's *Unofficial Guide to Cruises.* She not only describes the good and bad points of each cruise line but tells you the kind of passengers you are likely to find aboard. And she gives in-depth descriptions of accommodations and amenities on each ship in the line.

For singles, Showker recommends smaller ships: "It is easier to mix, and the staff takes greater care to ensure that you are part of the ship's social life," she says. Among smaller ships, she advises that expedition and educational cruises are the best choices. "A camaraderie develops quickly among passengers who share common interests and a certain sense of adventure," she points out. "For single women, the number of unattached men is likely to be higher than on traditional cruises."

### The Single Supplement

One of the big deterrents to cruise travel for singles has been cost. Some cruise lines impose surcharges that double the price in order to occupy a cabin alone; the most common policy is 150 or 160 percent of the double rate. Pricing does vary, and some lines give more of a break. The pricing for singles is always stated in the ship's brochure.

### Guaranteed rates

A guaranteed single rate means you pay a set price, usually comparable to a mid-range double fare, and the cruise line assigns your cabin at the time of departure. You don't get a choice of rooms, but you do get privacy. Since the cheapest and most expensive cabins usually sell out first, your chances are good of being placed in a decent mid-range accommodation. If you don't travel in high seasons, such as winter in the Caribbean, you may even luck out with a nice outside cabin.

Below are cruise lines offering a guaranteed fare at press time; check current information since policies do change. Also, other lines may offer these rates for cruises with light bookings even if the catalog does not say so, so be sure to ask.

The (GS) notation for some lines means they also offer guaranteed shares.

## NORWEGIAN CRUISE LINES
95 MERRICK WAY, CORAL GABLES, FL 33134;
(800) 327-7030.

They offer popular-priced cruises to the eastern and western Caribbean, the Bahamas, and Mexico. Many are theme cruises—jazz, country and western, magic, big bands, 50s, and so on. (GS)

## ROYAL CARIBBEAN CRUISE LINE
9035 SOUTH AMERICA WAY, MIAMI, FL 33132;
(305) 379-2601.

They offer popular-priced cruises to the Caribbean, Bermuda, Alaska, and the Mexican Riviera. (GS)

### Low single supplements
These lines have low single supplements, (25 percent or less). Some are top luxury ships, so you'll be paying top dollar but little penalty for being single.

## CRYSTAL CRUISES
2121 AVENUE OF THE STARS, LOS ANGELES, CA 90067;
(310) 785-9300.

This company's luxury ships sail from Los Angeles and Acapulco via the Panama Canal to San Juan and Fort Lauderdale, and also to Alaska, the Mediterranean, Northern Europe, and the Baltic Sea.

## ORIENT LINES
1510 SE 17TH STREET, FORT LAUDERDALE, FL 33316;
(800) 333-7300 OR (305) 527-6660.

This line boasts in-depth travel through Asia, Australia and New Zealand, the Mediterranean, and the Suez Canal and Egypt. They offer longer than average stays in port, and stays in cities at either end of the trip are included in the rates. Orient's Marco Polo has been named "Best Cruise Value" by the World Ocean and Cruise Liner Society. On certain routes, they drop even the normally low single supplement.

## SEABOURN CRUISE LINE

55 SAN FRANCISCO STREET, SAN FRANCISCO CA 94133;
(415) 391-7444 OR (800) 527-0999.

This line is characterized by small, luxurious ships with understated elegance; no tipping is allowed. Itineraries include Southeast Asia, the Panama Canal, the Caribbean, South America, the Mediterranean, the Baltic, Alaska, Africa, New England, and Canada. Single supplements can be as low as 10 percent, and the line is said to take special care of solo passengers.

## SILVERSEA CRUISES

110 EAST BROWARD BOULEVARD, FORT LAUDERDALE, FL 33301;
(800) 722-9955.

This company also offers small, luxurious ships; all of its cabins are suites with ocean views. It offers cruises to Europe, South America, the Far East, and the South Pacific.

### *Guaranteed shares*

Like tour operators, many cruise lines will try to match you with a suitable cabin mate. If no one is available, you get the cabin to yourself—but at the double rate. The odds are more in your favor in the off-season. The following lines offer guaranteed shares:

## ROYAL OLYMPIC CRUISES

ONE ROCKEFELLER PLAZA, SUITE 315, NEW YORK, NY 10020;
(212) 397-6400 OR (800) 872-6400.

This line offers moderately priced and luxury cruises on smaller ships to the Mediterranean, the Greek Islands and Turkey, Egypt, the Black Sea, South America, and the Red Sea. Royal Olympic occasionally has waived single supplements entirely on some cruises.

## CARNIVAL CRUISE LINES

5225 N.W. 87TH AVENUE, MIAMI, FL 33178;
(305) 599-2600.

Here you'll find popular-priced cruises to the Bahamas, Caribbean, and Mexico. Carnival's "Fun Ships" attract singles. Share rates are guaranteed, but only in quad rooms. You could wind up with one to three roommates.

## HOLLAND AMERICA LINES

300 ELLIOTT AVENUE WEST, SEATTLE, WA 98119;
(206) 281–3535 OR (800) 426–0317.

This line offers upscale cruises to the Caribbean, the Panama Canal, Alaska, the Mediterranean, and Northern and Western Europe.

### Single cabins

Single cabins are disappearing (new ships don't have them), but a few older ships still have this option. Among them are Carnival Lines' *Festivale;* Cunard Lines' *Sagafjord* and *Vistafjord;* Holland America's *Rotterdam;* P & O's *Canberra* and *Sea Princess;* and Regency's *Regent Rainbow.*

## Comparing Rates

To compare prices of similar cruises, divide the total cost by the number of full days on board. Arriving in home port at 8:00 A.M. hardly counts as a day at sea. In calculating the cost of any cruise, remember that you must figure at least $7.50 per day for tips. The recommended sums are $3.00 per day for room stewards and waiters, $1.50 for busboys. If you order drinks or use the barber shop or beauty salon, figure a 15 percent tip on each tab. Tips for shipboard personnel who provide special services are at your own discretion.

If you plan to take group tours ashore, be sure to include that cost in your calculations, as it can be considerable. The more ports, the more added expense.

To save money booking a cruise, you are better off reserving very early or very late. Early birds get advance booking discounts. Since the advent of so many new mega-ships with huge capacities, some lines are offering better pricing for single passengers who are willing to wait until 30 to 60 days before the sailing date for confirmation. And some offer standby fares for those who will take unfilled space close to the sailing date.

For this reason, passengers are wise to deal with a travel agent who specializes in cruises and is up-to-date on all the current possibilities. Larger cruise specialists also can frequently offer their own discounts, passing along the reductions they get from the cruise lines for being favored customers who buy space in bulk.

Dealing with someone who is familiar with the industry will also give you an edge in choosing a ship where you will be happy, regardless of the price. Single passengers come in all demographics and tastes as do any other cruise passengers. A company such as Carnival has become the largest afloat by going after first-time cruisers who may have little travel experience. They offer lots of participatory activities and costume parties (such as male beauty contests for husbands wearing their wives' nightgowns). These are right on target for many of their passengers, who thoroughly enjoy the high jinks. But sophisticated travelers may prefer a more conservative ambience, even if the tab is higher. Paying extra usually means getting better food as well.

### Among the knowledgeable agencies that specialize in cruise travel and also offer discounts are:

#### WORLD WIDE CRUISES
8059 WEST McNAB ROAD, FORT LAUDERDALE, FL 33321;
(305) 720-9000 OR (800) 882-9000.

They have a special Singles Desk and a computerized roommate-matching service devoted to serving single passengers.

#### THE CRUISE LINE INC.
150 NW 168TH STREET, NORTH MIAMI, FL 33169;
(800) 777-0707.

This company publishes a free magazine, *World of Cruising*, with cruise news, tips, and listings of current discount offerings.

### Agencies offering discounts on late bookings are:

- SPUR OF THE MOMENT CRUISES, (800) 343-1991 OR (310) 521-1070.
- POST HASTE TRAVEL; (800) 881-7690 OR (954) 966-7690.

Whichever cruise you choose, you are putting out a sizable sum, so don't fail to protect yourself with travel insurance. Read the regulations carefully: The two important things to cover are the cost of your fare if you must cancel or the cruise is interrupted, and the potentially large cost of major medical expenses away from home, especially in an emergency that would require evacuation from the ship. Almost all cruise lines offer insurance, as do travel agencies and independent insurance companies, so compare prices.

If you are traveling to an area that your own health insurance does not cover, you may need supplemental medical insurance as well. You will find more on travel insurance on page 316.

Kay Showker offers another word of warning: Always pay for a cruise with a credit card. If you go through a travel agency, see that the charge is run through the cruise line's account rather than the agent's, protecting you in case the agency should go under with your money in the till. Paying with a credit card also allows you to cancel payment if the cruise is not provided as promised.

........................................................

# River Cruises

Ocean voyages are not the only way to go to sea. Check out the interesting and offbeat itineraries offered by smaller ships sailing scenic rivers at home and abroad.

## CLIPPER CRUISE LINE

7711 BONHOMIE AVENUE, ST. LOUIS, MO 63105,
(800) 325-0010.

The *Yorktown Clipper* (138 passengers) and the *Nantucket Clipper* (100 passengers) travel the inland waterways of the Americas on more than twenty separate itineraries. On the Pacific Coast, the *Yorktown Clipper* sails from Alaska's Inside Passage to Baja's Sea of Cortez, and then to Costa Rica, the Panama Canal, the Lower Caribbean, Venezuela's Orinoco River, and the Grenadines/Windward/Leeward Islands. The *Nantucket Clipper* voyages from Canada's Prince Edward Island to

Florida on the Atlantic coast, plus the Great Lakes and the U.S. and British Virgin Islands. On-board naturalists and historians play an important role in enhancing the enjoyment of the places visited. Trips in Holland and along other European waterways are planned. The ships charge a flat rate for singles. You may pay more than the double rate, but you have a choice of cabins and guaranteed privacy. The owners report that many singles, especially older women, are frequent passengers, enjoying the informal and inclusive atmosphere of the ships.

## DELTA QUEEN STEAMBOAT COMPANY

30 ROBIN STREET WHARF, NEW ORLEANS, LA 70130;
(800) 543–1949 OR (504) 586–0631.

This line keeps alive the 150–year-old tradition of cruising the Mississippi River through the heartland of America on picturesque steam-powered paddle wheelers. The 138-passenger *Delta Queen* is listed on the National Register of Historic Places. Her sister ships, the *Mississippi Queen* and *American Queen* are larger, accommodating more than 400 passengers. Three- to fourteen-day cruises sail from New Orleans to Memphis, St. Louis, Minneapolis, and St. Paul, or branch out on the Ohio River to Cincinnati and Pittsburgh or on the Cumberland River to Nashville and the Ohio to Louisville. This is a nostalgia trip, offering an ambience of homespun, old-fashioned Americana. Though the average passenger is over 50, all ages seem to enjoy these leisurely, relaxed journeys. About one-third of the passengers are repeat guests. Old-fashioned entertainment such as Dixieland jazz and barbershop quartets and many festive special events (such as the Great Steamboat Race, the Kentucky Derby cruise, and Mardi Gras or Cajun Christmas celebrations) keep things lively. The line offers a guaranteed share program.

## KD RIVER CRUISES OF EUROPE

2500 WESTCHESTER AVENUE, PURCHASE, NY 10577;
(914) 696-3600 OR (800) 346–6525 IN THE EAST
AND (800) 858–8587 IN THE WEST. (E–EE)

Small ships of about 100 passengers sail the Rhine, the Moselle, the Seine, the Danube, and other beautiful European rivers from April to November. Daily stops are in the great cities of the continent as well as smaller towns and countryside you might otherwise miss. Rates are reduced by as much as 20 percent in April and May, which can be a delightful time to travel. KD has a 25 percent supplement in many room categories and will try to arrange shares.

........................................................

# Barge Cruises

A placid, comfortable way to see Europe is along its waterways, with congenial small groups and plenty of time to sight-see at each stop. The barges cruise at about 4 miles per hour, so it's easy to get off and bicycle, walk, or jog along towpaths or go into nearby villages and catch up with the ship at its next stop.

## EUROPEAN WATERWAYS/BARGE FRANCE
140 EAST 56TH STREET, NEW YORK, NY 10022;
(212) 688–9538 OR (800) 217–4447.

The company arranges trips on rivers and canals in France, Holland, Brussels, and Scotland.

........................................................

# Freighter Cruises

If you have the time for long voyages, freighter travel is an adventurous way to visit foreign ports at a reasonable cost and in surprising comfort. Many retired people and teachers and others with long vacations sign on. Trips may range from twenty to seventy days.

Most cargo vessels accommodate no more than twelve passengers, so the experience is very personal. Staterooms are spacious and have views, and, unlike cruise liners, many freighters have large, single cabins. This is travel for the self-sufficient, for there are no shipboard activities and evening entertainment usually means conversations, cards, and games. Rates may average as little as $100 a day, including meals shared with the ship's officers. Passengers may also use the lounge and deck. Possible destinations include Australia and New Zealand, the Norwegian coast, South America, the South Pacific, Africa, Europe, and the Orient.

### To learn about freighter travel, contact

**TRAVELTIPS CRUISE AND FREIGHTER TRAVEL ASSOCIATION,**
163–07 DEPOT ROAD, P.O. BOX 580188, FLUSHING, NY 11358;
(800) 872-8584 OR (718) 939-2400.

A modest membership fee is credited toward the first voyage. Members receive the *TravLtips* magazine, which includes firsthand accounts of other members' journeys. These stories provide great armchair adventures. There is also a listing of upcoming freighter itineraries as well as discounts on special-value regular cruises. A free pamphlet is available, answering many questions about freighter voyages.

........................................................

# Sailing Cruises

The best bet if you are looking for single company on a ship is to board a sociable, no-frills windjammer sailing cruise, where many passengers are unattached. (See page 108 under Adventure Vacations for more details.) A more luxurious option is

**WINDSTAR CRUISES**
300 ELLIOTT AVENUE WEST, SEATTLE, WA 98119;
(206) 281-3535 OR (800) 258-7245.

The beautiful tall-masted luxury sailing yachts of this company accommodate 148 passengers and attract sophisticated, active individuals ages 25 to 65. Destinations include the Caribbean, the Mediterranean, and French Polynesia. These trips are less expensive than you might expect, but singles do pay a 150 percent supplement.

Also note that Club Med now has its own sailing ship—the world's largest—but it is designed for couples rather than singles.

........................................................................

# Cruise Expeditions

Small ships that are able to get off the beaten path to such exotic locales as Antarctica, Africa, Polynesia, Micronesia, Melanesia, and Indonesia offer exciting excursions for adventure-minded travelers. These trips are expensive, but they are also once-in-a-lifetime experiences. Since the numbers of passengers are small and the visits are thrilling, the groups quickly become close, making these seemingly remote excursions very easy to enjoy on your own. Some of my most memorable travel experiences have been on expedition cruises. Operators report that many passengers come by themselves.

The following are among the great expedition cruises I can personally recommend:

### Cruising the Nile

A trip on the Nile is an unforgettable experience, offering a chance to see life on the banks of the river and to visit the astonishing ruins and the tombs of the pharaohs with expert guides. The narrow ribbon of gentle river allows a close-up view of village life at the same time providing a graphic illustration of the Nile's importance—beyond the border of green irrigated by the river, barren desert begins.

Longer cruises begin in Cairo; shorter ones begin in Luxor or Aswan (reached by plane from Cairo). The major sights lie between the cities. Sight-seeing stops include the Temple of Luxor and the awesome ruins of the Temple of Karnak as well as the Valley of the Kings, where the tombs of Tutankhamen and other pharaohs were found; you will also see the Valley of the Queens and the Tombs of the Nobles, which contain some of the most important art of ancient Egypt.

Besides the many international expedition cruise companies, a number of local Egyptian operators run cruises, as do the major Cairo hotels.

Among the most popular operators for Americans are these familiar names:

## HILTON INTERNATIONAL NILE CRUISES
c/o MISR TRAVEL,
605 THIRD AVENUE, NEW YORK, NY 10158;
(212) 973–2200 OR (800) HILTONS; OR P.O. BOX 257, CAIRO, EGYPT,
OR CALL (800) 448–4782 OR (212)697–9370.

## SHERATON NILE CRUISES
4 AHED PASHA STREET, GARDEN CITY, CAIRO, EGYPT.

For information in the U.S. call (800) 325–5353 or contact MISR Travel listed above.

## *The Coastal Express: Cruising the Fjords of Norway*

The ads call this "The World's Most Beautiful Voyage," and it's hard to argue as you cruise along Norway's breath-taking coastline. Wending into steep and narrow fjords, gliding past glaciers, farms, and fishing villages and crossing the Arctic Circle, the Coastal Express fleet goes where larger cruisers cannot venture. Though cabins are comfortable and newer ships in the fleet are a bit more luxurious, these are not ordinary cruise ships. They are working cargo ships, the vital lifeline for the hardy fishermen and farmers in the more remote northern villages along the coast. As they pick up and deliver mail, supplies, and passengers at thirty-five towns and villages along the way, the ships provide a true close-up of local life. Talks on board tell a lot about the country and its people.

The sail is all the more fascinating because the panoramas change daily on the way to "the top of the world." From the home port of Bergen to Kirkenes at the end of the line, trees give way to Arctic tundra, mountains to flats, and depending on the season, the light may change from night and day to all night or all day. The strains of Edvard Grieg on the loudspeaker announce the most dramatic entry into the narrow, steep-walled Trollfjord, where mountains loom almost close enough to touch.

Tromso, the gateway to the Arctic, and Trondheim, Norway's third largest city and one of the oldest, are major stops with many sights to see. Other ports are so tiny it takes no more than five minute to walk the town, but often there is a pleasant surprise—a whimsical statue, a little park, or simply the chance to watch fishing boats and people going about their daily routines. The final stop in Bergen is best of all. Cradled by steep mountains, filled with cobbled lanes and quaint wooden houses, Bergen delights everyone.

There are no floor shows on the Bergen Line and no midnight buffets. Meals are not extravaganzas, but they do feature absolutely delicious fresh seafood. Don't sign on if you want the usual cruise ship experience; do come aboard for the experience of a lifetime. If you can't spend the entire twelve days, fly to Tromso and take the homeward voyage to Bergen.

For information, contact Bergen Line, Inc., 405 Park Avenue, New York, NY 10022; (212) 319–1300 or (800) 323–7436.

### Cruising the Sepik River, Papua New Guinea

Papua New Guinea is like nowhere else on earth, a fantastically varied island, a bird and flower lover's paradise still widely unblemished by humans. The country's finest native art, such as masks, carvings, and bark paintings, can be found in villages along the Sepik River. This route is served by two modern and comfortable small boats, the *Melanesian Discoverer,* a catamaran accommodating forty-two passengers that departs from the port of Madang, and the *Sepik Spirit,* an eighteen-passenger vessel that leaves from the art-filled Karawari Lodge, the country's oldest and best-known tourist lodging. The *Sepik Spirit* comes highly recommended, being owned by Bob Bates, who does a superb job of running tours from his lodges, both Karawari and the Ambua Lodge in the highlands.

The serpentine Sepik River provides the only route of transportation in this region. Its twists and turns provide a new vista around every bend—exotic birds, luxuriant vegetation, families traveling by dugout canoe, and thatched-hut villages where you can go ashore to see traditional ceremonies. Some itineraries also include the Trobriand Islands, whose culture is unique.

While Papua New Guinea is remote, it is a perfect add-on to a visit to Australia and a truly unforgettable travel experience. It is one of the few remaining places on earth where you can see tribes living as they have since the Stone Age. In many areas, they have had contact with the Western world for less than fifty years. The cruise can be combined with a land package for further exploration in the beautiful highlands.

The best source of current tour and cruise information is Air Niugini at 5000 Birch Street, Suite 3000, West Tower, Newport Beach, CA 92660; (714) 752–5440.

Finally, cruising the Galápagos Islands is one of the ultimate travel experiences. Read about it under Nature, page 130.

### Expedition cruise operators

Better-known cruise companies that roam the globe from the Arctic to the Amazon using smaller ships include:

### LINDBLAD SPECIAL EXPEDITIONS

720 FIFTH AVENUE, NEW YORK, NY 10019;
(212) 765–7740 OR (800) 762–0003.

### ESPLANADE TOURS

581 BOYLSTON STREET, BOSTON, MA 02116;
(617) 266–7465 OR (800) 426–5492.

This office handles voyages from a number of top operators.

### ABERCROMBIE AND KENT/CONTINENTAL WATERWAYS

1420 KENSINGTON ROAD, OAK BROOK, IL 60521;
(312) 954–2944 OR (800) 323–7308.

### QUARK EXPEDITIONS

980 POST ROAD, DARIEN CT 06820;
(203) 656–0499 OR (800) 356–5699.

### AMAZON TOURS AND CRUISES

8700 WEST FLAGLER STREET, MIAMI, FL 33174;
(305) 227–2266 OR (800) 423–2791.

## SOCIETY EXPEDITIONS
2001 WESTERN AVENUE, SUITE 300, SEATTLE, WA 98121;
(800) 548–8669 OR (206) 728–2301.

## DISCOVERY TOURS
## AMERICAN MUSEUM OF NATURAL HISTORY,
CENTRAL PARK WEST AT 79TH STREET, NEW YORK, NY 10024–5192;
(800) 462–8687 OR (212) 769–5700.

## *Cruise References:*

### The Unofficial Guide to Cruises
KAY SHOWKER, MACMILLAN TRAVEL, NEW YORK.

### Berlitz Complete Guide to Cruising and Cruise Ships
DOUGLAS WARD, BERLITZ PUBLISHING, OXFORD, ENGLAND.

Hey! Want to make friends easily?

Let 'em know you're connected with AVIATION!

# The Singles Scene

ith the number of single travelers growing so rapidly, it is only natural that enterprising folks will find ways to serve them. This chapter is a potpourri of advice, events, and services of interest to singles—tours and resorts where singles mingle, publications aimed to help the single traveler, and ideas for finding a compatible roommate to beat the high cost of traveling solo.

Because younger travelers might prefer the company of their contemporaries, there is a section on age-specific programs for the 20-35 age group that get a high percentage of single participants. The growing number of trips and services just for women is detailed in the next chapter, followed by a survey of the scene for seniors—a burgeoning list of possibilities for those over age 50.

Let's look at some of the possibilities for all ages.

## Newsletters

The best way to keep track of current special opportunities for solo travel is with a newsletter. Subscription rates change, so be sure to inquire about current prices before sending a check!

*Travel Companions,* published bimonthly by the Travel Companion Exchange (see page 194), is valuable even if you have no interest in finding travel partners. It is chock-full of travel news and bargains, including special deals for singles, and good advice on traveling alone and on travel in general. Annual subscriptions are $48; a sample copy is $5, applied to the full price if you subscribe.

*Connecting...News for Solo Travellers* (1996 West Broadway, P.O. Box 29088, Vancouver V6J 5C2, BC Canada; 604–737–7791) was begun in

1989 by Diane Redfern, a Canadian whose purpose is to form a world-wide network of single travelers to share hospitality, tips, advice, and encouragement. Her twenty-page, bimonthly publication includes a wealth of helpful information including upcoming trips for singles, reports from readers on their recent travel experiences, and suggestions for singles-friendly lodgings. Those who share information receive an extension on their subscriptions. Ads include notices from singles offering hospitality to travelers and from people seeking travel companions.

Subscribers also get a valuable extra, the "Singles-Friendly Travel Directory," which is a current listing of cruise lines and tour operators offering a "guaranteed share" program or charging no single supplement. Readers' recommendations for lodgings are also included. Subscriptions are $25; sample issue, $5.

*Going Solo* (P.O. Box 123, Apalachicola, FL 31329; 904–653–8848) was founded in 1990 by Jane Doerfer, a sophisticated traveler whose good taste and tips make for interesting reading. In her publication, she details tours and lodgings appropriate for (but not limited to) singles, a varied lot from walking the British Isles to fly-fishing to spa vacations. Each issue also features news and good deals for singles. Doerfer details her own travels, sharing such discoveries as England's Wolsey Lodges, which are historic homes where the hosts are in residence and provide you with dinner as well as lodging. Annual subscriptions are $29.

*Single Traveler* (P.O. Box 682, Ross, CA 94957; 847–714-1334) is a bi-monthly publication with good information on singles-friendly destinations, lodgings that give singles a break, and the latest news on trips for singles. Subscribers can also join Single Travel Connections, a network for meeting other single travelers of all ages. When they feature tour operators, this newsletter gives information much like the charts in this book, with group size, age range, percentage of singles, and male/female ratios. Subscriptions are $29.

····················································

# Travel Companions

For many solo travelers, one of the most useful resources is The Travel Companion Exchange (Box 833, Amityville, NY 11701; 516–454–0880 or 800–392–1256). An organization started in 1982 and dedicated to pairing travel-minded single people. The goal is to avoid the discriminatory supplement for singles while meeting new friends at the same time. Members are also resources for homestays for travelers. A six-month membership is $99 and includes a subscription to the TCE newsletter mentioned in the last section.

Founder Jens Jurgen says the organization has served more than 12,000 members across the United States and Canada and has current members representing every state. There are other matching services (some listed below), but none comes close to the numbers or reliability of this group. Most members are age 40 or over, but ages can range from 20 all the way to 85. The male/female ratio is almost even, Jurgen reports.

The Exchange provides information; members do their own contact work. Applicants fill out a profile form describing themselves and their travel interests, then place a  short "personal" ad in a newsletter that is circulated to all members, with an abbreviated description, including age, and where they hope to travel. Those who are interested can send for the longer profile, and, if the interest remains, can contact the person directly for a meeting before deciding to make travel plans.

Even if the vibes are good, Jurgen recommends spending time together on a weekend or short trip before setting off on a long excursion. Since the listings specify where the person lives, you can look for someone close enough to meet before you make further plans.

While some members wish to be matched with members of their own sex, others are equally interested in meeting partners of the opposite sex, and Jurgen reports that many  compatible traveling mates have turned into lifetime companions. Here are samples of recent ads:

*Ted: 41, 5'11", SWM (single white male), NS (nonsmoker). Quiet, practical professional w/sense of humor. Enjoy most fine arts, current events, good food, learning about other cultures. Seek MTC (male traveling companion) 20-70. Considering trip to Mideast or North Africa, but flexible. Home: So. California.*

*Marie: 32, 5'4", 140, SWF, NS. Banker. Easygoing, good sense of humor, well-traveled, love European sight-seeing, museums, castles, dining. Other int: tennis, reading, classical music, making new friends, weekend trips. Home: Philadelphia.*

*"L": 65, 5'10", 148 DWM (divorced white male), NS. Enjoy tennis,*

# Smaller Companion-Finding Services

- Partners for Travel, *(P.O. Box 560337, Miami, FL 33256; 800–866-5565),* formed in 1992, offers profiles of members who match your travel preferences, a newsletter, and travel discounts. Most members are over age 45, so the membership of roughly 500 tends to be in Sunbelt locations. A six-month membership is $60.
- Travel in Two's Inc., *(239 North Broadway, Suite 3, North Tarrytown, NY 10591; 914-631–8301)* is both a matching service and a travel agency. It helps find a traveling partner of the same sex, then helps plan the trip. There is a $10 enrollment fee.
- Single Person's Travel Club *(10395A Folsom Boulevard, Suite 134, Rancho Cordoba, CA 95670; 800–865-0732)* is basically a nonprofit group with seven chapters in California. It holds socials, discussions, weekend outings, and some trips. Members, mostly in their 40s and 50s, receive a monthly newsletter. At press time, they were in process of taking over Partners in Travel, an organization for single travelers seeking partners; Californians can check the current status. Club membership is $35.

reading, hiking. Seek F/MTC 40-70, college grad with enthusiasm for life. Good conversational skills a must. Pix. Home: Grosse Pointe, MI.

There is also a shorter listing in this newsletter for specific travel plans. These are recent examples:

DWF, 45, NS. Seek MTC 50–65 to explore Spain/Portugal, rent condo and use as home base. No. California.

SWM, 51, NS. Like hosting FTC 34–52, smoker ok, wkds for Tanglewood concerts, also NYC, Cape Cod & fall in New Engl. CT

For a women-only matching service, see page 211; for a service for older travelers, see page 225.

······························································

# Trips for Singles

One way to ensure meeting other single people is to sign up for a tour designed expressly for singles. These offerings change from year to year, and many singles tour operators listed in the first edition of this book are no longer in business. This list is limited to those who have been operating some time. Many are operators listed in other sections of the book but who offer, in addition to other programs, special trips designated for singles. All of these groups will try to arrange for shares, but there may be a surcharge if you request single occupancy. Here are some of the possibilities:

## THE SINGLE GOURMET
133 EAST 58TH STREET, NEW YORK, NY 10022;
(212) 980-8788. (EE)

This nationwide organization dedicated to good eating and sociability started in 1982 and now has chapters in more than a dozen U.S. locations, three Canadian cities, and London. Restaurant outings are arranged regularly in each city, and a few trips are offered to all members each year. The trips include a full sight-seeing agenda but concentrate on dining, visiting the very top restaurants in each location. Lodgings are also deluxe. Recent trips included San Francisco and the Napa Valley, New Orleans, and a New Year's Eve journey to Spain. Travelers are paired at no charge. Members may attend dinners in other member cities when they travel. The age range of membership is from 20 to 60, with most age 40 or older. Women outnumber men 5 to 2. Many of the trip participants are from the Northeast, but there is a representation from all the chapters. Members say the trips are well run and sociable, and the days are flexible enough to allow for free time. Chapters are found in New York and its suburbs; Chicago; Philadelphia; Minneapolis/St. Paul; Norfolk and Richmond, Virginia; and in San Diego, Orange County, and Los Angeles, in California.

## AMERICAN JEWISH CONGRESS
(SEE PAGE 163)

The highly respected cultural organization offers several tours for singles only to Israel and other destinations. Tours are divided by age groups for under 40, 25–45, and 35–55. See page 164 for more information about their tours.

## SOLO FLIGHTS
10 GREENWOOD LANE, WESTPORT, CT 06880;
(203) 256–1235 OR (800) 266–1566 OUTSIDE CONNECTICUT. (M)
WILL TRY TO ARRANGE SHARES.

Well past its twentieth birthday, this travel center for singles offers a variety of tours in Costa Rica, Europe, and the United States, plus cruises, Club Med reservations, and occasional specialty trips such as a scuba diver's excursion to Belize.

## BACKROADS
(PAGE 97)

Offers many walking and biking trips for singles in the U.S., Europe, Asia, and the Pacific. The itineraries are identical to regular offerings and offer a choice of camping or inn stays.

## ROADS LESS TRAVELED
(PAGE 103)

Combines biking and hiking with rafting and horseback riding on singles trips to the Colorado Rockies and the Southwest. Singles tours attract younger participants, with 35 the most common age.

## BICYCLE ADVENTURES
(PAGE 100)

Specializing in bike trips in the Pacific Northwest, offers one departure each month just for singles and gets high marks from former participants.

## NANTAHALA OUTDOOR CENTER
(PAGE 36)

Holds a three-day singles weekend focused on sociability and fun for kayakers and canoeists of all levels. Things start off with a welcome party.

# Regional Organizers of Trips for Singles

**Singles Adventure Club** (Escapes Unlimited), 626 East Chapman, Orange, CA 92666; (800) 243-7227.

**Adventures for Singles, Inc.;** 640 Denards Mill, Marietta, GA 30667; (770) 956-0437 or (800) 706-7481.

**Traveling Singles Inc.,** 1600 Preston Road #306, Dallas, TX 75248; (800) 997-8717 or (214) 991-1822.

The next day the group divides on the river according to skills but comes together for meals and evening sessions.

## WINDJAMMER BAREFOOT CRUISES
(PAGE 109)
Sets aside several cruises each year for singles. They cut off registration when one gender reaches 50 percent, so there's always an even mix.

## TENNIS CAMPS LTD.
(PAGE 12)
Offers special weeks for singles, as does **Topnotch at Stowe** (page 13).

..................................................................

# For Young Singles

The following tours for younger travelers report that at least half of their participants are traveling solo. Both tours will arrange shares.

## CONTIKI HOLIDAYS

300 Plaza Alicante #900, Garden Grove, CA 92640;
(800) 466–0610 or (714) 740–0808. (I)

For more than thirty years, Contiki has served adventure-minded passengers ages 18 to 35 with trips to Europe, Africa, Australia, New Zealand, the continental United States, and Hawaii. Most participants are in their 20s; 70 percent are single, and they come from English-speaking countries all over the world. The average male/female ratio is 40/60, but according to one insider, males outnumber females on many U.S. and South Pacific tours, while European trips tend to be more heavily female. The trips are by motor coach. For trips labeled "Superior," accommodations are in hotels and resorts. Budget travelers stay in Contiki-owned chalets and villas, cabins, and hotels, sometimes four to a room. All rooms have private baths. Said one young woman recently returned from her first trip to Europe: "I can't think of a better way to go."

## CLUB 21–35, TRAFALGAR TOURS

21 East 26th Street, New York, NY 10010;
(800) 457–6891 or (212) 689–8977. (I)

"Fast-paced coach tours through Europe for younger travelers who want to see as much as possible on a budget," say the managers of this program, which has offices around the world, providing an international mix to the group. Itineraries to Europe range from twenty to thirty-eight days, with lodgings in hotels. The male/female ratio is close to even.

# Resorts Recommended for Singles

## CLUB MED

Club Med is the place where swinging young singles go for wild partying, right? When the first North American club was born in Guadeloupe in 1967, that image might have been accurate, but three decades later, it is out of date. Club Med's original guests have grown up, and so has the club. Now there are clubs designated for families, special programs for single parents, and discounts for guests over age 55.

Does that mean Club Med is no longer a good choice for solo vacationers? Not at all. The greatest appeal of Club Med remains. The first resorts to cater to singles remain beach vacations where you can be absolutely comfortable by yourself and never have to dine alone. Singles still make up a big percentage of the membership, and many of them welcome the fact that the social pressure at many clubs is less than it used to be.

Those who knew the Club Meds of old will be pleasantly surprised at new and remodeled clubs with larger and better appointed rooms. Columbus Isle in the Bahamas is the most lavish of the new breed, filled with fabulous folk art and antiques; it even offers TV and telephones in the rooms, a far cry from the Spartan original Club Meds. Paradise Island is undergoing a similar transformation, complete with marble bathrooms, and is due to be complete in 1998.

Many clubs have kept up with the times by offering aerobics classes and fitness centers with the latest in exercise equipment. And you can learn anything from sailing, scuba diving, and windsurfing to tennis and skiing to circus skills like juggling, acrobatics on a trampoline, or tricks on a trapeze. With the exception of scuba diving, horseback riding, and golf, sports instruction is included in one all-inclusive price, along with three lavish meals a day and wine or beer for lunch and dinner.

While many guests still prefer to save by having a roommate assigned, single rooms are now available with an added supplement; this can be a modest 10 to 20 percent off season or as much as 100 percent during holiday weeks. At Buccaneer's Creek, which is largely for singles, you can request a single room without a surcharge during certain periods. The Paradise Island makeover includes forty-one single-occupancy rooms with queen-size beds.

The best deal at Club Med is to take your chances with the Wild Card option. You pick the week for a set, money-saving price; they pick the place. Vacationers reap the benefits of allowing Club Med to even the numbers at its various resorts. Singles are never sent to family-oriented clubs.

Because Club Med is such a well-known choice for single vacationers, it deserves special space and description, pro and con.

## Life at Club Med

L ife at Club Med villages is meant to be carefree. There's no cash to worry about. You are given a card when you arrive that allows you to charge any expenses and settle up at the end of your stay, so your money can go into the safe until you leave. Rooms usually aren't provided with clocks, so old hands know to bring a watch and an alarm clock. Lessons are scheduled at specified times, and if you don't get there on time, you'll miss out.

With the many activities offered, days can be jam packed—or you can ignore all the activities and find a quiet spot on the beach. Meals are all-you-can-eat extravaganzas with dozens of choices. Some dishes are better than others, but if you don't like your first selections, you can always go back and find reliable alternatives, such as roast beef, lamb, or turkey served from carving stations.

A hostess seats everyone at big round tables, making it very easy to meet people. You can then make reservations to dine together with your new friends in the smaller specialty dining rooms.

But Club Med is not for everyone. If you hated summer camp and you are not turned on by the idea of group lessons, line dancing, and the "Hands Up" song with hand motions, you may not be Club Med material. "Olympics Day" is really a grown-up version of a "color war"—everyone is divided into teams for competitions that include everything from basketball to beer drinking.

In all fairness, though, no one forces you to do anything. You can stay under a palm tree with a book if you like and go for a walk on the beach after dinner, but you can't avoid the music and activity around you or the sound of the loudspeaker announcing daily in English and in French contests like volleyball and water polo tournaments.

The voice belongs to a GO (*gentil organisateur*), one of the bouncy, good-looking young men and women who do everything they can to make their enthusiasm contagious to their flock of GMs (*gentils membres*). The GOs work hard, giving sports instruction, being sociable, lead-

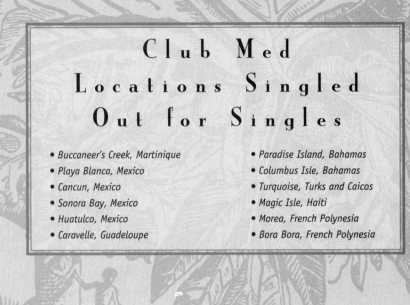

# Club Med
## Locations Singled
## Out for Singles

- Buccaneer's Creek, Martinique
- Playa Blanca, Mexico
- Cancun, Mexico
- Sonora Bay, Mexico
- Huatulco, Mexico
- Caravelle, Guadeloupe

- Paradise Island, Bahamas
- Columbus Isle, Bahamas
- Turquoise, Turks and Caicos
- Magic Isle, Haiti
- Morea, French Polynesia
- Bora Bora, French Polynesia

ing trivia contests before dinner and group dances afterward (no partner necessary). Then they put on the evening entertainment, which can be surprisingly good for amateurs. Sophisticated? Not really, but you have to admire their energy. After the show the disco opens, and dancing goes on well into the night.

## Choosing a Club

If you decide to give Club Med a try and look at their big catalog, you'll see plenty of tempting properties. After all, two of the club's main attractions are great locations and interesting architecture. Management makes it easier by pointing out which clubs are primarily geared to families and which to couples and singles. In the latter group, two are singled out as primarily for singles. They are Buccaneer's Creek in Martinique and Playa Blanca on the Pacific coast of Mexico. The club encourages younger singles to go to Buccaneer's Creek by offering special prices for ages 20 to 25 during winter and spring break weeks. This is said to be the one club that still resembles the swinging Club Meds of old.

If you have a particular sport or activity in mind, one way to ensure that you'll enjoy the week is to choose Club Med villages with a specialty. Intensive tennis and horseback instruction are offered at Sonora Bay, and dedicated diving centers are found at Columbus Isle, Turquoise, and Sonora Bay. Golf is available at half a dozen locations at an added fee, and some clubs offer free instruction. Turquoise has the most intensive circus program. You'll find more current offerings in the catalog.

Theme weeks are recent additions at the clubs and have ranged from "Renew Yourself," aimed at stress reduction and offering instruction in yoga and tai chi, to stargazing astronomy workshops or "Ocean Awareness" weeks featuring marine ecologists to better your understanding of coral reefs or whales. The "Legends of Tennis" week brings in champions such as Bjorn Borg and Rosie Casals for exhibition matches and expert instruction. Food and wine festivals feature famous chefs and vintners, and "Comedy Club Month" brings professional comedians and magicians to spice up the nightlife.

If you don't want kids around or want to better your chances of finding more single adults, avoid the clubs especially recommended for families. These are the Sandpiper in Florida, Eleuthera in the Bahamas, Punta Cana in the Dominican Republic, St. George's Cove in Bermuda, and Ixtapa in Mexico. (Some of these are definitely recommended for single parents, however; see page 287).

Sociable singles might also want to think twice before choosing Columbus Isle or Paradise Island, which are listed as appropriate for singles but are also designated as primarily for couples.

One final bit of personal advice: Don't choose a club with a location that requires several plane changes or long bus rides. The journeys are tiring and expensive and use up valuable vacation time. Check travel time carefully when you make your plans; times from the airport are listed in the catalog. Club Med one-week packages via charters save time and money; you'll probably save even if you have to pay for an overnight in the departure city in order to make connections.

The ambience at the various clubs depends entirely on the current crop of GOs (they shift assignments every six months) and the makeup of the guests, which changes from one week to the next. Like any vacation, you take your chances on who you will meet when you choose a Club Med location—but judging from the enormous number of people who return time and again, the chances are good that you will make friends. The club reports that more than 40 percent of their guests are repeaters.

To enroll in any Club Med, you must pay a one-time initiation fee, and there is an annual fee thereafter. The travel sections of major newspapers frequently carry ads from tour operators who buy space in bulk and promise discounts on rates, so check before you reserve.

For more information and a catalog, contact any travel agent or Club Med direct at (800) CLUB–MED.

_COMMENTS: EB: I recently spent a week at Club Med Turquoise, wanting to see first hand the changes since my last visit to a Club Med several years ago. This remains the best beach vacation I know for a single person. The general atmosphere is very friendly; by the time you've had a few meals and taken part in a few activities, you know a number of people. Many of them are interesting and have diverse professions, and since Club Med is international, guests come from all over the United States, Canada, and Europe._

_Turquoise attracts many singles in their 20s and early 30s, but the age range went well into the 60s when I was there, so no one needed to worry about feeling out of place. Some of the younger guests were intent on drinking and partying, but other than creating a few noisy tables in the dining room, they didn't affect the other guests._

_Undoubtedly, those who get the most from the Club Med experience are the sociable, fun-loving types who enjoy the line dancing and group songs and who take advantage of the many sports available. But there was ample room to escape on one of the loveliest beaches in the Caribbean, and even a section of quieter beach where classical music was piped in each afternoon._

_The most positive change I found was the food. The choices were really impressive. At every lunch and dinner, there were half a dozen meat and poultry entrees, two kinds of pasta, and nearly twenty kinds of vegetables. Each night featured a different theme—French, Italian, Caribbean, and Tex-Mex, to name a few. Seafood night brought caviar, smoked salmon, crab legs, and tons of shrimp—and these were just the appetizers! Every_ *meal offered bountiful fruit and cheese displays, a tempting array of desserts, and breads so delicious, they were a peril to the waistline.*

*The entertainment was also better than I remembered, thanks to a clever choreographer who knew how to make the most of his amateur cast. Some of the most exciting entertainment came on the night when guests showed off what they had learned at the circus workshop, displaying high-wire balancing and acrobatic feats that were nothing short of amazing. The circus emphasis adds to the spirit of fun at this particular club; wherever you go, you find people practicing juggling and other tricks.*

*I had only one criticism: Drinks between meals priced around $5 seemed quite expensive, and excursions were also pricey, anywhere from $40 to $75. The excursion prices are listed in the catalog, so take a look before you go, and come prepared to spend a bit if you want these extras. Remember also to add in the cost of departure taxes and transfers from the airport to the club.*

*Most of the people I met had been to several clubs and planned to come back again. Why do they keep returning? Here were some of the comments:*

*"No surprises. I know the food will be good and the staff will be great."*

*"I come for the diving. It is much more reasonable than at other resorts, and since I don't do it often, I like the fact that I am so well supervised."*

*"I like meeting people from all over."*

*"I like having so many sports options without having to worry about what they cost."*

*"So easy to meet people, so friendly."*

........................................................

# Superclubs:
# Hedonism II and
# Jamaica, Jamaica

Beautifully located in Negril, Jamaica, along a 7-mile swath of beach, Hedonism II lures many singles. Its attractions are similar to those offered by Club Med—rates that include all meals, plus tennis, sailing, water-skiing, windsurfing, volleyball, a Nautilus gym, squash, snorkeling, scuba diving, bicycling, horseback riding, aerobics, and arts and crafts classes. In addition, they offer an open bar all day and night and night-time entertainment that includes top local bands and performers. The long beach at Negril is shared by several hotels, convenient if you want to take a walk into town or sample the local nightlife.

Hedonism's unique lure is the free-wheeling Jamaican spirit and conta-gious reggae beat that permeate the island. "Let's party" is the motto, right from the rum punch you are handed as you arrive. All this attracts a young crowd, averaging between 21 and 35 and about 65 percent single. There is a nude beach and a "prude" beach. One observer noted with sur-prise that it was the young who tended to be covered; older guests, who ranged into their 60s, seemed to be on the nude beach, unconcerned with appearances.

Much of the food is grown locally, and menus feature a lot of native fruits and vegetables. All-you-can-eat meals include treats such as grilled lobster.

The same owners operate Jamaica, Jamaica, a resort on Runaway Bay, near Ocho Rios, another all-inclusive resort with a slightly more sophisti-cated ambience. Though the single population may often be as high as 50 percent, there are more couples here. Tennis clinics are a resort specialty. For more information, contact International Lifestyles at (800) 858–8009 or (516) 868–6924.

# For Women Only

ONE OF THE MOST NOTICEABLE TRENDS IN TRAVEL IS THE growth of activities for women only. There have always been spas for women, and as mentioned, almost every major ski area has begun offering special ski weeks for women. But the desire for comfortable, noncompetitive, nonpressured travel has spawned a dramatic increase in options for women, and there are more publications and organizations than ever to encourage women to take to the road. There's even a mail order company, Christine Columbus, that specializes in travel gear for women.

The most popular women-only trips fall into the active, adventure category. These trips are challenging, but they supply a supportive atmosphere and eliminate the need to keep up with macho males. The companionship and sharing on strictly female trips is another major lure; participants report firm friendships that last long after the trip ends, a big plus for participants whether single or not.

Carole Jacobs of *Shape* magazine aptly describes the appeal of these journeys. "Women-only adventure travel is more than a girl's night out . . . There's no better place to find yourself than on top of a mountain, no better time than when you're climbing a cliff to discover that your better half is not the one you left behind, but the one you found within."

Here are some of the varied resources and trips available for women:

## Publications for Women Travelers

*Journeywomen* magazine (50 Prince Arthur Avenue, Suite 1703, Toronto M5R 1B5 Ontario, Canada), a quarterly, describes itself as a networking magazine for female travel enthusiasts. Subscribers come from all over North America and from as far afield as Europe, Hong Kong, Israel, Vietnam, and Turkey, making for a wonderful exchange of travel tips and stories. This magazine is chock-full of valuable information and resources, from hotels welcoming singles to tours for women. Many of the advertisers are American. An article on "Safe and Solo in Turkey" includes suggestions on dining, names a Turkish bath reserved for women only on Tuesdays, and reminds that women must cover their heads on entering a mosque. A story on Tucson tells of a women-only golf instruction program, social hikes for those over 50, and women-led desert walks. A sample issue is $6.

*Sports Traveler* magazine (167 Madison Avenue, Suite 405, New York, NY 10016, 212–759–1357) is a slick publication filled with articles and ideas for the active woman. Biking, tennis, hiking, horseback riding, golf, sailing—name your sport and you'll find it here, along with travel ideas, outdoor clothing, and much more. Trip suggestions and ads are coed as well as for women only. Phone for subscription information.

# Female Traveling Companions and Hostesses

## SHARED ADVENTURES—A WOMAN'S TRAVEL NETWORK

FAIRVIEW TRAVEL SERVICE
FAIRVIEW PLAZA
420 WEST 75TH STREET, DOWNERS GROVE, IL 60516;
(630) 852-5533.

In 1987 this travel agency formed a club to help women find compatible traveling companions, and the group quickly gained more than 300 members, mostly from the Chicago area. As word spreads, the reach has expanded from Florida to California. When members request travel partners, a "network alert" goes out in the form of postcards and direct calls to those who have already indicated interest in the destination. There is no fee to join, but the agency does expect to make the travel arrangements for those it pairs. All ages have enrolled; the majority are between 30 and 55.

Fairview Travel also plans trips for women only. Recent itineraries have included weekend trips to Charleston or Mackinac Island, an Asian journey to Bangkok, Singapore, and Hong Kong, and an African safari. They recommend a weekend trip for prospective travel partners before they take a longer journey together.

## WOMEN WELCOME WOMEN

C/O BETTY SOBEL, USA TRUSTEE,
10 GREENWOOD LANE, WESTPORT, CT 06880;
(203)259-7832

Was formed in 1984 to foster international friendships by enabling women of different nations to visit one another. There are some 1,600 participants from sixty countries, ages 16 to 90. Each new member fills out a form asking to be a hostess, a traveler, or both. Questions on the form include age, occupation, religion, politics, and languages spoken. Details from these applications are included on a world-wide membership list, divided by countries. Visits are arranged individually, initiated by travelers writing to prospective hostesses. The organization recommends continued correspondence to become acquainted a bit before an actual visit and suggests that the first stay be short, in case expectations are not met.

Members also sometimes arrange to get together. Thirteen women from the U.S., England, Australia, Scotland, Holland, and Belgium gathered a few years ago in Westport, Connecticut, with each woman housed in a volunteer's home. Such gatherings are publicized in a newsletter published three times a year with news of forthcoming events, reports of members' travels, and requests for touring companions.

This is purely a voluntary organization, funded by its members' dues and donations. Minimum dues are $30.

# Women's Tour Operators

As with any program, before you sign on to one of these tours, ask for reference names and numbers of former participants.

## THE WOMEN'S TRAVEL CLUB

21401 NE 38TH AVENUE, AVENTURA, FL 33180;
(305) 936-9669 OR (800) 480-4448

With more than 1,000 members nationally, ages 30s to 70s, this club offers at least one small-group trip per month with room shares guaranteed to destinations from Paris to Ecuador, Thailand to Russia. Weekend trips are also on the agenda to U.S. locales like New Orleans and Charleston. Membership is $35, which includes a monthly newsletter.

## ISIS WOMEN'S TRAVEL ASSOCIATION

3313 SUPERIOR LANE, BOWIE, MD 20715;
301-262-2384 OR 800-432-8258

A new organization founded in 1996, it offers "innovative, interesting, and secure travel." Membership is available through a limited number of travel agencies nationwide. Roommate matching is one of the benefits of membership, along with a quarterly newsletter. Trips have included Hawaii, skiing in Aspen, an ecological tour of Costa Rica, and cruises.

# Women-Only Adventure Travel

## WOMANTREK

1411 EAST OLIVE WAY, P.O. BOX 20643, SEATTLE, WA 98102;
(206) 325-4772 AND (800) 477-TREK. (I–E)

O ff-the-beaten-path adventures for small groups of women only (with female guides) run the gamut from biking, rafting, sea kayaking, trekking, skiing, llama pack trips, and leadership courses to deluxe tours. Ages range from

| | |
|---|---|
| YEARS IN BUSINESS: | 12 |
| AGE RANGE: | 22–80 |
| MOST COMMON AGE: | 35–65 |
| PERCENT ALONE: | 75 |
| NUMBER OF PARTICIPANTS: | 300 PER YEAR |
| MALE/FEMALE RATIO: | ALL FEMALE |

the 30s to the 70s. Destinations include Peru, India, Nepal, Greece, China, Nova Scotia, Africa, Mexico, Thailand, the Galápagos Islands, and Tibet. Ski trips are in Washington and New Mexico. The organization offers camaraderie and the opportunity of a lifetime for women who are looking for experiences of personal importance and who wish to see the world, says the brochure. Some white-water trips include workshops on management, leadership, and personal renewal.

COMMENTS *Female, 40s: I've gone on three trips, alone and with a friend. The groups were made up of very intelligent people, and I formed lasting friendships with women from age 20 to 60. The guides are knowledgeable and the programs first-rate.*
*Female, 60s: I went on a safari alone and it was fine. The groups were small, only seven on my tour. The women's ages ranged from the 30s to 60s, but most were in their 40s and single, and mainly from the West Coast. Everyone got along well. It was a wonderful experience.*

## RAINBOW ADVENTURES

15033 KELLY CANYON ROAD, BOZEMAN, MT 59715;
(406) 587–3883 OR (800) 804–8686. (M-E)

W orldwide adventures for women over 30 range from "Play hooky weekends" to three-week world journeys. Trips are rated easy, moderate, or "moderate-high energy." Many trips are designed for beginners who want to enjoy

| | |
|---|---|
| YEARS IN BUSINESS: | 15 |
| AGE RANGE: | 30–79 |
| MOST COMMON AGE: | LATE 40S, EARLY 50S |
| PERCENT ALONE: | ALL WOMEN; OWNER SAYS THE MAJORITY ARE OR HAVE BEEN MARRIED AND HAVE CHILDREN |
| NUMBER OF PARTICIPANTS: | 10–20 |
| MALE/FEMALE RATIO: | ALL FEMALE |
| NO SINGLE SUPPLEMENTS | |

adventure travel within a supportive and noncompetitive environment. Activities include cross-country skiing, river-rafting, canoeing inn to inn, horseback treks, hiking, and fly-fishing in the western United States plus a walking holiday in England, trekking in Nepal, and sailing the Greek Isles.

COMMENTS   *Female, 40s: I've gone hiking in the UK, staying in small family hotels and sharing rooms. I've also gone cross-country skiing in Wisconsin and camping on a glacier in Alaska. The women have diverse backgrounds, but share a love for adventure. They come from all over the U.S., but predominantly from Illinois and Wisconsin. Good organization; will go again.*

     *Female, 70s: I've taken four trips, including hiking and canal boating in England. The trips are well organized, and I've always made good friends with women of all ages.*

## SHERRI GRIFFITH EXPEDITIONS

(SEE PAGE 111)

This group offers rafting trips labeled *Women at Play: No Experience Necessary.* These are sojourns into nature with spectacular scenery to quiet the soul and white water for excitement. The adventure is described as a supportive, noncompetitive setting to learn outdoor skills taught by well-trained and personable riverwomen.

### Other adventure groups to investigate include:

## WOMBATS

AN ACRONYM FOR WOMEN'S MOUNTAIN BIKE AND TEA SOCIETY

P.O. BOX 757, FAIRFAX, CA 94978

Runs a variety of women's biking tours from weekend excursions to "two-week two-wheel treks." Members get a quarterly newsletter.

## WOMANSHIP

THE BOATHOUSE, 410 SEVERN AVENUE, ANNAPOLIS, MD 21401;
(800) 342-9295

Provides sailing instruction and sailing cruises on Chesapeake Bay and in San Diego, New England, the Pacific Northwest, the Caribbean, Greece, Ireland, and other destinations.

## WOODSWOMEN
25 West Diamond Lake Road, Minneapolis, MN 55419;
(612) 822–3809 or (800) 279–0555

This organization is devoted to supportive and challenging learning opportunities. It sponsors many outdoor travel adventures, from dogsledding to backpacking, bicycling, walking, sea kayaking, canoeing, and other outdoor endeavors. Members get a quarterly newsletter.

## ADVENTURE ASSOCIATES
P.O. Box 16304, Seattle, WA 98116
(206) 932–8352
Organizes trips from Nepal to Bali to the Greek Isles.

## ADVENTURE TRAVEL FOR WOMEN
P.O. Box 672, Hood River, OR 97031;
(503) 386–2111
Arranges multi-sport vacations around the globe.

## WOMANPOWER ENTERPRISES
2551 Sumac Circle, St. Paul, MN 55110;
(612) 773–0937 or (800) 879–1696
Provides in-depth, women-only safaris to Kenya.

........................................................

# Women's Travel Gear

Christine Columbus (P.O. Box 2168, Lake Oswego, OR 97035; 800–280–4775) addresses the special needs of women travelers. Along with handy safety items and handsome accessories, this mail-order catalog features items you won't find in other places. For instance, a half-slip with zippered pockets keeps jewelry and money secure. "Bathroom friendly" gear includes such items as twill pants with a hidden zipper in the crotch seam and nylon shorts with a two-layer, pull-apart crotch, both very handy when the facilities are less than posh. Her chic leather tote bag has a hidden compartment in the bottom to stash sneakers and double as a hideaway for wallet and passport.

TRAV

# The Golden Age: 50 and Over

WHY A SPECIAL CHAPTER FOR OLDER TRAVELERS? Age is no deterrent on the great majority of the group trips mentioned in this book, and adventurous seniors in their 80s are happily roaming the globe on their own right this minute. So what's so special about the older traveler?

To begin with, there are more of them. With those much-publicized baby boomers entering their fifties, the number of so-called seniors is mushrooming and everybody wants their attention. Latest figures in the *New York Times* in 1996 reported that the 55- to 74-year-old group accounts for 39.9 percent of the population; by 2006, it is expected to be nearly 50 percent.

These are people who tend to have more disposable income and more time to spend it, so it isn't surprising that many people want to tap into that market early. No longer do you have to be 65 to reap discounts. Age 50 has become the "golden age" for many travel benefits.

The American Association of Retired Persons has lowered its age requirement to 50, opening a whole range of travel discounts to those who reach the mid-century mark. Learning opportunities geared to older adults are growing rapidly. Elderhostel, the wonderful educational program for seniors, has changed its age limit from 60 to 55—with companions as young as 50. Programs such as Senior Ventures offer not only classroom learning but European tours and the chance for tennis enthusiasts to travel together to the luxurious John Gardiner Tennis Ranch or take in the matches in Wimbledon.

On an active trip, sometimes even the fittest traveler of a certain age may welcome a gentler pace and the comforting knowledge that you don't have to keep up with thirty-year-olds. A growing number of operators are meeting this need with "soft adventures" geared to healthy, active over-50s.

For many older singles, especially once-married individuals who find themselves considering solo travel for the first time in their later years, the company of contemporaries may seem reassuring. Numerous group tours labeled "over 50" may be of interest to these travelers.

So a special chapter for the over-50 generation seems in order just to recap all the privileges that come with age! Let's look at some of the trips that you can't take unless you're over 50!

## ELDERHOSTEL
75 FEDERAL STREET, BOSTON, MA 02110;
(617) 426–8056. (I)

Since 1975, this remarkable program has provided intellectual stimulation and good company for adults over age 55 and their companions over age 50 who want to continue to expand their horizons. It offers inexpensive, short-term academic programs at educational institutions around the world. The topics? Cicero to computers ... politics to poetry. More than 1,800 institutions participate, providing programs in every American state and Canadian province and forty-five other countries. Some 250,000 travelers take part each year; about 40 percent of them single. Typical U.S. programs offer three courses that meet daily for 1 to 1½ hours each. Most living/dining accommodations are in dormitories, and participants have the use of the campus recreational facilities. The charge for an average six-night program in the U.S. is under $400. Besides classroom courses, programs include bicycling trips, cross-country skiing, stays in country houses and private homes, trips to other countries, and study cruises, all at reasonable rates. Put yourself on the mailing list, and three times each year you'll get a 150-page newspaper-sized catalog crammed with possibilities. A land-sea program in Alaska, a stay at Trinity College in Wales, a spring sojourn in the Great Smoky Mountains, a jazz course in New Orleans, or a stay in New Delhi—it's enough to make younger folks want to hurry up and age!

## SENIOR VENTURES
SOUTHERN OREGON STATE COLLEGE, SENIOR PROGRAMS OFFICE,
250 SISKIYOU BOULEVARD, ASHLAND, OR 97520. (I)
APRIL TO OCTOBER

Since 1983, colleges in four western states have co-sponsored these one-to-four week educational adventures providing education, recreation, and travel opportunities for "lifelong learners" age 50 and over.

Each school plans its own offerings. In Ashland, Southern Oregon State College puts its emphasis on the well-known Oregon Shakespeare Festival, with the chance to study plays and see them produced. Central Washington University programs run the gamut from Chinese customs and festivals to the American presidency, Yiddish literature to tennis tips. Programs may include river floats and a Puget Sound cruise. The Desert Southwest Cultural Institute in Arizona features Southwestern archaeology, Indian cultures, and national parks, plus some special treats for tennis buffs—a week at John Gardiner's Tennis Ranch and a trip to Wimbledon. Western Oregon State College organizes RV trips in the U.S. as well as cruises and European tours that have included Turkey and England, Scotland, and Wales.

## INTERHOSTEL

UNIVERSITY OF NEW HAMPSHIRE DIVISION OF CONTINUING EDUCATION
6 GARRISON AVENUE, DURHAM, NH 03824;
(603) 862-1147 OR (800) 773-9753. (E–EE)
JUNE TO MID-SEPTEMBER PLUS SOME CHRISTMAS PROGRAMS

Another education-oriented group operating since 1979, Interhostel study tours for adults over age 50 (and companions 40 or older) are held in many countries abroad, in conjunction with local sponsoring host universities and educational institutions. More expensive than Elderhostel, these trips still are good value, often utilizing dormitory space at cooperating colleges and including all meals and airfare in the fee. Several programs feature Christmas abroad. The most recent catalog lists more than fifty options, from Paris to Florence, Prague to Beijing. Faculty of schools in each city give insight into the history, politics, natural environment, and culture of the region. Excursions to sites of historic or cultural significance supplement classroom learning, and the itinerary includes social activities.

Interhostel tries to find roommates, but if no share can be found, there is a single supplement, often no more than 10 percent to 15 percent more than the double rate.

## SENIORS ABROAD

12533 PACATO CIRCLE NORTH, SAN DIEGO, CA 92129;

(619) 485-1696.

This is an international exchange program for adults over age 50, much like those that young people enjoy. Participants stay with families in New Zealand, Australia, and Japan, and in return  provide hospitality in their own homes for travelers to the U.S. A typical tour includes short homestays in several locations around the country; some tours may also intersperse a few days at hotels or B&Bs.  These are not bargain tours—the cost of administration of a program like this is high— but they do provide a unique opportunity for an in-depth look at another culture and an ideal option for single travelers who want companionship and the opportunity to meet contemporaries in other lands. Some 3,500 people have participated since the program began in 1984.

## MOUNT ROBSON ADVENTURE HOLIDAYS

BOX 687, VALEMOUNT BOE 2Z0, BRITISH COLUMBIA, CANADA;

(604) 566-4386.

MAY TO SEPTEMBER

Older travelers who want a taste of outdoor adventure at a relaxed pace may want to look into these "gentle adventures," three- and four-day programs that include hiking, rafting, and sight-seeing in the heart of the Canadian Rockies. Lodging choices include camping or cabins, and there is often a lodge to lodge canoeing trip. The operators say that there are many single participants. The single supplement is low.

## ELDERTREKS

597 MARKHAM STREET, TORONTO M6G 2L7, ONTARIO, CANADA;

(416) 588-5000 OR (800) 741-7956.

(I-E, PLUS AIRFARE)

YEAR-ROUND; GUARANTEED SHARES

Promising "exotic adventure for the young at heart," these in-depth programs take small groups to Sumatra, Bali, Thailand, Nepal, Vietnam, India, Ecuador, Turkey, New Zealand, and many other fabulous destinations, exploring local culture and scenery on foot and by boat. There is always emphasis on meeting local people.

## WALKING THE WORLD: OUTDOOR ADVENTURES FOR PEOPLE 50 AND OVER

P.O. Box 1186, Fort Collins, CO 80522;
(970) 225–0500 or (800) 340–9255. (M–E)
Will try to arrange shares

Name a beautiful place and chances are this group will take you hiking there. Designed for active, outdoors-oriented older travelers, this group, founded in 1987, features worldwide destinations including New Zealand and Ireland, Tuscany and the Scottish Highlands, Banff and Jasper National Parks in Canada, Hawaii, Wales, and the Devon Coast. Closer to home, walking tours range from the coast of Maine to Arches National Park in Utah. Hiking is not difficult but does cover some high elevations. Trips are from nine to eighteen days; distances covered daily range from 5 to 8 miles daily on some trips to 7 to 10 miles on others. Depending on the destination, accommodations may be bed-and-breakfasts, hotels, motels, or country inns; a few trips involve camping, with shared responsibilities for setting up camp and cooking.

## OVERSEAS ADVENTURE TRAVEL

(SEE PAGE 92)

In 1995 Grand Circle Travel, one of the over-50 tour operators (page 224), purchased this company in response to growing interest among clients for adventure travel. While all ages can and do sign on and many trips remain challenging, their catalog now says that OAT trips are designed for active, mature travelers.

## ALASKA WILDLAND ADVENTURE

(SEE PAGE 95)

Senior Safaris, seven- or nine-day itineraries, promise all the thrills of Alaska's national parks and wildlife refuges—and in-room bathroom facilities. June through August. (EE)

## INTERNATIONAL BICYCLE TOURS
(PAGE 102)

Flat, picturesque terrain and a leisurely pace characterize these special 50+ tours to Holland. The company reports that all of its trips attract many older bicyclers.

## BALLROOM DANCERS WITHOUT PARTNERS
c/o LUXURY WORLDWIDE CRUISES AND TOURS,
2750 NE 187TH STREET, NORTH MIAMI BEACH, FL;
(800) 778-7953.

This Miami travel agency caters to single men and women over 50 who enjoy dancing. It offers dance-oriented cruises on ships on major cruise lines and on the *Delta Queen.* The programs include dance instruction. At least one man is signed on for every five women; if enough men don't sign up, gentlemen hosts are recruited. Cost depends on the cruise selected.

## *Travel Companions*

## GOLDEN COMPANIONS
P.O. BOX 5249, RENO, NV 89513;
(702) 324-2227

This group was established in 1987 to serve older travelers seeking travel partners. Members get a bimonthly update and newsletter. Membership is $94 per year.

# Tour Operators Serving Seniors

If you want to see the world with fellow travelers in your own age group, consider these tours aimed at those who have passed their fiftieth birthdays. (Also note that the majority of travelers on many tours listed on pages 218–22 are over age 50).

## GRAND CIRCLE TRAVEL

347 Congress Street, Boston, MA 02210;
(800) 221-2610 or (617) 350-7500. (M-E)
Single supplements vary; many are low and they are waived entirely
on some departures and several cruises.

Begun in 1958 to serve members of the AARP, Grand Circle opened its trips to all in 1980 and boasts that 95 percent of their passengers say they will travel with them again. Tours take in the U.S., Mexico, all of Europe, and parts of Asia, including cruises and interesting itineraries such as "The Great Trains of Europe" and London theater.

## SAGA INTERNATIONAL HOLIDAYS

222 Berkeley Street, Boston, MA 02116;
(800) 343-0273. (M)
Will try to arrange shares

Founded in 1980, this leader in tours for mature travelers, has recently lowered its age qualification from 60 to 50. An extensive catalog of trips is offered across the United States, Canada, Mexico, Europe, and Latin America. "Road Scholar" programs are partnerships with local museums and universities to make these tours an in-depth learning experience. The catalog assures that they will go out of their way to make singles feel welcome and part of the group.

## MATURE TOURS

63 High Noon Road, Weston, CT 07883;
(800) 266-2566 or (203) 256-1235. (I-M plus airfare)
Will try to arrange shares

This is a sister company to long-established Solo Flights (page 198) concentrating on "youthful spirits over 50." Cruises on the Panama Canal and the Mississippi River, escorted trips to London, Israel, Spain, Costa Rica, and New York City, and New England fall foliage tours are among the recent offerings.

# Taking Advantage
# of Senior Discounts

- Join the American Association of Retired Persons as soon as you turn 50. AARP dues are small, and membership entitles you to many benefits, including discounts at every major hotel, motel, and car rental chain in America.
- Even if you don't belong to an organization, always ask hotels if they offer senior discounts. They won't bring it up unless you do; they have no way to know your age.
- Ask for the discount when you make your reservation; many places won't honor it later. At hotels, remind the clerk of your discount when you check in.
- Carry your driver's license or other proof of age when you check in, just in case you are asked.
- Compare rates. Sometimes special promotions at hotels are a better deal than the senior discount.
- Check with your auto insurance company; many companies offer a discount on car insurance after you pass your fiftieth birthday. Ditto for banks and retailers like Sears.
- Ask tour operators and resorts whether they offer a senior discount. Among the many who do are Club Med (page 200) and American Wilderness Experience (page 90).
- Are you a skier? Recognizing that older skiers are good business, almost every area now offers discounts, with the qualifying ages ranging anywhere from 50 to 60. Aspen Ski School has begun a special program called "Fit Over 50," aimed to help seniors continue to improve their skills. Call (800) 525–6200 for information.

# More Perks at 62

Getting a bit older definitely has its advantages:

- When you reach age 62, you are entitled to a 10 percent discount on airlines—all you have to do is ask! Also check with major airlines about money-saving coupon books and other good deals available to senior passengers.
- Amtrak takes off 15 percent of its lowest fares for passengers 62 and over.
- For $10, you can buy a Golden Age Passport that admits you to all the national parks, forests, refuges, and monuments free for life. Seniors get half off on fees for camping, parking, and tours, as well. Passports are sold at all parks. For details write to the National Park Service, P.O. Box 37127, Washington, D.C. 20013.

## 50 PLUS CLUB,
## A.J.S. TRAVEL CONSULTANTS, INC.

177 BEACH 116TH STREET, ROCKAWAY, NY 11694;
(800) 221–5002 OUTSIDE NEW YORK OR (718) 945–5900. (I–M)

Some 70 percent of the travelers on A.J.S. tours are single people over age 50, with the average age of travelers 60 and up. Small group trips of ten to fifteen people are offered to Israel, Switzerland, and northern Italy. Past participants report that the guides are excellent, the itineraries well-designed to give lots of time in one location and to avoid constant packing and unpacking, and that along with sight-seeing there are nice surprises, such as picnics beside scenic lakes.

# Section Two

## Solo TRAVEL Know-how

# Some General Advice

**I**f I'd traveled with a group or even another person, I wonder what memories I'd have missed. Would the man with the box of pigeons at his feet on the Polish train have offered to show me his town? The man at the tiny restaurant in Switzerland probably wouldn't have invited me to polka, and I am quite certain the hotel owner in Saba wouldn't have joined me for dinner, his treat.

—Letters to the Editor, *Travel Holiday*

Group vacations may provide great experiences and wonderful companionship, but many independent souls still prefer to set their own pace and agenda. If you've always wanted to see the Statue of Liberty or the Eiffel Tower or the Duomo in Florence, there's absolutely no reason why you cannot blaze your own path, design your dream trip, and happily do and see exactly what you please. One of the special privileges of solo travel is being able to tailor a trip to your own special likes and dislikes. Sleep as late or get up as early as you please. If you love antiques or bookshops or offbeat museums away from the main tourist track, you can indulge to your heart's content. If you want to savor a sunset, no one will say "Let's go." If you hate cathedrals, you need see nary a one!

It will take more planning to go your own way, yes—but often that very planning is a part of the fun of travel. Pre-trip research is the best way to start learning about your destination. The more you know in advance, the more you will get out of your trip.

Will you meet people on your travels? Probably more than if you were with a partner. You'll try a little harder to make friends than if you had a built-in companion, and you will be more approachable than if you were deep in conversation with your friend or spouse.

What are the best destinations for a first trip on your own? Whenever anyone asks me that question, my answer is, "Head for a city." Every great city has its own intriguing rhythms and personality, and often you can actually sense these best when you are alone, when you have no distractions and plenty of time to stroll, eyes wide open and antennae turned on high. Staying in one place also gives you a chance to get your bearings and begin to feel confident about getting around.

The best time to plan a city trip alone is during warm weather, when sociable outdoor cafes are in high gear. But, if you can avoid it, don't travel alone during the peak vacation season in July and August. Hotels and restaurants are least happy to see single guests during these months because this is when they are busiest and best able to fill tables and rooms with two or more instead of one. All the sights you want to see are also most crowded in high season. Late May, June, September, and early October are the ideal times to enjoy good weather without meeting up with hordes of tourists.

Pick your city carefully. Don't go alone to places like Los Angeles where you must drive unfamiliar streets or freeways to get around. Choose towns with a vital, walkable center and plenty of intriguing neighborhoods that can be explored on foot, plus an efficient and inexpensive public transportation system to get you from one place to another so that you won't need a car. Cities fitting this description usually meet another important criterion that makes for easier travel on your own— they have large single populations and many informal neighborhood restaurants to serve them.

Among the cities in the United States that meet these qualifications well are Boston, New York, Philadelphia, Chicago, Seattle, and San Francisco. Charming historic smaller cities like Charleston and Savannah are also easy to cover on foot. The best bets in Canada are Montreal, Toronto, and Vancouver. Almost any major city in Europe is a likely candidate, though places where English is spoken are probably the best choices for a first foreign venture. This doesn't mean you must limit yourself to London, wonderful city though it is. Think also of Dublin or Edinburgh, where English comes with a delightful brogue, Amsterdam, where the multilingual Dutch will welcome you in your own tongue, or Copenhagen, where English is the second language. I'll zero in on some of my favorite cities in the next chapter, but first let me share some techniques that work for me when I get ready to visit any new town.

.......................................................................

# S i z i n g   U p   a   C i t y

If you allow yourself to arrive alone in a new city without specific plans, you can feel lost and confused. To feel in control, your days should be mapped in advance. Start at home by contacting the local tourist office for information and maps of city streets and transit systems. Next, get the best guidebooks you can find and, if possible, a copy of the city's local magazine. If you don't have access to a newsstand that sells out-of-town publications, get the address and phone number of the magazine from the tourist office and order a copy by phone. If your community does not have a good travel bookstore, order by mail from those in the resource list on page 319.

When you have assembled your materials, read the brochures and books to learn about the character of the city and its special attractions for tourists. Use the magazine to find out what the people who live there are doing and where they are going right now.

Now make a list of the places you most want to see, and circle them on the street map. Though it is hard to get an accurate sense of scale from a map of a strange city, you can easily see which attractions are close together and plot your days by grouping places in the same geographic area. Check the transit maps against the street map to see which places can be easily reached by bus or tram.

Next, make a tentative day-by-day schedule of what you hope to do and see, ranking the sights each day from most to least important. That way, if something proves fascinating, you can find extra time by dropping the least important items on the agenda. If a top choice turns out to be a disappointment, you have plenty of options to fill your time.

In a brand-new city, I always start the first day with a local sight-seeing tour. This gives you a quick sense of the locations of important sites and streets. These tours often include inconvenient areas that you may not get back to easily on your own. Sometimes when I actually get a look at a place that sounded wonderful in the guidebooks, I realize it is not so great in reality, and I strike a further visit off my list.

I also like to leave time on my schedule for guided walking tours in interesting or historic areas of the city. Walking tours have fewer people than bus tours and are far more personal and interesting; they are an excellent way to meet people. In foreign cities, walking tours with English-speaking guides are the best way to seek out fellow travelers as well as a welcome respite from struggling to speak the language. With a really knowledgeable local guide, you'll get colorful inside information that isn't found in any book. The best current walking tours aren't always listed in guidebooks, but they are usually included in city magazines. You can also ask about these at your hotel or the local tourist office after you arrive.

Schedule plenty of time just to wander when you explore a new city—this is one of the great pleasures of solo travel. As long as you stay in safe neighborhoods, don't worry about getting lost. (Ask at your hotel about parts of the city that should be avoided.) Some of the best discoveries may lie on little side streets that don't show on the map. Even in a foreign city, if you write down the name and address of your hotel and mark it clearly on the street map, you will be able to get directions or find a cab when you want to return. One of the pleasant discoveries when you travel alone is that people everywhere seem particularly willing to go out of their way to help a solo visitor.

When you go exploring, you may find you get more out of your journey by pretending that you are travel writer who will want to bring the place alive for your readers. Take your time, look closely, window-shop, talk to people, ask questions, take mental notes, and make written ones. Make lists of the unusual shops and galleries you pass, take photos, and keep a nightly journal of your impressions. A journal is fun—it keeps you company, and it will vividly bring back the pleasures of your trip every time you open the pages back home. If you return to the city in the future, your journal will become your personal guidebook leading you back to the best places.

How much time you allot to shopping beyond souvenirs for friends and family depends on your own disposition. If you are like me and seldom find time for relaxed shopping at home, an afternoon to yourself for browsing stores in a new city is a treat. When I buy clothing or unique local handicrafts on a trip, they come with a bonus of happy memories.

# City Smarts:
# An Assortment
# of Tips
# on U.S. Cities

- San Francisco has an exceptional number of small, well-priced hotels. Especially recommended for solo travelers are the Kimpton Hotels. These lodgings are attractive, conveniently located, and moderately priced, and their complimentary wine reception each afternoon provides a chance to mingle with other guests. Many also offer coffee or a continental breakfast in the morning. The hotels I've personally inspected include the Monaco, Monticello Inn, Triton, Villa Florence, Vintage Court, Juliana, and the Tuscan Inn.

- New York's Gotham Hospitality Group hotels offer breakfast and sometimes afternoon refreshments (see page 278).

- In Chicago, the choicest hotel location is on or near North Michigan Avenue's "Miracle Mile," where fine dining and most of America's top retailers are found within a twenty-block stroll, and buses can be boarded to all the city museums. Surprisingly situated in this posh neighborhood is a high-rise Motel 6, one of the city's best buys.

- Charleston, one of America's most beautiful strolling cities, is an ideal destination for solo travelers since most of the lodging, dining, and sight-seeing is in the easily walk-able Historic District. If you can afford the tab, Charleston Place, a luxury hotel in the center of things, is ideal. Their restaurants (including the four-star Louis' Charleston Grill) offer a Single Diner program to encourage solo guests to come to dinner, including special wine and appetizer tastings and special visits by the manager and chef on duty. They even present a silver tray with a selection of magazines, papers, postcards, and books to keep you occupied between courses. Among dozens of appealing smaller inns, my top recommendation (when the budget allows) is 2 Meeting Street.

- Wherever you go, look for multi-day passes on city transit systems; they invariably save money.

Some of my favorite souvenirs have been paintings or folk art purchased on my travels. Looking for them invariably means talking to people and learning a lot about the local scene.

........................................................

# Choosing a Place to Stay

The circles you've marked on a city street map will help you choose a convenient area for your lodging. There are a few ways to consider accommodations when you are alone; the ultimate choices are dictated by budget and personal preference—and whether you are in the United States or abroad.

## U.S. Accommodations

If you can afford the splurge, it's a special pleasure to stay at a top hotel when you are traveling alone. Being surrounded by luxury is even more of a treat when you are by yourself, and the better hotels offer an important practical advantage as well: the concierge.

Now found widely in hotels in the United States as well as Europe, the job of the concierge is purely and simply to make your stay more pleasant. Besides taking care of all your transportation and ticket arrangements, a good concierge should know the city inside out—the best places to shop, the best ways to sight-see, and the places where single diners will feel comfortable. Well-connected concierges provide a lot of business to the city's restaurants, and when they phone in a reservation and say a good word, you can be sure that you won't be shunted to a cramped corner or ignored by your waiter. A good way to determine the quality of the concierge service in advance is to find out whether the head concierge wears the golden keys of Le Cle d'Or, the prestigious international concierge association.

At the other end of the scale, the small, charming budget hotels available in Europe just don't exist in most cities in the United States. With a few exceptions, our budget lodgings are at best impersonal and at worst, shabby and dreary. Luckily, now that the bed-and-breakfast craze has moved into big American cities, there is a cheerier choice when funds are limited. A bed-and-breakfast apartment or a home in a pleasant neighborhood provides an insider's advice on the city from your host, plus someone to talk to at breakfast and when you get home at night. As a bonus, you get a better sense of the real life of the city away from the business district. Dining is almost always more reasonable in the neighborhoods than in the business center of town—if you have fellow lodgers, you may even wind up with company for dinner.

Bed-and-breakfast reservations can be made through services that handle a large number of locations in each city. You'll find a sampling of these services in the box on page 237, and there are plenty of books with further suggestions. The lodgings themselves vary from lavish to modest, with either private or shared baths. Be very specific about your needs and desires when you make your reservation. Most of all, be sure the location is convenient to public transportation. If you think there may be times when you will return to your lodging late at night, find out whether cabs are readily available from midtown and the approximate fare to your destination.

Another plus for bed-and-breakfast accommodations is that, unlike hotels, they often give a generous break to single travelers. It isn't that hotels don't like singles, but the overwhelming majority of their rooms are designed for two people, and they seem to feel it is not good business to lose the extra revenue. That means one guest pays a "single supplement," making the rate almost the same as for two.

When you do get a single room in a hotel, it may be the smallest and least attractive in the place. Don't be afraid to speak up and ask for a better one.

The single supplement remains the biggest gripe of solo travelers, so perhaps if enough people write to hotel managers or major hotel chains to complain, some savvy hotels will begin to change this discriminatory policy.

While they may not have done much about improving their single rates, a number of U.S. hotels have begun offering a few services that make life pleasanter for their guests who are traveling alone. These amenities are aimed at attracting business travelers, but they are equally welcome to vacationers. One innovation commonly available in large hotels is a special "executive floor" where continental breakfasts and complimentary hors d'oeuvres are served in a special lounge. You pay extra for a room on this floor, but the lounge is a very easy setting for finding company, and the complimentary breakfast and snacks are pleasant money-savers. Executive floors also tend to provide extra security, with floor concierges on duty and special elevator keys.

## European Accommodations

Bed-and-breakfast homes have long been available in Europe, but, unlike in the United States, there's also a good chance of finding small and reasonable hotels that have local character and at least a modicum of charm. I favor staying in a hotel in a city where I don't speak the language, because I feel more secure in a central location when I don't know my way around. Most tourist offices, as well as guidebooks, offer listings of both small hotels and bed-and-breakfast lodgings.

By choosing smaller accommodations you can hold down the cost of traveling on your own, but you may have to make arrangements yourself by mail, fax, or phone. Travel agents are business people, after all, and these time-consuming reservations usually pay no commission. It's a simple matter to make your own arrangements, and the fax makes it easy to make contact. If you must communicate by mail, allow plenty of time for letters to make their way across the ocean and back.

If you are willing to make a move after you arrive, you can try another technique. Make a hotel reservation for the first night or two, and then take a morning to check out a list of small, less-expensive hotels in person, reserving a room in your favorite for the rest of your stay. If you find that you have booked a hotel that is disappointing, do the same—pay for the first night and look for a more pleasant alternative. Having the option to look around for lodgings is another reason to avoid traveling during busy peak seasons when desirable hotels are likely to be filled.

When you are hotel-shopping, don't hesitate to ask to see rooms—or to ask if a less expensive room is available. Contrary to what many people think, room prices are often negotiable if the hotel is not filled.

# U.S. City
# Bed-and-Breakfast
# Registries

- **New York**

  City Lights B&B Ltd., P.O. Box 20355, Cherokee Station, New York, NY 10021; (212) 737–7049.
  Urban Ventures, 38 West 32nd Street, Suite 1412, New York, NY 10001; (212) 594–5650.
  At Home in New York, P.O. Box 407, New York, NY 10185 (212) 956–3125.

- **Boston**

  Bed & Breakfast Associates, Bay Colony Limited, P.O. Box 57166, Babson Park Branch, Boston, MA 02157; (617) 449–5302.
  Greater Boston Hospitality, P.O. Box 1142, Brookline, MA 02146; (617) 277–5430.

- **Chicago**

  Bed & Breakfast, Chicago, P.O. Box 14088, Chicago, IL 60614–0088; (312) 951–0085.

- **Washington, D.C.**

  Bed & Breakfast League/Sweet Dreams and Toast, P.O. Box 9490, Washington, D.C. 20016; (202) 363–7767.

- **Philadelphia**

  Bed and Breakfast Connections/Bed and Breakfast of Philadelphia, P.O. Box 21, Devon, PA 19333; (610) 687–3565 or (800) 448–3619.

- **San Francisco**

  American Family Inn/Bed & Breakfast San Francisco, P.O. Box 282910, San Francisco, CA 94128; (415) 931–3083.{SB end}

For a list of reservation services in other cities, contact The National Network (TNN), Box 4616, Springfield, MA 01101.

# Making Your Own Travel Arrangements

## Saving on Airfare

If you are making your own travel arrangements, one way to save on transportation costs is to investigate some of the consolidators who offer bargain airfares. You'll see ads from these companies in almost any big-city newspaper, listing fares to major cities that are far below the going official rate. How do they do it? They buy blocks of seats that the airlines do not expect to be able to sell themselves, mostly on international routes. A good example: Air India flies to Bombay from New York with a stop in London. There are often empty seats on the New York–London leg that will be occupied in London. Consolidators can offer the trip to London at a big discount.

Some of these companies may specialize in specific regions such as Hawaii or the Orient. Rates and dates vary from one firm to another, so comparison shopping is essential.

There can be drawbacks to dealing with a consolidator. It is more difficult to get a refund, and you may not always get frequent-flyer mile credit. You may not be transferred to another carrier in case of cancellation or delay of a flight, and you may have to juggle your dates to coincide with the flights that are available.

Consolidators are not recommended for inexperienced or nervous travelers who might panic if complications arise. For those who feel confident about coping in case of emergencies, however, the consolidators offer flights on regular scheduled airlines at a very substantial savings.

Dealing with a reputable consolidator is important. Some  who come well recommended are:

### TFI TOURS
34 WEST 32D STREET, NEW YORK, NY 10001; (800) TAKE–TFI OR (212) 736–1140.

### BARGAIN AIR
655 DEEP VALLEY DRIVE, SUITE 355, ROLLING HILLS, CA 90274;
(213) 377–2919 OR (800) 347–2345.

# Savvy
# Travel Tips
# for Solo Travelers

- *Always ask for the corporate rate at a hotel, even if you don't work for a big company. It usually saves you 20 percent. Few hotels ask for I.D. when you arrive, and if you do, a business card is usually all you need to show.*

- *Don't call the 800 number to reserve at big hotel chains; they don't always know about local specials.*

- *Don't accept the first rate offered at a hotel; always ask if something cheaper is available. If they aren't full, most hotels are amenable to a little bargaining. Be sure they incorporate lower weekend rates into your bill.*

- *In the United States, big savings are available from hotel discount services, sometimes as much as 50 percent off the published rate. Two major services are Express Reservations (800–356–1123) for New York and Los Angeles, and Quikbook (800–789–9887) for Atlanta, Boston, Chicago, Los Angeles, New York, San Francisco, and Washington, D.C. Hotel Reservations Network (800–96-HOTELS) handles hotels in London and Paris, as well eleven U.S. cities.*

- *No rooms available at the hotel? Call back after 6:00 P.M.; that's when rooms saved for no-shows become available.*

- *Can't get through to the airlines during a fare sale? Try calling at 7:00 A.M. or after 11:00 P.M., when you're less likely to get a busy signal.*

- *During bad weather months, avoid delays by flying early in the day and choosing nonstop flights. When you must change planes, look for winter hubs like Dallas, Atlanta, or Las Vegas rather than northern cities such as Chicago, Denver, or Detroit. Don't book the last flight of the day; if it is canceled, you are out of luck.*

- *To avoid getting stuck in the middle seat on a plane, always ask for seat assignments when you reserve your ticket. Check in at least twenty minutes before departure in order to hold your seat.*

- *Always pay for tickets and tours with a credit card; it is your insurance in case the airline or the tour company goes out of business.*

## GLOBAL DISCOUNT TRAVEL SERVICES

4052 SOUTH INDUSTRIAL ROAD, LAS VEGAS, NV 89103; (800) 497–6678.

If you are looking for discounts within the U.S., the outfit with the dubious name of **Cheap Tickets, Inc.** does deliver them; I've used them myself. Call (800) 377–1000.

Remember also that many tour operators offer independent tours that do not require traveling with others. They simply give you the benefit of a group rate for airfare and hotels and sometimes a free sight-seeing tour. The hotels tend to be commercial, but you may want to compare these group rates with those you are quoted on your own.

# Traveling by Train in Europe

European trains are a pleasant surprise for first-time American travelers. They are fast and comfortable; they run frequently and are almost always on time. Trains like the TGV, running on new high-tech tracks, travel 130 to 170 miles per hour—so smoothly that you can hardly believe how fast you are moving. They allow you to relax and see the sights and to arrive at a central location where both taxis and public transportation are usually available. There are no guarantees, but trains can sometimes be a way to meet people, as well

The Eurailpass is one of Europe's best buys. For a specified period, fifteen days to three months, it allows unlimited first-class travel on speedy trains that go almost everywhere in seventeen countries. Since distances are small and trains run often, you can cover a lot of ground in a short time. The pass must be purchased in this country before you leave; it is not available in Europe.

If you want to base yourself in cities and do day or overnight trips, the Eurail Flexipass is ideal, allowing a certain number of travel days within a twenty-one-day period. For those under the age of 26, the Eurail Youthpass offers economy second-class travel. But there is nothing second class about those second-class seats—they are perfectly comfortable and recommended for anyone who wants to save a bit of money on travel.

You can adapt a train trip to almost any kind of European itinerary. I had a wonderful journey recently, seeing Swiss mountain villages on day trips from Lausanne, then whizzing to Paris in 3½ hours on the TGV, that amazing high-speed superliner. After several days in Paris, a 1½-hour train ride took me to Blois, which became my home base for an excursion into the Loire Valley chateau country. I didn't need a car in Blois—there were daily bus excursions from the railroad station to the great chateaus of Chambord, Chenonceau, and Amboise. Blois itself was a charming, small medieval town with its own famous chateau within walking distance of my hotel.

Stays in the countryside also provide a way to stretch your budget, since hotels and restaurants are far less expensive than those in big cities. In Blois I stayed at a stylish, modern, three-star hotel where three-course gourmet dinners were half the price of comparable meals in Paris.

Each European country has its own national railroad featuring special money-saving passes; you can learn about these from the local tourist office. If you plan to visit only one country, these may be a better choice than a Eurailpass.

A great thrill is taking the Eurostar, the train that runs through the tunnel beneath the English Channel to whisk you from the center of London to midtown Paris or Brussels. It is just as quick as flying (if you include time getting to and from airports) and much more fun since you can watch the countryside as you whiz by; the actual time in the underground tunnel is very short. BritRail, the British rail service, has excellent packages that include the "Chunnel" trip. They also issue passes for unlimited train travel in Ireland, Scotland, Wales, and a round-trip ferry crossing of the Irish sea.

Because trains in Europe run more frequently than they do in the United States, it is possible to tour short distances with almost as much flexibility as you would by car, and train stations are often centrally located for sight-seeing in the old parts of the cities.

My first European travel on my own, in fact, was a one-week, low-budget train trip through Holland, a compact country that is ideal if you want to see a lot in a short time. I used a suitcase small enough to fit into station lockers, and traveled much the way I might have by car. Fifteen minutes out of Amsterdam, I got off the train, checked my bag, and went

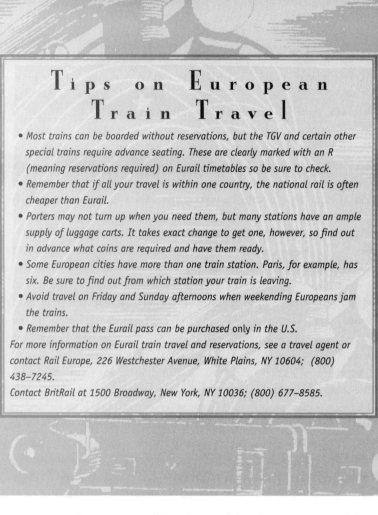

# Tips on European Train Travel

- Most trains can be boarded without reservations, but the TGV and certain other special trains require advance seating. These are clearly marked with an R (meaning reservations required) on Eurail timetables so be sure to check.
- Remember that if all your travel is within one country, the national rail is often cheaper than Eurail.
- Porters may not turn up when you need them, but many stations have an ample supply of luggage carts. It takes exact change to get one, however, so find out in advance what coins are required and have them ready.
- Some European cities have more than one train station. Paris, for example, has six. Be sure to find out from which station your train is leaving.
- Avoid travel on Friday and Sunday afternoons when weekending Europeans jam the trains.
- Remember that the Eurail pass can be purchased only in the U.S.

For more information on Eurail train travel and reservations, see a travel agent or contact Rail Europe, 226 Westchester Avenue, White Plains, NY 10604; (800) 438-7245.

Contact BritRail at 1500 Broadway, New York, NY 10036; (800) 677-8585.

out to see the charming city of Haarlem, walking the old square and visiting the Franz Hals Museum. (Finding your way is a cinch in Holland, since the VVV, the local information office near each train station, provides walking maps and has an English-speaking staff.)

After lunch in the square, I reboarded the train for the old university town of Leiden, another short ride away, where I did more browsing. Later, I boarded a train for The Hague, where I settled in for a couple of days. From there, day trips by train took me to Delft, Gouda, and Rotterdam, and a trolley ride brought me to the seaside resort of

Scheveningen. The entire journey was inexpensive and easy, and I never felt nervous for a minute.

Famous scenic tours can be taken by train. The Bernina Express and the Golden Pass Route in Switzerland, the Bergen Express in Norway, and Loisrail in France follow routes through magnificent scenery that you can sit back and enjoy from your picture window. Most long-distance trains have either a dining car or will serve meals at your seat. You can also reserve a sleeper—your own little bedroom—and use the train as your hotel, making the most of your travel time.

You'll find that train travel is not intimidating in most foreign countries. Signs in stations are easy to read; pictures point out lockers and checkrooms. Reservations offices are marked with a big R and information offices with a big I. In larger cities there is always someone in either of those offices who speaks English. The trains, their track numbers, and departure times are clearly listed on big boards. Even in countries where you can't understand the loudspeaker announcements, you need only spot the track number, line up at the right place, and you'll know when to board when you see the crowd starting to move.

With most major trains, it's hard to make a mistake, since the side of each car bears an identification panel showing the name of the city where the train originated, the final destination, and the major stops in between. Trains sometimes switch cars en route, so always check the destination on your car. First- and second-class cars are identified with large numbers, and a smaller number clearly identifies the cars with reserved seats.

## Traveling by Train in North America

Amtrak trains are an underrated resource for people traveling alone in the United States. Getting to and from centrally located train stations is much easier than the hassle of traveling to airports. Seats are wide and comfortable, and you can walk to the lounge car for refreshments or conversation if you get restless.

Trains can also substitute for driving alone when you want to tour. Well-priced All Aboard America fares are good for a thirty-day period in one of three regions (the eastern, central, or western U.S.) with three stopovers permitted. Amtrak offers its own tour packages using local hotels, as well. Trips crossing regions can be arranged for an extra fee.

Roomettes and single slumbercoaches designed for one adult allow you to save money and time by using the train as a hotel and covering many miles while you sleep. Fares include all meals while you are on board; tea, coffee, or fruit juice and a newspaper are complimentary in the morning.

Along the eastern corridor, Boston, New York, Philadelphia, Wilmington, Baltimore, Washington, Fredericksburg, and Richmond are a straight run from conveniently located midtown stations. The trains run often, making for easy city tours.

You can also let Amtrak do the driving while you enjoy the scenery on some fine fall foliage routes. The *Montrealer* runs from Washington, D.C., through New York's Adirondack Mountains to Montreal. The *Vermonter* goes through the Green Mountains. Both the Vermonter and the *Ethan Allen Express* can take you to Vermont ski areas, avoiding the worry of winter driving to the slopes.

In the western U.S., bilevel superliners allow you to sit back and enjoy the scenery through big picture windows, and Sightseer Lounges with windows extending all the way into the roof are great places to meet people.

Canada's Rocky Mountaineer offers one of the most spectacular train routes in the world—the journey from Vancouver to Calgary through Jasper, Banff, and the Canadian Rockies. You can also tour comfortably on VIA, the national railway, from Montreal to Quebec City to Toronto at a speedy 95 miles per hour. Canrail passes allow twelve days of travel within a thirty-day period, allowing for plenty of sight-seeing time. Like Eurail passes, these must be purchased before leaving home.

For information on AMTRAK service, call (800) USA–RAIL; for Rocky Mountaineer, (800) 665–7245; for VIA Rail Canada, (800) 561–3949.

### Some excellent guides to train travel include:

*U.S.A. by Rail* by John Pitt, Globe Pequot Press, Old Saybrook, CT.
*Traveling Europe's Trains* by Jay Brunhouse, Pelican Publishing

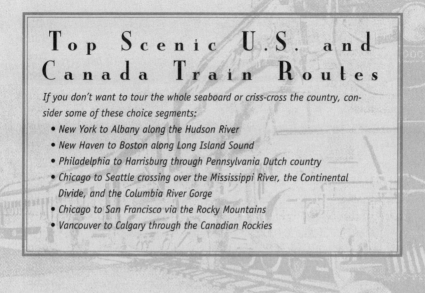

## Top Scenic U.S. and Canada Train Routes

*If you don't want to tour the whole seaboard or criss-cross the country, consider some of these choice segments:*

- *New York to Albany along the Hudson River*
- *New Haven to Boston along Long Island Sound*
- *Philadelphia to Harrisburg through Pennsylvania Dutch country*
- *Chicago to Seattle crossing over the Mississippi River, the Continental Divide, and the Columbia River Gorge*
- *Chicago to San Francisco via the Rocky Mountains*
- *Vancouver to Calgary through the Canadian Rockies*

Company, Gretna, LA.

*Europe by Eurail* by George and La Verne Ferguson, Globe Pequot Press, Old Saybrook, CT.

*Britain by BritRail* by George and La Verne Ferguson, Globe Pequot Press, Old Saybrook, CT.

..................................................

# Meeting Local People Abroad

Spending time in a new country is always far more meaningful if you are able to meet and really talk to the people. When you are traveling alone, the chance to visit with local residents is doubly welcome. A few organizations help make this possible.

## U.S. SERVAS COMMITTEE, INC.

11 JOHN ST., NEW YORK, NY 10038; (212) 267-0252.

This nonprofit, interracial, and interfaith group is affiliated with the United Nations as a nongovernmental organization. Its purpose is to promote peace through person-to-person understanding and friendship, which they do by opening doors for travelers to "homes and hearts" in more than 100 countries.

Servas maintains a roster of approved hosts abroad (and throughout the United States) who welcome foreign visitors to stay in their homes, usually for two nights; no money is exchanged. To apply for membership, each applicant fills out a detailed form, which subsequently serves as a letter of introduction to hosts. This form must be submitted with two letters of recommendation. A personal interview by a volunteer is required before a new applicant is accepted for the program. If approved, members pay an annual fee plus a refundable deposit for host directories in specific countries. Travelers then write or phone these hosts to ask for hospitality, giving each reasonable notice.

Members are asked to learn as much as possible in advance about the customs and cultures of the places they plan to visit. They are also requested not to stay only in major cities since hosts in suburbs and smaller communities often have more time to welcome visitors. The purpose of visiting is to share yourself, your country, and your interests, and travelers are urged to be respectful of their hosts' values and customs. When the program works well, lifelong friendships can be formed, and many hosts eventually visit former guests.

### FRIENDS OVERSEAS

68-04 DARTMOUTH STREET, FOREST HILLS, NY 11375; (718) 544-5660 (BETWEEN 9:00 AND 11:00 A.M. OR 5:00 AND 7:00 P.M., EASTERN TIME).

American tourists can write to this organization if they would like to meet Scandinavians, couples or singles, during their visits to Denmark, Sweden, Norway, and Finland. American participants receive the names and addresses of Scandinavian members who are eager to meet compatible Americans and begin a correspondence before the visitor leaves the States. This can lead to invitations to an evening out or a day

## Meet the People

*Several tourist offices keep lists of local people who are happy to meet with visitors and spend a few hours showing them the city. Usually there is a match with someone who has an occupation or interests similar to the visitor; in foreign countries, these friendly volunteers are bilingual. Local tourist offices can put you in touch with these organizations, which include:*

- *Big Apple Greeters (New York City)*
- *Meet the People Program (Jamaica)*
- *People to People Program (Bahamas)*
- *Japan Goodwill Guides Program*
- *Zurich Tourist Office*
- *Chatterbus Tour Office (Brussels)*
- *"In Dialogue" programs (Germany)*

of sight-seeing, and perhaps an invitation to visit a home. Sometimes accommodations in homes may be offered. Send a self-addressed, stamped, business size envelope for full information.

**FRIENDS OVERSEAS—AUSTRALIA,** at the address above, is a meet-the-people program that introduces Americans to residents of Australia who are willing to give advice by mail and personal guidance in their country.

## AMERICAN INTERNATIONAL HOMESTAYS, INC.
P.O. Box 1754, NEDERLAND, CO 80466; (303) 642-3088 OR (800) 876-2048.

Since 1988 this organization has organized homestays with English-speaking families in somewhat unusual destinations abroad. About 200 American travelers ages 40 to 70 take advantage of this opportunity for in-depth and inexpensive travel each year. You can choose bed-and-breakfast arrangements or have a home-cooked dinner with your host family each night. There is a choice of staying in one place for three nights or more or following a pre-planned itinerary on two-night stays through countries of Central Europe and the Baltics, as well as Russia, China, India and Nepal, Australia, New Zealand, and Tahiti.

## WOMEN WELCOME WOMEN
(SEE PAGE 211)
Offers homestays for women in many countries around the world.

## Dining Alone

The one part of traveling solo that people seem to dread most is dining alone. Even the most worldly travelers may hate it. Some people refuse to travel by themselves just to avoid it.

In part, this is understandable since it is undeniably a lot pleasanter to share a meal. But often the reluctance is strictly a matter of point of view. When *Travel & Leisure* magazine talked to business people who frequently travel alone, many of them said that after a hectic day it is actually a relief to be able to relax and not have to make conversation with strangers. Many also considered a room service dinner a wonderfully indulgent luxury.

The same can be true after a busy day of sight-seeing. It really isn't so bad relaxing over a drink by yourself and thinking back over the day—unless you think it is. Some diners are so self-conscious they bury themselves in a book, thereby missing out on the pleasure of people-watching in the restaurant—or maybe even starting up a conversation with someone at the next table.

One of the reasons that solo diners may feel ill at ease is that busy restaurants don't always seem pleased to see them. It's that same old problem—most tables are designed for two. The smaller tables inevitably seem to be stuck back near the kitchen. And, understandably, it may be true that waiters would be happier getting tips from two instead of one. If you make the effort to be friendly, however, explaining that you are a solo traveler, and enlisting advice about the menu and even about what to see and do in the city, you may find a staunch ally in your waiter.

Sometimes I shift my schedule so I can eat an early dinner before restaurants are filled and when I know they are happier to see a solo diner. Often I'll have this early meal in the neighborhood where I spent the afternoon, which gives me a chance to try places in areas I might not venture into on my own later in the evening.

When I want to eat at a really posh place by myself, I usually go for lunch. This is not only cheaper than evening dining but usually leaves me

## American Youth Hostels: Travel on a Shoestring

Short of travel funds? Not to worry. If you don't demand luxury, you can still travel happily on a tight budget. American Youth Hostels (AYH) are not only for the young. Many a canny traveler takes advantage of their rock-bottom rates for dorm rooms (divided by sex) and shared cooking facilities. Lodging goes for $8 to $25 per night; in some locations, you can even splurge on a private room usually occupied by couples and still save a bundle over other lodging choices. Ante up $25 a year to join AYH, and you can make reservations with a credit card at 150 U.S. locations and take advantage of nearly 5,000 hostels in seventy countries around the globe. (Hostels are open to nonmembers, as well, for slightly higher fees per night.)

In the U.S., AYH uses many interesting converted historic sites such as an ironmaster's home built in 1827 in Pennsylvania, an 1810 townhouse in Baltimore, a Victorian mansion in Sacramento, an old lifesaving station on Nantucket, and an art deco hotel on Miami Beach. Some locations even have recreational facilities. The organization has won the National Preservation Honor Award from the National Trust for Historic Preservation for its contributions to preservation in saving these historic properties.

If you will be sharing a dorm with strangers, it only makes sense to leave valuables at home and to keep your money and camera with you at all times. With a bit of care, hostels can be a sociable and money-saving opportunity.

wanting very little for dinner that night. I've found that if you stop by in advance and explain to the captain that you are in town alone and ask which day they might best be able to accommodate you for lunch or dinner, you'll likely get a more cordial reception—and a reservation. Don't try this visit during the height of the lunchtime rush.

I have a female friend with another technique. She phones to reserve tables for one under the name of "Dr. Glenn." Somehow the title seems to do the trick; she isn't turned down, and she is welcomed when she arrives.

Though you don't want to miss out on some of the really great restaurants in a new city, as a rule, when you travel alone, it is a lot more comfortable going to smaller, more casual dining places. The less formal dining rooms in large hotels are always a good bet for single travelers, since management is quite used to serving them; you'll notice that these rooms tend to have a lot of small tables. You don't have to be staying in a particular hotel to take advantage of its dining facilities, so you can have a number of comfortable evenings simply by surveying the local hotel scene.

If I am looking for variety and I have no concierge to guide me, I always scout the blocks around my hotel during the day for promising little places within walking distance. This may or may not be successful, depending on the neighborhood and the city.

A surer technique is to seek out the trendy city neighborhoods that attract a lot of browsers. Usually as you stroll along you can count on finding small cafes in these areas. Watch for outdoor terraces with empty tables or little cafes with lots of small tables by the windows or along the walls. These are often used to serve single diners; you will probably spy some who have arrived before you.

Other best bets in every city are restaurants with serving counters. These are not necessarily coffee shops or luncheonettes, as you'll see from some of the places listed beginning on page 251. Sushi bars are always fine for dining alone, as are restaurant bar areas and wine bars in many cities that also serve light meals. I've found that Chinese restaurants tend to be relaxed places where single diners need not feel self-conscious.

Good sources of ideas are the Zagat restaurant surveys, which are made up of opinions from local residents and always include suggestions for dining alone as well as listings of places where local singles gather. The Zagat guides are available for most major U.S. cities. For ordering information contact Zagat Survey, 4 Columbus Circle, New York, NY 10019; (800) 333-3421 or (212) 977-6000.

One other option: take an evening sight-seeing tour that includes dinner and you'll definitely have company. That's the way I saw San Francisco's Chinatown for the first time.

Wherever you go, you'll be better received in a restaurant if you are reasonably well dressed. I met one traveler who told me she always dresses up when she goes out to dine by herself. She also carries a notebook and asks lots of questions about the restaurant and the menu. She hopes she will be mistaken for a food critic, and so far, she says she has been treated well wherever she has tried her little game.

Another way to find dining companions in a city in the United States is to look into the meeting dates of the local chapters of any professional organization or alumni club you may belong to, or the scheduled dinners of the local Single Gourmet group. Contact the national Single Gourmet organization listed on page 197 for local addresses. And don't hesitate to look up friends of friends.

The best way to find nightlife is to read local publications. If you are 35 or under, look for alternative papers such as the *Boston Phoenix*, or the magazine *Time Out* in New York. If you are hesitant about venturing alone, check into nighttime tours.

Singles bars still exist, but they are far less attractive to travelers in this age of AIDS. A brief romance in a strange city once might have seemed romantic, but today it is a bit like playing Russian roulette. A good rule for females always is to pay your own way at bars or in restaurants. If you are meeting someone you don't know well, always do so at a public place, never at your hotel.

For those who prefer specific dining destinations to browsing, here are some solo suggestions from restaurant critics who were kind enough to share their expertise on three major U.S. cities:

## *Boston*

Mat Schaffer, restaurant critic for *Boston Magazine*, offers these suggestions:
### GALLERIA ITALIANA
(77 TREMONT STREET; 617–423–2092) is known for the superb Northern Italian fare of award-winning chef Barbara Lynch. Order a full meal (the

pasta is homemade) or graze on antipasto at Miss Kitty's Salon, the crimson-curtained wine bar area at the front of the Galleria. The party atmosphere is contagious; the owners make you feel as if you're a member of the family.

## DAILY CATCH

(313 Hanover Street in the North End; 617-523-8567) specializes in seafood, especially squid—fried, stuffed, sautéed, even minced into marvelous meatballs served in tomato sauce over linguini. Located in the city's Italian neighborhood, the tiny dining room is conducive to meeting diners at adjoining tables.

## JAE'S CAFE

(520 Columbus Avenue; 617-421-9405) has a Pacific-Rim menu of Thai, Korean, and Japanese dishes. If you dine at the sushi bar downstairs, you're guaranteed to strike up a conversation with the person next to you.

## CHARLIE'S SANDWICH SHOP

(429 Columbus Avenue; 617-536-7669) is a neighborhood breakfast and lunch spot where everyone shares tables. Be ready for long lines on Saturdays, and be sure to order the turkey hash.

## GRILL & CUE

(256 Commercial Street; 617-354-6559) offers American bistro food on the first floor. The outstanding bread basket is a meal in itself. Sit in the bar, and you'll likely find someone to challenge to a game of eight ball on one of the six purple felt-topped Black Crown billiard tables on the second floor.

## STEPHANIE'S ON NEWBURY

(190 Newbury Street; 617-236-0990) dishes out terrific American comfort food, sandwiches, and salads to a fashionable clientele in a *très chic* setting. Alfresco dining on the sidewalk out front features some of the city's best people-watching.

## HAMERSLEY'S BISTRO

(553 Tremont Street; 617-423-2700) is nationally recognized as one of Boston's finest restaurants. The roast chicken is spectacular. Chef Gordon Hamersley is the lanky guy in the open kitchen with the red hair and ever-present baseball cap. The intimate seating makes it virtually impossible not to spark up a conversation.

## BREW MOON

(115 STUART STREET; 617–523–6467) is one of the city's most popular brew pubs. The food is cutting-edge eclectic and is designed to complement brewmaster Tony Vieira's excellent beers. The bar is popular with singles after work and on weekends.

## LALA ROKH

(97 MOUNT VERNON STREET; 617–720–5511) is a Persian restaurant in the basement of a Beacon Hill townhouse. Allow the well-informed wait staff to guide you through the pleasures of an exotically delicious cuisine with influences from the Near East to the Far East.

## RIALTO

(IN THE CHARLES HOTEL, HARVARD SQUARE, CAMBRIDGE; 617–661–5050) serves the foods of southern Spain, France, and Italy. Make a reservation—Jody Adams is rightfully considered one of Boston's most accomplished chefs. The lounge is a good place to meet the local intelligentsia.

## MR. & MRS. BARTLEY'S BURGER COTTAGE

(1246 MASSACHUSETTS AVENUE, CAMBRIDGE; 617–554–6559) is a Harvard Square landmark that has been serving huge hamburgers to Harvard students forever. Every other customer dines solo—many with their head in a book.

---

COMMENTS *E.B.: When I am in Boston alone, I always head for the bar/counter at* Legal Seafoods, *27 Columbus Avenue, 617–426–4444, behind the Park Plaza Hotel. There are waiting lines, but a single diner sometimes gets a seat while couples wait. The seafood is super; the chowder is heaven.*
*Another possibility is* Durgin Park, *a longtime landmark in the North Building of Quincy Market, 617–227–2038, where diners are seated at long communal tables and served big portions of roast beef and other hearty American fare by waitresses renowned for their grumpiness. It's definitely touristy, but do it once anyway.*

---

## *Chicago*

Penny Pollack, Dining Editor of *Chicago Magazine,* recommends:

## BERGHOFF

(17 WEST ADAMS; 312–427–3170) is a genuine Chicago institution serving traditional German cuisine and house-made brews since 1898!

## BENKAY SAKE BAR

(IN THE HOTEL NIKKO, 320 NORTH DEARBORN; 312–744–1900) invites you to choose from twenty-four kinds of sake while nibbling appetizer portions of vegetables, seafood, chicken, and beef grilled in front of you.

## BIG BOWL CAFE

(159½ WEST ERIE; 312–787–8927) is a casual, fun Asian cafe created in the noodle-house tradition. Simple, fresh noodle-based dishes under $10 are the mainstay here. An interactive stir-fry bar adds to the fun.

## ED DEBEVIC'S SHORT ORDERS

(640 NORTH WELLS AT ONTARIO; 312–664–1707) provides 1950s nostalgia, burgers served to the blare of rock and roll, and a gum-cracking, smooth-talking wait staff.

## FRONTERA GRILL

(445 NORTH CLARK; 312–661–1434) serves the most sophisticated Mexican food in town. Single diners may want to sit at the four-stool counter hidden in the back.

## BLUE CRAB LOUNGE

(21 EAST HUBBARD; 312–527–2722) is under the same roof as Shaw's Crab House. It offers raw-bar items plus a few more ambitious entrees served mostly at high stools along the bar. If you prefer table seating, Shaw's is a good choice, too.

## CAFE SPIAGGIA

(980 NORTH MICHIGAN; 312–280–2764) treats you to all the flavors of Northern Italy in a casual-chic setting overlooking Michigan Avenue—and for considerably less money than in its elegant next-door sibling, Spiaggia.

## CAFE GORDON

(110 EAST CHESTNUT; 312–280–2100) is a snazzy in-town cafe with an easy-to-like menu. Gordon's signature flourless chocolate cake is the dessert of choice.

## SEASONS CAFE

(AT THE FOUR SEASONS HOTEL; 120 EAST DELAWARE; 312–280–8800) provides a cozy nook off the main dining room where you can enjoy expertly prepared soups, grilled fish, pastas, and salads.

## BISTRO 110

(110 EAST PEARSON; 312–266–3110) serves typical bistro standards accompanied by crusty baguettes at this lively spot just off Michigan Avenue.

## MITY NICE GRILL

(AT WATER TOWER PLACE; 835 NORTH MICHIGAN AVENUE; 312-335-4745) has the decor and feel of the forties and the comfort food of the nineties. The perfect stop after shopping on Michigan Avenue.

## MRS. PARKS TAVERN

(AT THE DOUBLETREE GUEST SUITES AT 198 EAST DELAWARE; 312-280-8882) is a sophisticated spot in a sophisticated neighborhood. The kitchen benefits from the talent and style upstairs at the pricier Park Avenue Cafe.

## FARRAGO

(733 NORTH WELLS; 312-951-7350) is a gallery-district storefront eatery that features an inventive menu drawing on world cuisines.

## BRASSERIE JO

(59 WEST HUBBARD; 312-595-0800) is a sizzling, bustling River North hot spot for robust Alsatian food and custom-brewed beer.

## CHEESECAKE FACTORY

(IN THE JOHN HANCOCK CENTER AT 875 NORTH MICHIGAN AVENUE; 312-337-1101) sports eclectic, over-the-top decor and provides great people-watching, an enormous California-style menu, and delectable cheesecakes.

---

COMMENTS   *E.B.: Chicago pizza is not to be missed. I haven't tried them all, but I'll vouch for Giordano's, (at 747 West Rush Street; 312-251-0747 or at 1840 North Clark Street; 312-944-6100). It's the place that made "stuffed pizza" famous. Also worth noting is Gordon, (500 North Clark Street; 312-467-9780), one of the city's better restaurants, it recently has featured "Gordon's Table," where solo diners gather. Such features don't always last, so call to be sure before you go.*

---

## *San Francisco*

Patricia Unterman, respected restaurant reviewer for the *San Francisco Chronicle,* suggests these singles-friendly places:

## CHINA MOON

(639 POST STREET; 415-775-4789) is a stylish Chinese cafe with a counter; owner Barbara Tropp has a loyal local following.

## IL FORNAIO

(1265 BATTERY STREET; 415-986-0100) a bustling Italian trattoria with a comfortable counter.

## LITTLE JOE'S

(523 BROADWAY; 415-443-4343) is a busy, old-fashioned Italian restaurant known for its pasta and veal; it's inexpensive and has a counter.

## HAYES STREET GRILL

(320 HAYES STREET; 415-863-5545) specializes in fish and has a number of smaller tables for singles. Zagat says this place has the best fish in the city.

## STARS

(150 REDWOOD ALLEY BETWEEN POLK AND VAN NESS; 415-861-7827) offers both counter seating and an informal cafe in a large au courant restaurant in the Civic Center; owner Jeremiah Tower is a culinary star.

## VICOLO PIZZERIA

(201 IVEY STREET; 415-863-2382) is an upscale pizzeria with counter seats and small tables.

## VIVANDE

(2125 FILLMORE STREET; 415-346-4430) is a wonderful Italian deli and cafe with a counter and small tables. Note that it is open only until 7:00 P.M.

## TADICH GRILL

(240 CALIFORNIA STREET; 415-391-1849) is a venerable downtown tradition serving absolutely fresh seafood at fair prices.

## RUBICON

(558 SACRAMENTO STREET; 415-434-4100) seems to be a must on the off-chance of spotting owners Robert de Niro or Francis Ford Coppola. The chef is quickly becoming a star as well.

## HAWTHORNE LANE

(22 HAWTHORNE STREET; 415-777-9779) is in an ivy-covered building in the blooming SOMA area; it boasts a pair of former Postrio chefs. It's pricey but well recommended.

Ms. Unterman adds that many San Francisco restaurants now feature a bar or counter where you can stop in for a fine meal alone.

# Four Favorite Cities

**E**VERYBODY HAS HIS OR HER OWN FAVORITE CITIES. I'VE chosen Amsterdam, Montreal, Paris, and New York, not only for their beauty or excitement but because I have found them to be especially easy cities to be in by myself. My descriptions are not meant to be used as a substitute for a comprehensive guidebook—they are simply personal impressions to share what I've found most enjoyable when traveling on my own.

## Amsterdam

There's a fairy-tale quality to the tilty, gabled townhouses on the tree-lined canal streets of Amsterdam. Though apartments, boutiques, and cafes may hide behind the historic facades, the beautiful, old city has not changed since the seventeenth century. No matter how many times you walk along the canals, they are always enchanting, even in busy mid-day when traffic and whizzing bicycles dispel the old world illusion. The loveliest times for walking are on a silent Sunday morning or on a summer evening when the old facades are floodlit.

The contrasting aspects of this city equally well known for its Rembrandts and its red-light district are endlessly fascinating. Amsterdam is small, so you can cover most of it on foot, savoring such details as the charming, no-two-alike gables atop the houses, the growing number of kicky boutiques, the many art galleries, the tempting bakeries, and the masses of flowers in the colorful, floating flower market. Outdoor markets for everything from postage stamps to parakeets to "junk-tiques" are another intriguing part of the cityscape that you need no company to enjoy.

Amsterdam's polyglot population is another part of its appeal. The freewheeling atmosphere makes everyone, young and old, feel at home. The street music characterizes the happy spirit of the city. On one recent stroll in Amsterdam I counted six kinds of music from various music makers: a classical violinist outside the concert hall, a folksinger-guitarist near the van Gogh museum, a rock group in front of the train station, a carillon ringing from a church steeple, an organ concert wafting from an open church door, and the tinkly tunes of a barrel organ in Dam Square. All are typically Amsterdam.

Several things make Amsterdam particularly easy for solo travelers. First, everyone speaks English. Second, if you stay within the confines of the old city, you can easily walk to see the Rembrandts in the Rijksmuseum and the priceless collections in the Vincent van Gogh Museum, as well as to concerts and restaurants. If you tire, cheerfully clanging trolley cars are waiting on every major street. To save money buy the trolley tickets that are good for a whole day or get a strip of tickets good for a number of rides. Tickets are also available for individual rides if you think you won't make good use of the more economical multiple-ride tickets.

Because the center of the city is small, almost any hotel is conveniently located, but two with particularly sociable bars are the American Hotel, an art deco landmark at 97 Leideskade, and the Pulitzer, an amalgam of seventeenth-century townhouses at 315 Prinsengracht. The Ambassade at 341 Herengracht, (31–20–622–2333) made up of six patrician canal houses, is one of the more interesting luxury hotels. Among less-expensive canal-house hotels with special charm are the Canal House at 148 Keizersgracht, (31–20–622–9987); the Hotel Agora at 462 Singel, and Seven Bridges at 31 Reguliersgracht (31–20–623–1329).

What's best of all about Amsterdam when you are by yourself is that it is a city where people like to "hang out"—in sidewalk cafes in summer and in coffee shops and local taverns, known as "brown bars," in winter. There's always a place where you can comfortably have a cup of coffee, a drink, or a meal without feeling out of place because you are alone. And if you need to, it is easy to watch your budget. At dozens of restaurants, you'll see the knife-and-fork symbol indicating a tourist menu, which means a price-fixed three-course meal. You'll no doubt make your own dining discoveries as you wander, but here are some recommended spots:

The busy square called Leidseplein is the center of Amsterdam's nightlife, and together with the side streets perpendicular to its edges it offers a wide range of cafes from casual to chic. These cafes deserve special recommendation:

## CAFE-RESTAURANT AMERICAIN

(IN THE AMERICAN HOTEL AT 97 LEIDESKADE) is a high-ceilinged art deco rendezvous for everything from reading a newspaper over a cup of coffee to indulging in a full dinner menu. Theatergoers, actors, musicians, and tourists all can be found here or on the big terrace cafe outside. One of the city's most popular gathering spots, it's perfect when you are alone.

## OESTERBAR

(10 LEIDSEPLEIN) offers a top seafood restaurant upstairs with an informal, tiled dining room on the street level with tables and a counter.

You might also try these nearby restaurants:

## HAESJE CLAES

(275 SPUISTRAAT) is small, narrow, wood-paneled, atmospheric, and inexpensive.

## DE KNIJP

(134 VAN BAERLESTRAAT) offers a range of choices from quiches to six-course feasts in a pleasant spot with a garden.

## CAFE HANS & GRIETJE

(27 SPIEGELGRACHT) is a quaint place with an upstairs restaurant and a downstairs bar/cafe.

## PULITZER COFFEE SHOP

(IN THE PULITZER HOTEL AT THE CORNER OF KEIZERSGRACHT AND REESTRAAT) has rattan furnishings, contemporary art, and a menu that runs the gamut from snacks to substantial meals.

## CONTINENTAL SHERRY BODEGA

(246 LIJNBAANSGRACHT) is a timbered place known mainly as a wine-tasting spot. It serves light meals or tapas on the street level and rises floor by floor to more expensive fare. The bar is a popular watering hole.

## CASA DI DAVID

(426 SINGLE) is a family-run Italian restaurant overlooking the canal. It offers reasonably priced homemade pastas and pizza.

## PANCAKE BAKERY

(191 PRINSENGRACHT) is a restored canalside warehouse with more than fifty kinds of Dutch pancakes—great for lunch or a light dinner and very light on the pocketbook.

## L'OPERA

(27-31 REMBRANDTSPLEIN) is a split-level art deco restaurant-cafe and bar with a big, popular terrace.

## SAMA SEBO

(27 PC HOOFTSTRAAT) is the place to sample a multi-dish Indonesian rijsttafel.

## SALAD GARDEN

(75 WETERINGSCHANS), located near the Rijksmuseum, has much more than salads—light meals are served downstairs; formal dining is above. A perfect place for afternoon tea.

## HOLLANDS GLORIE

(220-222 KERKSTRAAT), longtime local favorite, serves up popular-priced food in a wonderful Old Dutch setting of copper and tiles.

For further information on Amsterdam, contact the Netherlands Board of Tourism (NBT) at 355 Lexington Avenue, New York, NY 10017 or call (800) 95-DUTCH. Recommended guides include, *Eyewitness Guide to Amsterdam,* Dorling Kindersley, London and New York. *Cadogan Amsterdam,* Cadogan Books, London.

# Montreal

Here's a touch of French *joie de vivre* right over the border—and you don't even have to know the language. Montreal is an easily manageable city of 1.8 million people with the life, charm, and sophistication of a city many times its size. Promenaders on the streets and laughter in the sidewalk cafes last well into the night!

The setting is unusual and scenic: an island in the middle of the St. Lawrence River, with a little mountain, Mont Royal, providing acres of greenery right in the middle of town. The street and shop signs, much of the food and the ambience are strictly French and foreign, yet almost everyone in Montreal is bilingual, so you'll not have to open your phrase book unless you want to.

The marvel of Montreal is its Metro, a subway system that is not only clean, safe, and speedy but a tourist attraction in itself. Buy six metro tickets at a time for a discount, and ask for a free pocket-sized map card of the city and the Metro system. Miles of the Metro's wide, well-lit, attractive corridors connect the city's main shopping complexes and offer hundreds of shops in the corridors themselves. The system provides something to do no matter what the weather. The entertainers who make your strolling and waiting time tuneful are top-rate musicians who have auditioned to compete for their spots.

The efficient train system also makes it easy to visit far-flung attractions such as the Olympic Stadium or the former site of Expo 67, now a complex of gardens, museums, and the elegant Casino de Montreal, housed in the former French Pavilion. The guided tour of the Olympic Park includes visits to the city's fine Botanical Garden, the second largest in the world, known for its Japanese and Chinese gardens. Other attractions are the unique Insectarium, the Biosphere (where the St. Laurence–Great Lakes ecosystems come alive), and the Biodome, which has four eco-systems under one roof.

Quaint Old Montreal on the banks of the St. Lawrence is the city's tourist mecca. Browsing is pleasant, though many of the shops are decidedly commercial. For a fascinating history tour of the area, take one of the walks given daily from late June through September with one of Guidatour's English-speaking guides. For information, call (800) 363-4021.

The city's history is displayed in the new Pointe-a-Calliere Museum of Archaeology and History of Montreal, located on the site on Place Royale where the city was founded. The upstairs cafe has a wonderful view of the port.

Self-guided walking tours printed in the free official Tourist Guide take you through some of the city's other neighborhoods—the elegant Sherbrooke Street area that boasts the city's top hotels and boutiques and the handsome McGill University campus; Saint-Denis, the lively "Latin Quarter" of student life filled with boutiques and cafes; Avenue Laurier, a burgeoning area of upscale shops, and Boulevard Saint-Laurent with its mix of nationalities, bistros, discos, and bars. Everywhere you go, you'll find sidewalk cafes where you can have a rest and a view of the passing scene.

On Sherbrooke, the Montreal Museum of Fine Arts is housed in two buildings; the spectacular newer pavilion was designed by noted Israeli architect Mose Safdie with a fourth-floor atrium that offers a grand view of the city. The collections range from Rembrandt to Rodin.

Shopping is one of this city's greatest pleasures, and one you need no company to enjoy. The fashions are French, and the prices are Canadian, a great combination for travelers with American dollars. Boutiques and department stores on Sainte-Catherine Street vie with the most elegant of those to be found at city shopping centers anywhere. Ogilvy's, for one, is an old-world treasure filled with five floors of lovely boutiques.

Two centers are modernistic dazzlers and good places for informal meals as well. Les Cours Mont-Royal, a former hotel on Peel Street, has been converted to a fourteen-level elegant mall of interior courtyards, skylights, fountains, and glittering chandeliers. The mall is shared by more than fifty fine shops, movie theaters, condominiums, and offices. Its black-and-white food court, called Noir et Blanc, has among its tenants one of the city's best restaurants, Guy et Dodo Mora.

Place Montreal Trust, between McGill College Avenue and Mansfield, boasts a number of cafes and 120 boutiques on its five multicolored levels, including such familiar names as Fendi, Rodier, Bally, and Crabtree and Evelyn, as well as dozens of shops featuring exclusive designer creations.

If you have dreamed of buying a fur coat for yourself or to give as a gift, Montreal is definitely the place. The selection and the prices are superior, and the American dollar goes far. The fur district is centered around Mayor Street.

Where to stay? The top-of-the-line hotels are on Sherbrooke West, the recently restored Ritz-Carlton Kempinski at 1228, (800–426–3135) and the Westin-Mont Royal at 1050 (514–284–1110). They are top-notch and conveniently located near the cafes on convivial Crescent Street. The more moderately priced La Citadelle is about six blocks away at 410 Sherbrooke West (800–449–6654). Chateau Versailles (1659 Sherbrooke West; 800–361–7199), a small hotel comprising four Victorian houses, is also a good value.

The safe and efficient Metro makes this an ideal city for bed-and-breakfast lodgings. For reservations, contact Montreal Bed and Breakfast, P.O. Box 575, Montreal H3X 3T8; (514) 738–9410.

When it comes to restaurants, you can hardly go wrong in Montreal. The gastronomic capital of Canada, it is a city all but dedicated to wining and dining. This is a sophisticated city, and no one raises an eyebrow when you enter a restaurant alone. Take your pick of the places in the following areas:

Crescent Street between Sherbrooke and Sainte-Catherine is a favorite area of Montreal's over-30 smart set. A host of good, informal choices await, many with outside terraces. Les Halles at 1450 Crescent is one of the city's gourmet landmarks; it's probably a better bet at lunchtime if you are alone. Nearby streets such as Bishop and Stanley have their own share of charming cafes. A few recommendations are:

## THURSDAYS
(1449 CRESCENT) French, with a lively young crowd.
## LE CHRYSANTHEME
(1208 CRESCENT) Interesting Chinese.
## LE MAS DES OLIVIERS
(1216 BISHOP) French.
## L'AUTRE SAISON
(2180 CRESCENT) A good lunching spot with super salads.

The lower part of Saint-Denis Street near the University of Quebec draws younger patrons to its wall-to-wall lineup of cafes of all nationalities. The farther up the hill you go, the more sophisticated the restaurants and the older the crowd. During the late-June Jazz Festival, the lower street sings with impromptu concerts. Suggestions in this neighborhood are:

## L'EXPRESS
(3927 SAINT DENIS) French bistro.
## TOQUE
(3842 SAINT DENIS ) "Vertical cuisine," a unique experience.
## ALLUMETTE
(3434 SAINT DENIS) French.
## LA SILA
(2040 SAINT DENIS; ) Italian.

Prince Arthur Street and Duluth Avenue, not far from the Saint-Denis area, are filled with Greek and other ethnic restaurants with big outdoor patios. They're all inexpensive and strictly BYOB —bring your own bottle of wine. Prince Arthur is also a pedestrian mall where guests enjoy street entertainment along with the modest dinner tabs. Just pick a place with an empty seat out front.

You'll find more tourists than locals in Old Montreal, but you'll also find street musicians and a host of outside cafes. This neighborhood is not my favorite part of the city, but I did enjoy a meal at Claude Postel (443 St. Vincent). It offers excellent French food.

Other good bets in Montreal are found in The Alcan Building (Maison Alcan) at 1188 Sherbrooke Street West. In the inner court of this interesting building are the Moby Dick Bar, where local journalists meet after work; Le Pavillon De L'Atlantique, a good seafood restaurant; and Le Tulipe Noire, a perfect place for lunch, light suppers, or desserts.

The Ritz Garden is nearby at 1228 Sherbrooke Street West. Don't miss the beautiful outdoor setting and delicious food. The gracious Ritz staff will make you comfortable, but if you are shy about dinner, come for lunch, a fabulous breakfast, or high tea. Also not far away are the restaurants in the Westin-Mont Royal Hotel at 1050 Sherbrooke Street West. **L'Apero**, located right off the lobby, is pleasant for a buffet luncheon, and **Zen** is a Chinese extravaganza with moderate prices.

For further Montreal information, send for the free Tourist Guide and other excellent materials put out by the Greater Montreal Convention and Tourism Bureau. Contact Delegation Generale du Quebec (17 West 50th Street, Rockefeller Center, New York, NY 10020-2201; 212–397–0200) or contact Tourisme Quebec at (800–363–7777. *Birnbaum's Canada,* (Houghton Mifflin Company, Boston) has a good chapter on Montreal.

..................................................................

# P a r i s

Can the most romantic city in the world really be a good place to be alone? I know none better. Paris is dazzling, incredibly beautiful, and interesting at every turn. There are never enough days to begin to cover all the neighborhoods to be explored, all the fascinating shops for browsing, and all the incredible museums to be visited. No matter how many times you go, there is always something new to see. The splendid new additions to the Louvre, the soaring d'Orsay Museum filled with Impressionist works, and the charming Picasso Museum are visual treats. The old Place de Vosges neighborhood grows more beautiful each year. And since there is always some controversial modern building going up, it's fun to have a look and form an opinion about places like the Pompidou Center, the new Les Halles, the pyramid entrance at the Louvre, and the Bastille Opera.

Of course, a visit to Paris may be more enjoyable if you speak a modicum of French. Some lessons before you leave home are helpful, and a phrase book is a necessity. On my last visit I noticed that a remarkable number of Parisians now are willing to speak some English, and I found residents extremely kind and helpful. The three-star restaurants may not be overly warm to American-speaking guests, but in the less-rarified stratas of the city, in my opinion, Paris no longer deserves its longtime reputation for coldness.

Unfortunately, you can't always count on the cab drivers to speak English. When I travel around Paris, I always carry the indispensable street guide, the little red *Cartes Taride,* which locates every single address in each of the city's *arrondissements* or districts. It also includes a detailed map of each arrondissement as well as maps of the Metro subway system and the bus routes. All you need to do is add an X to mark your spot, and you'll always be able to find your way. You can find the *Cartes Taride* in larger U.S. bookstores, or you can buy one when you arrive in Paris.

The Metro is simple to figure out. Stations are marked with a large M, and many have elegant turn of the century art nouveau entrances. You can buy *un carnet* ("uhn kar-*nay*"), a book of ten tickets good for train or bus at a discount. If you will be in town for five to seven days, a better bet is the Carte Orange that gives you a week of unlimited travel; come prepared—you'll need two passport-size photos of yourself. Whichever you use, remember to take your ticket when the machine returns it. You sometimes need it to exit.

To find the right train, find your destination on a Metro map and trace the line by following the color coding and the number of the line.

At the end of the line you will see the number of the last stop—it will guide you to the right train. The name of the last stop is also indicated on the platform.  Inside the train is a chart of all the stops, so you can follow your route. You'll find a neighborhood map at almost every Metro exit.

You might prefer to take your time and ride the bus, since every route in this city makes for a scenic tour. A bus map is available at the big tourist office on the Champs Elysée. Each bus is clearly marked with a route number and its final destination. Traveling across town by bus may require more than one ticket; ask the driver. Just a few of the outstanding sight-seeing routes are:

- LINE 24, WHICH CROSSES THE SEINE FOUR TIMES AND PASSES MOST OF THE CITY'S FAMOUS SITES.
- LINE 29 FROM THE OPERA TO THE BASTILLE.
- LINE 38 FROM LES HALLES ACROSS ILE DE LA CITÉ AND UP BOULEVARD SAINT-MICHEL TO THE LUXEMBOURG GARDENS.
- LINE 63, A LEFT BANK ROUTE THROUGH THE SAINT-GERMAIN-DES-PRES AREA.
- LINE 84 FROM THE MADELEINE UP RUE ROYALE, AROUND THE PLACE DE LA CONCORDE THROUGH THE HEART OF THE LEFT BANK TO THE LUXEMBOURG GARDENS AND AROUND THE PLACE DE PANTHEON.
- LINE 96 FROM MONTPARNASSE THROUGH SAINT-GERMAIN-DES-PRES TO SAINT PAUL.

Remember that bus service is limited on Sundays and evenings.

Not even the most magnificent ride will satisfy for long in a city made to order for walking. One of the best ways to get to know Paris on a first visit is on the Bonne Journée walking tours. There is a different one every day, taking in the Marais, the Ile de la Cite, Montmartre, and the Père-Lachaise Cemetery where Oscar Wilde, Edith Piaf, and Jim Morrison are buried. Theme tours include such walks as the History of Crime in Paris, which leads from prisons to gallows to the Police Museum, and "A Movable Feast," which follows the steps of Hemingway and explores the expatriate scene of Paris in the twenties. Bonne Journée can be contacted at 6, place Charles-Dullin, 75018 Paris; (33) (1) 46 06 2417.

It's also nice for those of us who haven't mastered French that the Louvre offers regular tours in English. Check at the information desk for the time schedule.

Besides tours, the many English-language bookshops afford an excellent way to find other English-speaking people in Paris. **Brentano's** (37, avenue de l'Opera) is the largest of these and a good place to pick up information through the little paper called *American in Paris,* which lists activities of interest to Americans. You might find such events as a "quintessential July Fourth party." Restaurants advertising in this paper are those where Americans living in the city are likely to be found.

My favorites of the English-language bookstores are **W.H. Smith's** combination restaurant, tearoom, and bookshop at 248, rue de Rivoli (also a fine place for a meal or a snack), and **Shakespeare and Company,** 37, rue de la Boucherie, an atmospheric gem of a used bookstore on the Left Bank. When I last visited the latter, you could borrow (they'll ask you to leave a deposit) a copy of *Pariswalks,* one of the best guides to self-guided walking tours, and have free tea upstairs on Sunday afternoons at 4:00 P.M. If you are staying in the city long enough, you might want to sign up for language lessons at the Alliance-Francaise, 101, boulevard Raspail, another place to meet your countrymen.

Of course you haven't come all the way to Paris only to meet other Americans, but when you have no companion in a city where few people speak your language well, it is a relief to take a break occasionally and talk freely to someone from home.

While you're in Paris, read all you can about the city to discover some of the special small pleasures that you might overlook, such as the concerts held at Sainte-Chappelle, illuminated by daylight through the church's glorious stained-glass windows. Check the "Bests" section in the guidebook *Paris Access* for other treasures favored by a number of noted Paris visitors. The "Star Sights" noted in the *Eyewitness Guide to Paris* offer a good roundup of special sights not to be missed.

Any guidebook can tell you about the grand hotels of Paris, but there are many small, reasonable hotels with some amount of charm (albeit small rooms) where you can be comfortable by yourself and not spend a fortune. One I've patronized is the Hotel Verneuil Saint-Germain (8, rue de Verneuil), a tiny charmer on the Left Bank. Others that have been recommended to me are: the Hotel de la Bretonnerie, 22, rue Ste-Croix de la Bretonnerie (48 87 7736), in the lovely Marais district; Hotel Des Deux Iles, 59, rue St. Louis En Lile (43 26 1335), on the Ile St. Louis; the Brighton, 218, rue de Rivoli (42 60 30 03), near the Tuilleries gardens; and the very simple Lenox Saint-Germain, 9, rue de l'Universite (42 96 10 95), on the Left Bank.

Unless you are determined to try the famous culinary palaces of Paris, dining alone in this city is a snap. There are cafes and bistros in every neighborhood, many with big outdoor terraces, and dozens of tiny eateries where solo diners are commonplace. Attractive tearooms are perfect places for lunch, as are wine bars. And though the street has become a bit tacky, the Champs-Elysées offers a lineup of reasonably priced cafes offering the traditional steakfrites (beef steak and French fries); lone diners are not at all unusual in this neighborhood.

An expensive but wonderful way to enjoy French cuisine with company—and to take home the ability to cook it yourself—is to sign up for the Gourmet Sessions at the famous cooking school, Le Cordon Bleu (8, rue Leon Delhomme). Courses are available from a half day to a month. A one-day class of particular interest for visitors is a visit with chefs (and an English interpreter) to a city market, followed by a light buffet and a cooking demonstration in the afternoon. Demonstration lessons are also open to the public. For a schedule and information in the U.S., phone (800) 457–CHEF. Le Cordon Bleu also supplies students with a list of hotels where they receive special rates.

Check the *Michelin Guide to Paris* if you want the latest count on star chefs in Paris; if you can afford the bill, you can probably eat better in this city than anywhere in the world. This small selection concentrates on atmospheric neighborhoods where you can roam and almost take your pick of comfortable spots to dine. Here are a few specific recommendations; broken down by neighborhoods:

### The Marais

#### LA GUIRLANDE DE JULIE

(25, PLACE DES VOSGES) has a prize location on the beautiful square and a fine chef.

#### BOFINGER

(5, RUE DE LA BASTILLE) is a lively and pretty landmark brasserie dating back to 1864.

#### JO GOLDENBERG'S DELICATESSON

(7, RUE DE ROSIER) is on the main artery of the old Jewish ghetto, a local landmark.

## Ile de la Cité

### NOS ANCETRES LES GALOIS
(39, RUE SAINT-LOUIS-EN-I'LLE) minute, charming.

### AU GOURMET DE L'ISLE
(42, RUE SAINT-LOUIS-EN-I'LLE ) simple and pleasant, with a prix fixe dinner.

## Saint-Germain

### LE PETIT SAINT-BENOIT
(4, RUE SAINT-BENOIT) is a no-frills tasty choice when the budget is low.

### LE PETIT ZINC
(25, RUE DE BUCI) is known for good food and always busy. The block of rue Gregoire-de-Tours between rue de Buci and boulevard Saint-Germain has about fifteen similar cafes.

The famous brasseries where Sartre, Hemingway, and other literary lions once assembled are now said by many to be overpriced and filled with nothing but tourists, but they are landmarks I wanted to see on my first visit to Paris and perhaps you will, too. You will find three on boulevard Saint-Germain: Aux Deux Magots at 170, Café de Flore at 172, and Brassierie Lipp at 151. La Coupole is at 102, boulevard du Montparnasse.

## Other Recommendations
You might also try:

### RESTAURANT DE PALAIS D'ORSAY
(62, RUE DE LILLE) is in the marvelous d'Orsay Museum and is open for lunch and dinner.

### CAFE DE LA PAIX
(12, BOULEVARD DES CAPUCINES, 9TH ARRONDISSEMENT) is a restored national landmark. Come for meals or tea between 3:00 P.M. and 6:00 P.M.

### FAUCHON
(26, PLACE DE LA MADELEINE, 8TH ARRONDISSEMENT). This is the best cafeteria in Paris. You'll eat standing up, but it's still a "don't miss" for lunch.

### LA FERME SAINT HUBERT
(21, RUE VIGNON) is next door to a cheese shop of the same name and specializes in cheese dishes; it's very popular.

## CAFÉ DROUANT

(18 RUE GAILLON) is the sibling of a famous restaurant and offers good value, given the quality of the food. The shellfish motif on the ceiling is famous.

**RUE DE LA HUCHETTE,** a Left Bank street near the Shakespeare & Company bookshop, is lined with inexpensive, small Greek restaurants—good to know about if your budget is running low.

If you are really low on cash and homesick, there are dozens of McDonalds and Burger Kings, plus scores of sound-alikes all over Paris. What is the culinary world coming to?

### Guides to Paris

**Eyewitness Guide to Paris,** Dorling Kindersley, London and New York. Wonderful photographs and guided walking itineraries.
**The Best of Paris,** by Gault/Millau (Prentice-Hall Press, New York). The best guide for restaurants and hotels; good for shopping tips also.
**Paris Access,** by Richard Saul Wurman (AccessPress, Ltd., 59 Wooster Street, New York, NY 10012). Detailed neighborhood walking tours that include sights, shops, and dining places where you need them.
**Michelin Guides, Paris.** The old standbys, with green for sight-seeing, and red, with those much-desired star ratings, for dining. The guides stay popular because they tell you what you need to know quickly, and the narrow size is easy to carry in your pocket or purse.
**Cadogan Paris,** Dana Facaros and Michael Pauls, Cadogan Books, London.

# New York

This is my city. Almost all of us who live here have a love-hate relationship with the place. We grumble about the traffic, the subways, the rents, the prices, and the crowds. What keeps us here, however, are the same elements that make New York a fabulous place to visit: It is one of the most diverse and exciting cities in the world, overflowing with cultural riches, theater magic, marvelous food, and wares from around the globe. The old saying is true: If you can't find it in New York, it probably doesn't exist.

The pace and pulse of the city are tangible, maybe daunting at the start but eventually drawing you in to pick up your step and share the excitement. If you can't have a wonderful time here, you just aren't trying.

The New York subway is intimidating to strangers and sometimes even to natives. To feel secure getting around the city, familiarize yourself with the bus system. Buses are slow but sure, and they provide a great way to see the sights as well as the natives. Also, they cost just $1.50 per ride. You won't mind the traffic nearly so much if you aren't watching a taxi meter tick. You'll need exact change before you board, and no bills are accepted, so bring lots of change with you. Better yet, go down into any subway station and buy a Metrocard, which is also accepted on all buses. You can buy the Metrocard in any denomination over $5; each ride is automatically deducted when you board and slide the card through a slot. The card is gradually replacing the old New York subway tokens.

Contrary to what many out-of-towners expect, getting your New York bearings is easy because most of Manhattan is laid out on a straight grid, with avenues running north to south and streets running east to west. The central business district is only about sixteen blocks wide, and you'll spend most of your time within eight to ten of them. Bus transfers are free if you need to change from a "crosstown" (east-west) bus to one heading uptown or downtown (or vice versa), but you have to ask for a transfer when you board the first bus, not when you are getting off.

Bus routes are clearly marked on maps at most bus stops. A bus map is also printed on the back of the subway maps available free at token booths at the main city stations, or you can write to the New York Convention and Visitors Bureau (see page 277).

No one should miss a heart-stopping, skyscraper-high view of the city at night. Nothing else shows you so vividly why New York is unique. The Empire State Building observatory is open until midnight, and the top floor of the World Trade Center is open until 9:30 P.M. You might want to have a drink in the lounge of the Rainbow Room on the sixty-fifth floor of the RCA building, at City Lights on the 107th floor of the World Trade Center, or atop the Beekman Tower Hotel at First Avenue

# Only-in-New York Pleasures

Some favorite New Yorkers' pleasures that can be shared by visitors include:

- Biking the car-free roadways on the weekend or jogging around the reservoir any day in Central Park (both activities recommended for daylight hours only).
- Sitting on the steps of the Metropolitan Museum of Art on Sunday afternoon and watching the street performers and the passing parade.
- Visiting the farmer's Green Market in Union Square on Wednesday, Friday, or Saturday.
- Weekend brunching and gallery-hopping in SoHo along Broadway, West Broadway, and the cross streets between.
- Wandering Eighth Street, West Fourth Street, Bleecker, and other Greenwich Village streets along with young and young-at-heart New Yorkers.
- Walking the promenade along the East River from the World Financial Center through Battery Park City, with the Statue of Liberty in view all the way.
- Evenings at the city museums. The Museum of Modern Art is open until 8:30 P.M. (voluntary donation after 5 P.M.) on Thursday and Friday; the Metropolitan Museum of Art to 8:45 P.M. on Friday and Saturday; the Whitney Museum until 8:00 P.M. on Thursday (free admission after 6:00 P.M.); the Guggenheim to 8:00 P.M. on Friday (voluntary donation) and Saturday, and the American Museum of Natural History to 8:45 P.M. on Friday and Saturday.

and 49th Street. A magical time to see the city from above is at dusk, when you can watch millions of city lights go on.

New Yorkers are champion walkers and they like exploring their city as much as visitors do, so when it comes to seeing specific neighborhoods on foot, you'll find a great choice of walking tours around almost every part of the city each weekend from late spring through fall. Some of these groups also offer bus excursions that make it easy to visit suburban attractions. Here are some of the leading organizations that offer guided walks and tours:

**MUNICIPAL ART SOCIETY,** 457 MADISON AVENUE AT 50TH STREET, NEW YORK, NY 10022; (212) 935-3960.
**92ND STREET Y,** 1395 LEXINGTON AVENUE, NEW YORK, NY 10128; (212) 996-1105.
**BIG ONION TOURS;** (212) 439-1090.

Central Park is one of the city's glories, a beautiful site and the best place to see a microcosm of city life from baby strollers to rock concerts. In summer it is the scene of free concerts by the Metropolitan Opera and the New York Philharmonic, free Shakespeare in the Park, and a whole series of popular and rock music known as Summerstage. The park is perfectly safe in daylight and is filled with hundreds of people. If you are nervous, however, join one of the guided Urban Park Ranger tours; schedules are available at The Dairy building in the park near 64th Street.

On a first trip to New York, Little Italy and Chinatown can be confusing and might well be better seen on a guided walking tour. But here are some suggested neighborhoods to roam safely on your own to get a sense of the city and its diversity (buy a book of self-guided walking tours to find out who lived where as you wander):

- THE POSH UPPER EAST SIDE RESIDENTIAL STREETS, ROUGHLY BETWEEN 70TH AND 90TH STREETS FROM FIFTH TO PARK AVENUES.
- THE CHARMING WEST SIDE NEIGHBORHOODS FROM CENTRAL PARK WEST TO WEST END AVENUE BETWEEN 68TH AND 86TH STREETS.
- THE CHIC MADISON AVENUE SHOPS FROM THE 60S TO THE 90S.
- THE OVERPRICED BUT ENTICING BOUTIQUES ON COLUMBUS AVENUE FROM 68TH TO 81ST STREETS.
- THE WINDING STREETS AND HISTORIC TOWNHOUSES OF GREENWICH VILLAGE, THE OLD HEART OF LITERARY NEW YORK.

Shopping is a favorite New York pastime. Besides the special merchandise carried by the hundreds of small shops, out-of-towners often find the variety of wares in the big department stores such as Macy's, Saks Fifth Avenue, and Bloomingdale's a revelation. Most of the branches in major cities can't compare with the home stores. And the advent of superstores like Bed, Bath and Beyond means stocks so enormous you can hardly get through the whole store.

If you are brave and you know your labels, you can venture down to bargain hunt on the crowded Lower East Side. Note that stores are closed on Saturday in this old Jewish neighborhood, and Sunday is the busiest shopping day. It is a good idea to go armed with one of the special shopping guides to the area sold in most bookstores.

Another pleasure not to be missed by book lovers is the city's trove of wonderful bookstores. Among the many stops providing hours of happy browsing are the beautiful Rizzoli store at 31 West 57th Street, specialty shops such as The Biography Bookshop at 400 Bleecker Street; Applause Theater Books at 211 West 71st Street; Kitchen Arts & Letters at 1435 Lexington Avenue between 93d and 94th Streets; The Military Bookman at 29 East 93rd Street, E. Wyhe Art books at 794 Lexington Avenue, and Murder Ink., two stores full of mystery novels at 1465 Second Avenue and 2486 Broadway. Check the Yellow Pages for addresses of the big Barnes and Noble superstores now found all over town, most with a coffee bar for browsers and favorite meeting spots for single New Yorkers. Remaindered books and bargains can be found at the original Barnes and Noble at 105 Fifth Avenue, and used-book treasures are available at the Strand at 828 Broadway at 12th Street, the Argosy at 116 East 59th Street, and the Gotham Book Mart at 41 West 47th Street. The Yellow Pages will guide you to dozens of other specialists for everything from comic books to collectors' volumes.

No trip to New York is complete without a visit to the theaters and concert halls. To avoid spending a king's ransom, take advantage of the TKTS booth (Times Square Ticket Center) at 47th Street and Broadway. Half-priced tickets for Broadway and Off-Broadway shows are sold on the day of the performance starting at 3:00 P.M., and at 10:00 A.M. for matinees on Wednesday, Saturday, or Sunday. If you happen to be sight-seeing downtown, there is a branch of TKTS, usually with much shorter lines, on the mezzanine at 2 World Trade Center. The hours are Monday to Friday 11:00 A.M. to 5:30 P.M. and on Saturday, from 11:00 A.M. to 3:30 P.M.

Contrary to another popular belief, everything in New York does not cost pots of money. Television shows are one favorite free pastime, but you must get your request in early—at least one month in advance and often as much as six months ahead for the hot shows. Some networks will mail out ticket requests received by phone; others ask you to send in a postcard. At times, standby tickets may be available the morning of the show. Singles have a good shot. You can also pick up same-day tickets on occasion at the New York Visitors Bureau at Two Columbus Circle. For up-to-date information on your favorite show; it's best to phone. Network numbers are: ABC, (212) 887–3536; CBS, (212) 975–2476; NBC, (212) 664–3055.

It won't cost you a cent to take in a master class or attend high-quality, free concerts by faculty and students at the noted Juilliard School; phone in advance for schedules and ticket information at (212) 799–5000, ext. 235. Thursday morning rehearsals of the New York Philharmonic at Avery Fisher Hall are open to the public for a modest fee.

There are numerous free concerts as well in building atriums (such as the glorious Winter Garden at the World Financial Center), museums, and outdoor plazas around the city. Check *New York* or *Time Out* magazines or phone the Convention and Visitors Bureau at (800) NYC–VISIT.

Any guidebook will list the city's leading hotels. If you can't afford the top listings, but you prefer a small hotel to bed-and-breakfast homes, here are a few inexpensive and moderate recommendations. All are area code 212.

## PICKWICK ARMS

(230 EAST 51ST STREET; 355–0300) offers no frills but a good, safe, East Side location.

## HOTEL METRO

(45 EAST 35TH STREET; 947–2500) is breezy and cheerful and offers complimentary breakfast.

## EDISON

(228 WEST 47TH STREET; 840–5000) is a refurbished hotel in the heart of the theater district; it saves searching for cabs after the show.

## WYNDHAM

(42 West 58th Street; 753–3500) provides big, pretty rooms, dated plumbing, and the best values in town. This is a favorite with show-biz people; reserve far ahead to get in.

All of the Gotham Group hotels are highly recommended for solo travelers. They include breakfast, a sociable ambience, and sometimes even evening dessert. These stylishly renovated older properties include the Franklin (164 East 87th Street; 369–8000), the Wales (1295 Madison Avenue; 876–6000), the Shoreham (33 West 55th Street; 247–6700), and the Mansfield (12 West 44th Street; 944–6050). The Wales and the Franklin are located on the Upper East Side, a bit far from midtown but convenient for museum visits.

Consider leaving the midtown business center and seeing New York like a native by taking advantage of the city's bed-and-breakfast registries. They'll show you what real life is like in the Big Apple, where in warm weather people sunbathe in the parks on Sunday and sit around in sidewalk cafes. Having checked out a number of these lodgings for a recent article, I was surprised at the lovely apartments available as B&Bs. It says a lot about the price of housing in New York that so many people are welcoming paying guests.

Where to dine alone in New York? There are plenty of options. If you want ambience, you'll find cafes even in some of the tiniest hotels. You'll no doubt make your own discoveries as you walk around, but some suggested havens for dining alone, by neighborhood, include:

## *Midtown*

### THE OYSTER BAR

(lower level in Grand Central Station, 42nd Street and Lexington Avenue) provides counter service and a number of small tables; it's tops for seafood.

### THE BRASSERIE

(100 East 53rd Street between Park and Lexington) is a recently refurbished old-timer; it has a long counter as well as small tables, a menu from onion soup gratinée to steak, and is open twenty-four hours a day.

### CARNEGIE DELICATESSEN

(854 Seventh Avenue between 54th and 55th streets) is a New York landmark

with wisecracking waiters, long, cramped tables, and legendary corned beef and pastrami sandwiches.

## CHEZ NAPOLEON

(365 WEST 50TH STREET) is a homey, family-run French bistro, convenient for theatergoers.

## CHINA GRILL

(60 WEST 53RD STREET AT THE CORNER OF 6TH AVENUE) is a trendy favorite with a French-Chinese menu and long dining bar.

## COMING OR GOING

(38 EAST 58TH STREET) is a tiny Italian/American spot, popular for lunch and quiet for dinner.

## MANHATTAN CHILI COMPANY

(1500 BROADWAY) is great for a pre-theater meal.

## EDISON CAFE

(AT THE HOTEL EDISON AT 228 WEST 47TH STREET) offers potato pancakes, blintzes, matzo ball soup, and the chance that show-biz biggies will stop in between shows.

## LA BONNE SOUPE

(48 WEST 55TH STREET) is good for a light dinner.

## PALIO

(151 WEST 51ST STREET) is an elegant Italian restaurant that serves meals at the knockout downstairs bar.

## THE PEMBROKE ROOM

(IN THE LOWELL HOTEL AT 28 EAST 63RD STREET) is a gracious hideaway serving a lavish tea that can double as supper. Hours are 3:30 to 7:00 P.M., with the last serving at 6:30 P.M.

## PEN & PENCIL

(205 EAST 45TH STREET; 212–682–8660), a business lunch favorite, offers cluster seating that encourages inter-table chatting among separately seated guests. Solo diners also receive a complimentary glass of the house pear grappa.

### Upper West Side

Browse Columbus Avenue and its side streets between 65th and 81st streets for limitless possibilities—just pick a cafe that doesn't have a line spilling out the door! If you aren't going to Lincoln Center, come after 8:00 P.M. when the crowds are smaller. A few recommendations:

## MUSEUM CAFE
(COLUMBUS AT 77TH) offers a pleasant ambience.

## VICTOR'S CAFE
(COLUMBUS AT 71ST) has been a longtime favorite for Cuban food.

## RIKYU
(COLUMBUS BETWEEN 69TH AND 70TH STREETS) is Japanese with a choice of small tables or a sushi bar.

## LINCOLN SQUARE COFFEE SHOP, RESTAURANT AND BAKERY
(COLUMBUS AVENUE BETWEEN 65TH AND 66TH STREETS) has a varied menu and a super salad bar.

### Upper East Side
Browse Second Avenue between 74th and 86th streets, and 86th Street east or west of Second Avenue and you'll have experienced a mini world tour of cuisines. Try one of these:

## PAMIR
(1437 SECOND AVENUE BETWEEN 74TH AND 75TH STREETS) is a pretty little spot with Afghanistan specialities, a delicious and delicate blend of Indian and Middle Eastern fare.

## MOCCA
(1588 SECOND AVENUE BETWEEN 82ND AND 83RD STREETS) is a European-style Hungarian cafe; it has good goulash and good prices.

## EMPIRE SZECHUAN
(1649 SECOND AVENUE AT 86TH STREET) is one of the neighborhood's many Chinese choices.

## RUSH'N EXPRESS
(30 EAST 86TH STREET) supplies borscht, blinis, and other delicious Russian treats for take-out or eat-in at wonderfully low prices. (Another location is at 303 Park Avenue South.)

## MANGIA, MANGIA
(1297 LEXINGTON AVENUE AT 87TH STREET) is a pleasant, reasonably priced Italian eatery.

## VIAND

(300 EAST 86TH STREET AND ALSO AT 1011 MADISON AVENUE AND AT 673 MADISON AVENUE) is an upscale coffee shop with wide-ranging diner-style menus and surprisingly good food. The upper Madison Avenue address is ideal if you are visiting the Metropolitan or Whitney museums.

### Greenwich Village/SoHo

Pick any block and you'll likely find tiny, welcoming restaurants. Here are some possibilities:

## CUCINA STAGIONALE

(275 BLEECKER STREET) produces Italian food that pleases both palate and pocketbook.

## JOHN'S PIZZERIA

(278 BLEECKER STREET) is generally agreed to be New York's best, as attested by the long lines. Come at an off-hour.

## WHITE HORSE INN

(HUDSON AND 11TH STREETS) is a 106-year-old neighborhood classic.

## ZOE'S

(90 PRINCE STREET; 212–966–6722) has popular counter where diners can watch the chef in action.

## CHEZ BRIGETTE

(77 GREENWICH AVENUE) is a hole-in-the-wall spot with counters—and incredible French food. Great for onion soup at lunch.

Don't leave the Village without sampling its coffee houses. Two suggestions are:

## PATISSERIE LANCIANI

(271 WEST 4TH STREET) located between Perry and 11th Streets, has a light menu in addition to coffees.

## CAFFE VIVALDI

(32 JONES STREET) offers incredible desserts.

### The East Village

Here's where young New York eats on a budget. A few favorites are:

**"LITTLE INDIA,"** covering all of 6th Street between First and Second Avenues, and spilling over onto First Avenue, is lined with tiny

---

# A Tip about Tips

*Most New Yorkers find it easiest to just double the tax (8¼ percent) on their restaurant bills and leave a 16.5 percent tip. The difference from the usual 15 percent is negligible, and it saves lots of mental arithmetic.*

---

Indian restaurants, most BYOB. There are at least a dozen to try.
**MITALI EAST** at 334 East Sixth Street, gets good reviews—or just pick the decor that pleases you; some people joke that they all use the same kitchen, anyway.

**CHRISTINE'S**
(438 SECOND AVENUE AT 25TH STREET) is a bit uptown but noted for inexpensive and hearty Polish home cooking.

**TERESA'S**
(103 FIRST AVENUE AT 6TH STREET) is another downtown Polish choice.

**UNION SQUARE CAFE**
(21 EAST 16TH STREET) is farther uptown and in another world. A stylish cafe that is one of the city's favorites, it has an innovative menu and a long bar where singles dine comfortably.

## Guides to New York
Recommended guides to the city are:
**Eyewitness Guide to New York,** (Dorling Kindersley, London and New York)
**Nooks and Crannies: A Walking Tour Guide to New York City** by David Yeadon (Charles Scribner's Sons, New York)
**AIA Guide to New York City** by Elliot Willensky and Norval White (Harcourt Brace, New York). A knowledgeable architectural guide for walking tours.

**The City Observed: New York,** A Guide to the Architecture of Manhattan by Paul Goldberger (Vintage Books, New York). Written by the *New York Times* architecture critic.
**Frommer's Irreverent Guide, Manhattan** (Macmillan, New York). An honest appraisal of what's good and bad round the city.

# Bring The Kids

**B**USY SINGLE PARENTS WHO TAKE DOUBLE RESPONSIBILITY FOR their kids most of the year really deserve a vacation. They most often want to share that vacation with the children. They look forward to rare relaxed and unscheduled time to have fun together, family time to really talk and share. Having kids for company actually solves certain travel problems, such as solitary meals.

Yet, while shared family vacations can be wonderfully rewarding, single parents also need a break. In fact, each generation benefits from time off for relaxing and socializing with people in their own age group. For parents, that doesn't necessarily mean looking for romance—just a bit of adult companionship and conversation. So, the most successful single-parent outings with the kids offer both the opportunity for togetherness and time to be apart.

For that reason, some traditional family vacations aren't really great for single parents. One parent trying to keep up with two or three kids at Walt Disney World might be exhausted instead of exhilarated. Car trips can be miserable with no one to share the driving or the disciplining of the children. And resorts with children's programs can be populated mostly by couples who are relishing time together while *their* kids are busy, and they are therefore not much company for a parent alone. Luckily, there are options that offer both togetherness and a chance for separate activities.

## Some Practical Pointers

**S**tart by planning something *you* really want to do, regardless of the kids. Ranches are wonderful places for family vacations, but if you hate the idea of getting on a horse, life on a ranch isn't going to be any more appealing just because the children are along.

As with any family outing, arrangements generally work out better if the youngsters are involved in the planning and are excited about the trip. If there are choices to be made, even preschoolers can look at color brochures and have some say in what looks great to them. Let the children help write for brochures and information, using their own names so that the mail comes back addressed to them. If you decide on a city vacation, have them participate in making lists of what you hope to do each day. Readers can make a trip to the library to get books about the area you will be visiting.

A productive pretrip activity is to have children put together a scrap-book with space for preplanning and a day-to-day diary with room to paste in souvenirs as you travel. It helps build anticipation beforehand and keeps them busy along the way.

Older kids can also help put together those tried-and-true travel games, such as making a list of states that can be checked off when their license plates are spied. Another family favorite is printing the alphabet down the side of a sheet of notebook paper for each child, with space to fill in ob-jects spotted for each letter. Don't forget to bring favorite books, toys, and other games to keep everyone happily occupied.

When you pack, choose comfortable, fast-drying clothing in dark col-ors so you needn't nag about keeping clothes clean on vacation. Be sure to include rainwear in case of bad weather.

Two issues that make for crabby tempers on family vacations are fa-tigue and hunger. Do your best to avoid both. Be prepared with snacks during travel times and in hotel rooms. Unfamiliar beds and schedules and the excitement of new places can wreak havoc with bedtimes, so plan time out for rest each day. It will do you good, too.

Keep traveling time to a minimum. Pack a small bag for each child with pajamas, toothbrush, toothpaste, and a favorite blanket and toy, so they can settle into a new place fast. If you need cribs and high chairs, call ahead to double-check that they are available and in place.

You'll find many more practical suggestions for traveling with children in the book *Great Vacations with Your Kids* by Dorothy Ann Jordan and Marjorie Adoff Cohen (E.P. Dutton, New York). The book also includes many vacation suggestions.

..........................................................................

# Singular Parent Choices

Some of the vacation choices recommended for single adults are equally comfortable for single-parent families. Active adventure vacations are wonderful for youngsters who are old enough to enjoy them. Almost all are appropriate for teens, and some can accommodate much younger children. Ask the operator about the ages recommended. Some groups that explicitly welcome children are listed below along with learning options that have separate programs for youngsters.

Ranch vacations are made to order for single parents, and all the guidance on page 23 is appropriate for families. Cruising from a family point of view is covered later in this chapter. See page 109 for information on windjammer cruises. Teenagers love the adventure of these big sailing ships, but restless younger children are not well suited to these trips. For them, stick to the oceanliners. If you want to go to a resort, check for tennis, sailing, or golf schools that are resort-based and have children's programs. Those arrangements will give you a focus, and you can make friends while the children enjoy their own brand of fun.

Here are a variety of vacation suggestions for single parents:

## CLUB MED

40 EAST 57TH STREET, NEW YORK, NY 10019;
(800) CLUB-MED. (SEE PAGE 200.) (M-E)

Club Med doesn't just tolerate children—they welcome them, and they welcome single parents, too. Five Club Med villages have been designated for families, and at two of these, Eleuthera in the Bahamas and Ixtapa in Mexico, there are "Single Parenthood" programs featuring a private cocktail party for single parents at the start of each week and a sign-up board to make it easier to find a partner for sailing, tennis, or golf.

Kids' programs entertain and teach children aged 1 to 12 with nonstop activities, meals, and amusements, supervised and coordinated by a special staff, all at no additional cost. Programs run from 9:00 A.M. to

9:00 P.M. daily, and there are optional kid-pleasing early lunches and dinners to give parents the chance to enjoy conversation with other adults at meals.

Other villages for families include Sandpiper in Florida, Punta Cana in the Dominican Republic, and St. Lucia in the West Indies. Each has Petit, Mini, and Kids Clubs divided by age and geared to ages 2 to 11 or 12. Kids can stop by for one favorite activity, for an hour, or for the entire day. Some villages have Baby Clubs with sitters for babies and toddlers ages 12 to 23 months. Sandpiper will take children as young as 4 months. Little ones get their own wading pools, and there is a private dining room with high chairs and furniture scaled to youngsters. Baby Clubs are equipped with cribs, playpens, and toys. Strollers, potties, and baby monitors can be borrowed at no extra charge. They even sell diapers in the boutiques. How family-minded can you get?

Activities vary from village to village. Among the fun possibilities are lessons in scuba diving (with mini-equipment in the pool), snorkeling, sailing, golf, and tennis, plus arts and crafts, archery, boat rides, picnics, puppet shows, swimming, carriage, pony, and horseback rides, and go-carting. Lots of children love the Club Med circus workshops where they learn juggling, magic, trampolining, and how to walk a tightrope (with a net right below, of course).

At certain times of the year, one child age 1 to 5 comes free with each adult. The time periods and the specific clubs offering this package may vary, so it's best to check for current information.

Teenagers have their own programs for ages 12 to 14 and 15 to 17 at Huatulco in Mexico and at Copper Mountain in Colorado.

## GOLF DIGEST INSTRUCTION SCHOOLS
5520 PARK AVENUE, BOX 395, TRUMBULL, CT 06611;
(800) 243–6121 OR (203) 373–7130. (SEE PAGE 20.) (EE)

Once a year this large golf program offers a special parent/child week. Open to youngsters ages 12 and up; the instruction is geared to both age groups. A sharing and learning experience that builds closeness as well as golfing prowess, the program is limited to sixteen parent/child teams. In the past the week has been held at Amelia Island, Florida, and Sea Island, Georgia; check for the current locations.

## SIERRA CLUB FAMILY OUTINGS
C/O SIERRA CLUB, 730 POLK STREET, SAN FRANCISCO, CA 94109;
(415) 776-2211. (SEE PAGE 90.) (I)

Introducing families to the joys of camping and the outdoors is one of the missions of the Sierra Club. Half a dozen outings each summer are designated especially for families, and the catalog notes that single parents as well as uncles, aunts, and grandparents are welcome. The difficulty of the trips varies. Some trips are lodge-based; others are at campsites. All offer opportunities for nature study, day hikes, fishing, swimming, and solitude. The group meets for breakfast and supper; lunch for outings is packed at breakfast. Most activities are informal and unstructured, and the group usually makes its own fun in the evening.

Among recent offerings were "Toddler Tramps" in state and national parks; these are appropriate for very young children. Other adventures included trips to Hawaii and wilderness adventures designated for children six years and older. The Sierra Club catalog also notes other types of trips that are suitable for families.

## FAMILY GOES TO CAMP
## SHERI GRIFFITH EXPEDITIONS
P.O. BOX 1324, MOAB, UT 84532;
(800) 332-2439 OR (801) 259-8229. (SEE PAGE 111.) (M)

The most exciting river runs are recommended for ages 10 and up, but this special five-day, four-night family trip of about 94 miles on the Green River through Desolation Canyon is full of big, rolling waves that are fun but not difficult and is open to children from age 5. Camping is on sandy beaches with plenty of beach toys and shovels and buckets for sandcastle building. Hiking excursions into side canyons (some with ancient Indian writings on the walls) are part of the trip. Meals take pint-sized tastes into account by including hamburgers as well as steak. After dark come campfires, roasted marshmallows, and plenty of talk and song.

Guides also take the children on separate outings. Parents can join in or take this time for themselves—for quiet relaxation besides the river, a leisurely walk, or a demanding hike. According to the operators, many of the adults are single parents.

## FAMILY RAFTING
## O.A.R.S. RAFTING ADVENTURES
Box 67, Angels Camp, CA 95222;
(209) 736-4677. (See page 113.) (I)

For families who want to be introduced to the fun and excitement of river-rafting, special discounts are offered on selected dates for trips on the many rivers this company navigates. The regular trips offered by this group also welcome children of specified minimum ages, starting at 4 years for some of the shorter, easier trips and starting at 14 years for the more rugged rivers.

## FAMILY RAFTING
## DVORAK'S RAFTING EXPEDITIONS
17921-B U.S. 285, Nathrop, CO 81236;
(800) 824-3795 or (719) 539-6851. (See page 113.) (I-M)

On specified family weeks, this outfitter invites one child under the age of 13 to come along free with an adult. These trips on the Green and Dolores rivers are planned with kids in mind. Reserve early—they fill up fast.

Other short trips suitable as an introduction to river-running offer discounts for families of three and up.

## CONSERVATION SUMMIT YOUTH PROGRAMS
## NATIONAL WILDLIFE FEDERATION
8925 Leesburg Pike, Vienna, VA 22184;
(703) 790-4363 or (800) 245-5484. (See page 120.) (I)

Most of the programs for adults offer separate supervised activities for children of all ages. "The Big Backyard," running from 8:00 A.M. to noon for three- and four-year-olds, is a nature discovery program including micro-hikes, touch-and-feel expeditions, and fun-with-nature crafts. "Junior Naturalists," for ages five to twelve, divide into age groups for nature hikes, stream studies, wildlife investigations, bird walks, folk-

tale hours, outdoor games, and arts and crafts. Their day runs from 8:30
A.M. to 3:00 P.M. A separate Teen Adventure program is adventure-ori-
ented, with the chance to learn hiking, orienteering, and rope skills.

## CORNELL ADULT UNIVERSITY
626 THURSTON AVENUE, ITHACA, NY 14850-2490;
(607) 255-6260. (SEE PAGE 47.) (I–M)

Though the title says adult, kids are far from forgotten here. More
than 100 youngsters from all over the United States enroll in the
Youth Program, having fun while their parents are learning on their own
level. Families always have breakfast and dinner together, but child supervision is available from 8:30 A.M. to 11:15 P.M. for those who want it.

Programming is provided for five age groups. Infants and tots under 3
have no formal schedule, but qualified baby-sitters are available. Li'l Bears
(ages 3 to 5) learn and play in a Cornell preschool facility. Art, music,
crafts, expeditions across campus, and time to rest are all part of their fun.
(Children enrolled must be potty trained.) Tykes, (five- and six-year-olds
who have been to school) have their own similar sessions.

Sprouts (ages 7 and 8) have a learning program as well as hikes, games,
sports, crafts, and cookouts. Junior Cornellians (ages 9 to 12) meet in the
morning for a choice of classes and have recreational activities, outings to
state parks, visits to campus facilities, and presentations and demonstrations by members of the faculty during supervised afternoon and evening
programs. They can choose from a variety of classes including cooking,
animal behavior, outdoor adventures such as ropes and wilderness hiking,
horseback riding, windsurfing, and sailing.

Teens (ages 13 to 16) have an even wider selection, and they have
their own reserved dormitory floor and dining place.

## CHAUTAUQUA INSTITUTION
CHAUTAUQUA, NY 14722;
(716) 357-6200. (SEE PAGE 51.) (I–M)

While parents enjoy the multitude of classes and cultural events during the summer at Chautauqua, youngsters can enroll in the diverse
children's programs offered. Programs are for one week to a full season.

Children's School, held from 9:00 A.M. to noon daily, is an early child-hood center for preschoolers from age 2½ to 6. It includes language en-richment, pre-reading, early math concepts, and exposure to the arts as well as creative free play. An afternoon Pre-Club for five- and six-year-olds who have attended the morning program includes beach activities, group games, arts and crafts, music, creative dramatics, and field trips. About 1,400 youngsters each summer take advantage of the Boys' and Girls' Club for ages 6 to 15. It is organized as a day camp where children get a full schedule of summer recreation such as swimming, sailing, ca-noeing, arts and crafts, drama, music, archery, basketball, soccer, volley-ball, and baseball. The group is divided into sections according to age.

For teenagers, the Youth Activities Center is open daily from noon to 11:00 P.M. It has its own beach (with diving board), a snack bar, amuse-ment machines, Ping-Pong equipment, swimming pool, table games, and color television. Dances, cookouts, guest speakers, and movies are offered at night. The center also is headquarters for the High School and College Clubs, each with activities planned by its own members.

## YOSEMITE FIELD SEMINARS
P.O. Box 230, El Portal, CA 95318;
(209) 379–2321. (See page 125).

A recent program planned especially for families has been a family backpacking expedition covering about 11 miles over three days and open to families with children ages 6 to 11. Catered family camping, open to ages 4 and up, is a program that provides an easy introduction to camping in Yosemite's lovely Tuolumne Meadow and features easy hikes and prepared meals.

## BACKROADS BICYCLING VACATIONS
1516 Fifth Street, Berkeley, CA 94710;
(800) GO–ACTIVE. (See page 97.) (I–M)

Several of this group's tours, both camping and with inn lodging, are designated as family outings. Recent destinations have included Washington State's Puget Sound, the Canadian Rockies, Maine,

Vermont, Nova Scotia, and excursions in France and Switzerland. Family weekend trips in California are also planned.

## ALASKA WILDLAND ADVENTURES

P.O. Box 389, Girdwood, AK 99487;
(800) 334–8730. (See page 95.) (EE)

A family safari each summer is designed for parents and children ages 6 to 11.

## RASCALS IN PARADISE

650 Fifth Street, Suite 505, San Francisco, CA 94107;
(415) 978–9800 or (800) U–RASCAL. (EE)

Hawaii and Honduras, Alaska and Africa, Florida and Fiji are among the far-flung family offerings of this California-based group. Age minimums vary with the difficulty of the trip and are as low as 3 years for many destinations. To make the experience easier for families, on many trips the group establishes one home base and goes exploring on day trips. Baby-sitters are available as needed. Kids have a separate menu, and mealtimes bring familiar foods even in remote climes. Groups are usually composed of four to six families; if four or more families sign up, an escort goes along.

The operators also specialize in booking family-oriented resort and ranch vacations. They can tell you which have special rates for single parents, and they are familiar with the differences in offerings at resorts in Jamaica (such as F.D.R. and Boscobel Beach) that specialize in family vacations.

# Family Cruise Vacations

Children love cruise ships. They love climbing the steps or riding the elevators from one deck to another; they like the pools and the gyms and all the activities and entertainment on board; they adore scampering down the gangplank to see a brand-new port. The constant parade of

# Questions for Cruise Lines

*Here are a few pertinent questions to ask when you compare family cruises:*

- Are cabins large enough to comfortably accommodate families? Are there any connecting cabins? Is there room for a crib if you need one?
- What are children's rates? Are there periods when these go down?
- Are there breaks for single parents?
- When can you count on supervised activities for children?
- How large is the children's staff? What training do they have?
- What is the average size of the group they supervise?
- Is there a children's center on board? What does it offer?
- Is there a separate center for teens?
- Are children's meals offered during the early sitting if parents are signed up for the later serving?
- Are booster chairs available in the dining room?
- Are any evening activities planned for young passengers?
- Are baby-sitters available in the evening?
- Is there any provision for baby-sitting for young children while the ship is in port?
- Are there any special shore excursions for youngsters? Any special children's rates on regular excursions?

food is a treat, especially since it usually includes familiar favorites like hamburgers and ice cream as well as sophisticated fare. Teens enjoy it too—provided they find company aboard. Some ships provide special video/disco centers where they can meet others their age.

Cruising certainly is not an inexpensive family vacation, but it can be a memorable one, and many of the problems of cruising alone are solved when you have your family along.

Almost any itinerary seems exciting, but Premier Cruise Lines (400 Challenger Road, Cape Canaveral, FL 32920; 800–327–7113 or 407–783–5071) is dedicated to family travel, with Warner Brothers' Looney Tunes characters like Bugs Bunny on board to assure a fun time. Single parents get special rates. The ships make three- and four-night cruises from Port Canaveral to Nassau and Port Lucaya in the Bahamas.

Most cruise lines today recognize that families are good business, and more than fifty ships now offer varying kid-sized amenities, from baby-sitters to foreign language lessons. Norwegian Cruise Lines, for example, publishes a special brochure on its children's programs; it lists special activities for four age groups, from ages 3 to 17. The ship includes a children's playroom and an ice-cream bar, and kids get their own newspapers—one for children and one for teens.

Costa Cruises has a Youth Center and a full-time youth counselor on board year-round, plus daily activities for children ages 5 to 12 and for teens. Kids on Royal Caribbean also have their own playrooms and supervised activities. They can attend pizza and ice-cream parties and other special events. Disney is also planning to launch a line of family cruise ships in 1998.

Many cruise lines allow children under 3 to share their parents' staterooms free of charge, and many have special children's rates or reduced fares for the third and fourth passengers in a cabin. Reduced rates and children's programs vary with the seasons, and some lines offer them only during school breaks. Choose carefully, so that you can look forward to smooth sailing on a family vacation at sea. An excellent guide for more information is *Cruise Vacations with Kids* by Candyce Stapen (Prima Books, Rocklin, California).

## S k i   W e e k s

Skiing is a wonderful family sport. Even the youngest children take to the slopes with glee, and thanks to nurseries and lessons for children, parents can find free time to take off at their own ability level. The bigger ski resorts typically have centers that accommodate children from infants to ages 6 or 8. You can leave the children for an hour or two or for the day.

As the kids get older, skiing allows for plenty of independence. After one or two family runs, everyone usually goes off to his or her own challenges, reuniting for lunch and at day's end. If the weather is uncooperative, parents can stay by the fire or read a book in the lodge while gung-ho youngsters brave the elements. In our family, skiing was the one family vacation that remained popular even after my children were in college and traveling on their own.

If you can afford it, the ideal situation for families is a lodge within walking distance of the slopes or one that has shuttle service to the mountain. This means eager beavers can be first on the slopes while parents get needed rest, and everyone can quit and go home when they are ready.

Another good bet is Club Med at Copper Mountain in Colorado, where special lessons are available for children ages 3 to 12. Younger ones get a basic initiation, those 6 to 12 have two hours of lessons in the morning and afternoon. Besides skiing, the Mini Club is open from 9:00 A.M. to 9:00 P.M. with staff-supervised activities and meals for the kids.

Every ski area offers money-saving ski week packages with or without lessons, and many have additional savings for children who stay in parents' rooms. Families also may choose less expensive, less crowded smaller ski areas while children are still young and need less challenge. The best plan is to pick several areas that interest you and write for current programs.

········································································

# Single Grandparents

Single grandparents and their grandchildren can make great traveling companions. Each generation widens the other's perspective, and a trip affords them a wonderful chance to get to know each other better and bond for life.

## GRANDTRAVEL, C/O THE TICKET COUNTER
6900 WISCONSIN AVENUE, SUITE 706, CHEVY CHASE, MD 28015;
(800) 247-7651 OR (301) 986-0790

Grandtravel was the first to make it easier to arrange this type of trip, usually scheduled during school breaks. These escorted tours take

care of all travel arrangements, and they provide time for each generation
to be alone with their peers as well as ample time together. The kids
might go roller skating while the grandparents go out for a gourmet dinner. The grandparents typically are in their 60s or early 70s, the grandchildren ages 7 to 14. Among the U.S. destinations are the western
national parks, Washington, D.C., Colorado, southern California, the
desert Southwest, and Alaska. Foreign itineraries have included New
Zealand, China, England, and Scotland, barging in Holland, and safaris
in Kenya.

There are now several other options for grandparents. The Sierra Club
(see page 289) has a special week in its family programs set aside for
grandparents, and Premier Cruise Lines (see page 295) is offering discounts for passengers older than 55 during certain periods. The B'nai
B'rith Center for Jewish Family Life has a GrandExplorers program to
help grandparents pass on family traditions and heritage. The major trip
is a ten-day vacation in Israel, but there are also trips to New York City
and Washington, D.C. For information, contact B'nai B'rith Israel
Commission, 1640 Rhode Island Avenue, NW, Washington, D.C.
22036; (202) 857–6577.

## City Safaris

Parents who prefer an outing solely for their own family would do well
to think about visiting a city. Kids really wax enthusiastic about pick-
ing a city and planning what to see and do. All you have to do to keep
everybody happy is to allot a fair share of time for activities that appeal to
youngsters as well as grown-ups.

For the happiest outings, plan an itinerary alternating your choices
with those of the children. Intersperse museum visits with trips to the
zoo, the beach, or an aquarium, for example. If you insist on shopping
with children along, reward them with a performance at a children's theater or a children's movie. Look for boat rides, major league baseball
games, and other sure-to-please treats everyone can share. While you are
researching reasonable family-priced dining, look out also for the best
local ice-cream emporiums. Above all, provide plenty of breaks such as

excursions to city parks where kids can run and play or use up excess energy on a rented bike. Parks offer a bonus for parents, for while the smaller members of the family are letting off steam, adults can gain a special perspective watching everyday local life they might otherwise have missed.

The growth of all-suite hotels with two rooms for the price of one is a real boon for families. These are equivalent in price to standard hotels and offer space, privacy, refrigerators, and separate TVs; some even have cooking facilities. While you may not want to spend your vacation cooking, having snacks, drinks, and breakfast ingredients on hand is a real money-saver. Some of the all-suite chains also include a free breakfast.

Most bed-and-breakfast facilities, however, are not good choices for families with young children. Healthy, noisy little ones often feel much too restricted in someone else's home. And somehow, even a budget motel seems more exciting, more of a special outing.

Almost any major city presents opportunities for family adventures, but those with easy and inexpensive public transportation systems offer a special advantage.

## Chicago

Chicago is my top pick for family fun. It is filled with kid-pleasing attractions, is easy to navigate, and is easy on the budget. You can stay in a high-rise Motel 6 in the heart of the city! Most of the city's museums have a free admission day, and the Lincoln Park Zoo is free whenever you visit. Too much sight-seeing? Take a break at Oak Street beach, right in town.

Navy Pier and its 150-foot Ferris wheel is almost reason enough for a visit. The revitalized 1916 pier, a city landmark, is a spectacular playground on the lake with more than 50 acres of parks, an old-fashioned carousel, ice skating in winter, and a big, bright children's museum.

Cruises leaving from Navy Pier and along the Chicago River, which runs through the city to the lake, are a wonderful way to appreciate the great architecture in this town where the skyscraper was born. The Chicago Architecture Foundation runs the most informative river trips, but kids may prefer the Wacky Pirate Cruise, an hour of singing and surprises that still manages to highlight the city's notable buildings.

Another popular perspective on the skyline is from the 103rd-floor sky deck of the Sears Tower, the tallest skyscraper in the world.

The Art Institute, home to many of the world's most famous works of art, has a wonderful interactive introduction to art for kids in the Kraft General Foods Education Center, where paintings are hung at kids'-eye level. Family Days are planned to highlight various parts of the collection.

Also fun for families is a walk past the veritable museum of outdoor sculpture around Chicago's downtown commercial center, known as The Loop. A free brochure, "Round & About the Loop," available at the city's three visitor centers, points the way to a hunt for treasures—works by the likes of Calder, Chagall, Picasso, and Miro.

Allow plenty of time for the Museum of Science and Industry, Chicago's most visited attraction, a vast building covering more than fifteen acres with more than 2,000 exhibits, including the chance to descend into a realistic reproduction of a coal mine, tour an actual U-505 submarine, and be strapped in for a simulated space shuttle flight.

Grant Park on the lakefront includes three major museums. The Field Museum of Natural History features a four-story brachiosaurus, the world's largest mounted dinosaur, and the Adler Planetarium has a special Sky Show for kids. Everyone enjoys visiting the beluga whales, sea otters, and penguins at the Oceanarium in the Shedd Aquarium.

Also located on the lake is Lincoln Park and its thirty-five-acre zoo, home to more than 2,000 mammals. There is a separate children's zoo where many baby animals can be seen and small animals like rabbits can be petted, plus the Farm in the Zoo, a working farm with the chance to see milking every day. All of this is free.

At dinnertime, sample Chicago's famous deep-dish pizza, drop in at Michael Jordan's place, or visit the one and only Rock 'N Roll McDonald's.

## Boston

Another of my favorite cities to visit with children is Boston, home of the New England Aquarium, with its exciting dolphin shows, a fabulous Children's Museum, and the country's only Computer Museum, a surefire hit with most youngsters. In Boston, kids can have a lively history lesson walking the red line of the Freedom Trail, tossing their own chest of tea overboard on the Boston Tea Party ship, and boarding "Old Ironsides," the USS *Constitution*. A visit to Paul Revere's home and the Old North Church in the North End can be followed by dinner at one of the area's many Italian restaurants, with unbeatable cannoli for dessert.

The famous swan boats are out in the Public Garden in warm weather, offering rides near the spot made famous by Robert McCloskey's classic children's picture book *Make Way for Ducklings*. Read the book before you go.

Kids also love visiting the food booths at Quincy Market, where lavish choices for every taste include pizza and brownies as well as a whole world of ethnic fare, all to be enjoyed at outdoor tables to the tune of free entertainment by street musicians. This is also a great city for sports lovers; especially popular are the baseball games at Fenway Park, one of the country's last classic arenas.

Don't overlook the Esplanade beside the Charles River, a great place for watching roller skaters, joggers, rowing crews, and sailboats in action. A walk up Beacon Hill is a wonderful way to see what cities were like in America a long time ago. Trolley tours and double-decker buses allow on and off privileges around the city all day, a good investment at least one day of your visit.

## Philadelphia

Children love Philadelphia—and vice versa. Besides the perennial attraction of the Liberty Bell and Independence Hall, this city makes youngsters welcome with many attractions. The "Please Touch" Museum was the first museum in the nation designed especially for children under age 7. Another surefire favorite is the imaginative Treehouse at the Philadelphia Zoo, where kids can find out how it feels to climb through a 35-foot-high honeycomb or hatch out of a giant egg in the Everglades swamp. The nation's oldest zoo also offers a separate Children's Zoo, where kids can board Noah's Ark to pet the furry passengers, see how cows are milked, ride a pony, or watch a sea lion show.

History, Philadelphia-style, becomes a hands-on experience at Franklin Court, a fabulous little museum devoted to Benjamin Franklin. A telephone hotline there allows you to call anyone from George Washington to John F. Kennedy to hear what they had to say about the remarkable Mr. F. At Dial-A-Witticism, you can call up a Franklin quip on almost any subject.

Not far away on the river, Philadelphia's waterfront is blooming, with a maritime museum, historic ships for boarding, and a boat that shuttles back and forth to the New Jersey Aquarium just across the Delaware River.

The big Franklin Institute ranks as one of the nation's great science museums. It is full of participatory exhibits that let you climb aboard a steam locomotive or take a walk through the chambers of a giant walk-through heart. The newest addition, the Meyer Center, is a whirring, blinking world of participatory exhibits that show what we can expect in the future from medicine to transportation to fashion. Even the youngest visitors can enjoy touring a space station and imagining themselves as astronauts. The museum offers a leaflet suggesting other exhibits that can be enjoyed by children under age six. Adults are as fascinated as the kids.

Philadelphia also offers the nation's largest city park, filled with diversions.

There is good eating both at the family restaurants near South Philly's colorful Italian Market and at Reading Terminal Market, where generations of Philadelphians have shopped for fresh produce and meat—and where knowing locals come for lunch at stands offering everything from freshly carved turkey sandwiches to Greek gyros or hot enchiladas. And don't miss a sampling of Philly's gourmet junk food, the cheese steak, at Jim's at Fourth and South Streets.

## Washington, D.C.

This city is guaranteed fun for both generations, though it is best to wait until children are old enough to be interested in the workings of government. The Tour Mobile allows you to get on and off all day, seeing the many monuments and sights without wearing out shoe leather. If you can, visit when Congress is in session. Get in touch with your Congressman or Senator in advance to request passes that admit you to the public galleries without being part of a tour. Stop into your representative's office, and you may get to meet your congressperson and/or learn from his or her staff just what goes on in an office in the Capitol. You can get a schedule of committee meetings and sit in on one to see your government in action.

The FBI tour is a special treat for most young visitors, and the Mall allows for stretching young legs. Every kid loves climbing on the prehistoric animals outside the Museum of Natural History and gazing at the spacecraft in the National Air and Space Museum. The National Museum of American History is another popular spot where you can salute the original "Star-Spangled Banner" or watch the earth rotate an inch or two under the Great Pendulum. Every kind of Americana is found here, from the original set of Sesame Street to the inaugural gowns of our First Ladies.

Many hotels are within walking distance of the main sights, but don't hesitate to save by staying outside the city, as long as your accommodations are near a stop on the Metro; it's the cleanest, quietest subway you'll ever ride.

## San Francisco

It almost seems that this city was designed with children in mind. Few amusement park rides can equal the fun of the trolly cars clambering up and down the hills of San Francisco, and harbor seals frisking around Fisherman's Wharf are the best free entertainment around. And how can you match the thrill of walking or biking across the Golden Gate Bridge?

San Francisco also has one of the nation's first and best museums for children, the huge Exploratorium, where you can explore science with dozens of imaginative participatory exhibits, from learning to "paint" on a computer screen to entering the Tactile Dome, a pitch black crawl through a variety of touch experiences.

Families can easily spend a day in Golden Gate Park. You can ride on an antique carousel, circa 1912, go boating on lakes, or watching miniature sailboats in action. You can visit the California Academy of Sciences, where the gem and mineral hall is a favorite, or enjoy the funny antics at the Steinhart Aquarium, home to more than 14,000 denizens of the deep.

Older kids think it is really cool to take the boat trip for a tour of infamous Alcatraz Island; reserve well in advance for this is one of the city's most popular excursions. Best of all, the places that kids love best in the city have almost equal appeal for moms and dads.

The special excitement of any of these great cities will make for meaningful, shared memories for everyone in the family—which is what family vacations are all about.

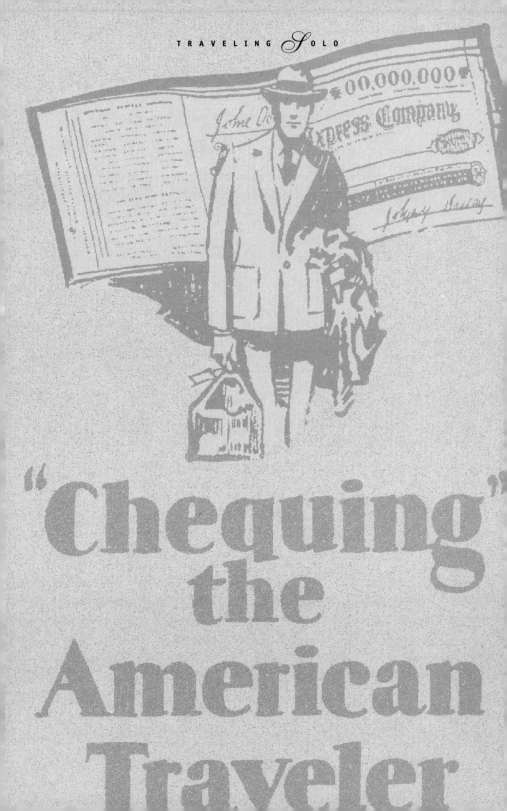

# "Chequing" the American Traveler

# Traveling Safe and Smart

**W**hether you are joining a group or traveling on you own, with or without children in tow, when you set out without another adult along, it is doubly important to be a smart traveler. Traveling alone carries some built-in stresses: no one to help watch the bags or read a map, no one can share the aggravations. But there are many practical steps you can take to keep yourself feeling confident and in control.

## Practical Packing

**R**edcaps never seem to be around when you need them most, so remember when you pack your suitcase that every item inside is something you may have to carry. Use the smallest suitcase you can get along with and pack a folding tote bag to hold any extras you might acquire on your trip. If you need a lot of clothing, two smaller bags or a small case on wheels and a garment bag that goes over your shoulder are easier to manage than a giant suitcase.

A soft-sided bag with a frame is the best combination I've found for both light weight and protection. Cordura is an excellent sturdy choice as a luggage material. Strong wheels make a bag easy to transport. The most stable bags are those with retractable handle across the wide side of the top and two big wheels that carry the weight when you tilt the bag. Suitcases on four wheels pulled by a strap are easy to tip over. If your luggage lacks wheels, a wheeled carrying cart can be a lifesaver.

Other helps are padded shoulder straps or bags that can convert into a backpack, freeing your hands for finding tickets or change. Don't keep valuables in a backpack, where you cannot see them when the pack in on your back.

Be merciless when it comes to paring your travel wardrobe. Unless you are going to a resort where dressing up is the rule, all a woman really needs for a week of normal travel is three dark skirts or slacks, three daytime tops and three tops for evening, a sweater, a jacket, and a raincoat, preferably one that easily folds up. Pack a folding umbrella, as well—the smaller the better.

A similar basic wardrobe suits men, who may add a tie or two for evening for some destinations. One pair of comfortable walking shoes (already broken in!) and one pair of dress shoes complete the picture for both sexes, unless you need to add a warmer coat for colder climates. If you need a coat, wear it or carry it, don't try to pack it.

Expect unexpected weather. Be prepared for a cold, rainy spell in July or a January thaw. For extra warmth, bring silk long underwear, the kind that skiers wear; it is lightweight, and can be rolled up into almost nothing when you pack. Avoid bulky items as much as possible. If you are going to a cold climate, think like those skiers and wear layers—underwear, cotton turtleneck, flat-knit sweater, wind-resistant jacket.

So many hotels have indoor pools these days that you may want to take along a bathing suit no matter what the season. Packing a couple of plastic bags to hold wet or soiled clothing is another good idea.

The best travel advice is that old adage: Bring half as many clothes and twice as much money as you think you'll need.

The most important item in your travel wardrobe is a pair of comfortable walking shoes with nonskid soles—a pair that has been broken in at home *before* your trip. Two important small items are a sewing kit for quick repairs and a travel alarm to be sure you don't oversleep.

Bring plenty of film with you. It's almost always cheaper at home, and you don't want to run out where there are no refills available. Don't trust airport x-ray machines with your precious vacation pictures. Buy a film-shield bag or hand your film (and camera if it is loaded) to the guard for manual inspection.

Before you set off on your trip, be sure your luggage is locked securely and clearly tagged, and remember to put your name, home address, and next destination address inside your suitcase as well. Tags sometimes get detached, and if your bag is lost, inside identification will help locate you.

It's also not a bad idea to jot down the brand, size, color, and any other

# Packing Tips

- Make a packing list. It will keep you from forgetting important items and will come in handy if your luggage goes astray and you need to account for the contents.

- Organize your wardrobe around one basic dark color (brown, black, or navy) to cut down on accessories.

- Transfer shampoo and lotions into mini-bottles of lightweight plastic. Don't fill them to the top: pressure may cause the contents to expand. Put spillables into a plastic bag, just in case.

- Pack heaviest items first; put shoes along the side of the bottom of the bag.

- Pack tightly; don't waste precious space. Fill in spaces with underwear, socks, and hose. Roll pajamas, sweaters, and other casual wear to fit into small spaces.

- Pack suits, dresses, shirts, and blouses in plastic dry-cleaner bags to cut down wrinkling, or put layers of tissue paper between garments.

- Drape slacks, dresses, and any longer garments across the suitcase with the ends hanging over the sides. Put shirts and blouses in the center and fold the long ends over. The center clothing acts as a cushion to prevent wrinkles.

- Pack some old clothes and discard them after you wear them, lightening your load as you go or leaving room for new purchases.

- Don't force your suitcase to close; it may mean broken hinges or zippers when you can least cope with them. If the suitcase won't close, remove a few items.

- Lock your luggage to avoid accidental opening and to discourage thieves. Wrap a tape around the bag to discourage them further.

- A bright piece of ribbon or yarn will help you spot your bag among the look-alikes on the luggage carousel.

- Remove old claim tags so baggage handlers won't be confused about your destination.

aides for identifying your luggage in case it is delayed or lost by an airline. They will ask you to write a description, and sometimes memories play tricks under stress.

Another important tip: Make copies of your tickets, confirmations of hotel reservations, passport, and other important documents, and keep them separate from the originals. The copies will be a big help should you need replacements.

Above all, never pack valuables, jewelry, travel documents, or medicines in luggage that you intend to check. Always put them in your hand luggage. Always pack one change of clothes in your carry-on luggage, just in case. If you arrive in a warm climate in winter clothes and your bag is delayed, you'll bless that one lightweight outfit!

Incidentally, if your bag is delayed more than a few hours, airlines often will advance you cash to buy a few necessities, so always ask; they may not volunteer!

# Easy Departures and Arrivals

Be sure to allow extra time for the airport. Check-in and baggage inspection lines are longer and slower now that airlines are taking extra security precautions; extra time means you won't feel panicked about missing your plane. Better to leave calm and collected than in a frantic rush.

Remember to take photo identification with you; you won't be allowed to board without it.

If you are traveling into an unfamiliar city from the airport alone, you'll find yourself a lot more confident if you know what to expect. Find out from your travel agent, tour operator, or hotel, airport, or airline personnel how long it takes to get into the city and the options for getting there. Is there a convenient bus or limo to your hotel? Does the hotel have courtesy van service? Are cabs plentiful? What is the difference in cost between public transportation and usual cab fare? The Airport Transit Guide, available through the Magellan Catalog listed on page 312, can give you much of this information on many cities.

If you take a cab, you will save hassles by knowing in advance the normal rate to town. *Before* you get into the cab, ask the driver what the fare will be. If it is out of line with the expected rate, wait for another cab.

As mentioned earlier, I've learned that, abroad and even sometimes in the United States, it is a good idea to write down the name and address of your destination clearly before you get into a cab and to mark the spot on a street map. You can't assume that foreign drivers know English or that all cab drivers know their cities well.

The more you know and are prepared in advance, the more you will have that all-important feeling of control in an unfamiliar place.

# Money Matters

Nobody likes to think of bad things happening on vacation, but the surest way to prevent them is to be prepared. Overladen single travelers juggling bags and bundles can be a tempting target. Money holders to hide your cash and guard against pickpockets give great peace of mind when you travel.

Protection comes in many forms. Some money holders are slotted to fit on a belt and tuck into your skirt or slacks; others have straps that either hang around your neck or across your shoulder like a holster or fit around the calf of your leg under trousers. For women, there are half-slips with zip-pockets in the bottom of the hem. Money belts have zip compartments hidden on the inside. There's even a waterproof plastic money holder on a neck cord that solves the problem of where to put your cash if you go swimming alone.

Many travelers use hikers' day packs or "fanny pack" that fit around the waist. These are convenient, but they identify you as a tourist so may not be the wisest choice. If you do use a fanny pack, look for a strong, wide belt; thieves have been known to come up behind and cut the straps. Always keep the pack in front, in your sight.

I often carry a lightweight but sturdy cloth tote bag with straps long enough to go over my shoulder but short enough that I can tuck the bag under my arm when I walk. It allows me to bring along a pad and pencil and an extra sweater or umbrella; I keep my wallet and camera in the very bottom of the bag, out of sight.

I picked up a great little tip from the Travel Companions newsletter for countries like Brazil where thefts from tourists are a big problem. A reader noted that a Brazilian friend had taught her to carry her camera and valuables in a supermarket plastic bag, which made her look like a native rather than a tourist.

No matter which of these safety measures you find most convenient, the point is to keep your cash, tickets, passports, and valuables safe—and preferably out of sight.

Travelers checks are still a standby to avoid losing cash, but the prevalence of ATM bank cash machines in the U.S. and Europe that accept Cirrus, Plus, and other common banking networks means you don't have to carry as much money with you as in the past. Not only can you get money easily twenty-four hours a day, but you get a preferred exchange rate abroad; the bank gets a wholesale rate that is not available to individuals. Most bank machines offer instructions in English. The fee charged for the transaction is also likely to be less than the hefty exchange charges abroad. It still makes sense, however, to keep transactions to a minimum since there is a charge each time you withdraw money.

Always use credit cards for large purchases; you get the preferred exchange rate, and you have someone to come to your aid if there are problems with the purchase.

If you use traveler's checks, you probably know to keep the receipts separate from the checks, in case you have to make a claim. It is also a good idea to separate your credit cards and cash into two wallets kept in two different places; if one disappears, you have another resource.

Another money suggestion before you set out: Be sure you have small bills for tips and enough change on hand to use the telephone or mass transit systems. If you are traveling to a foreign country, "trip packs" of foreign currency for this purpose can be bought in major U.S. airports. If you exchange money in the airport on arrival, remember to ask for small bills and change; the tendency is to hand out larger bills. If you use a cash machine, ask the hotel to give you smaller change as soon as you arrive.

The practice of tipping puzzles many travelers. If you are going to a foreign country, read up on local customs before you leave home. In

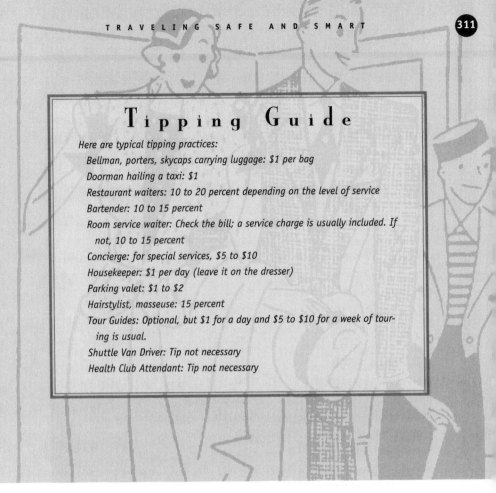

# Tipping Guide

*Here are typical tipping practices:*

*Bellman, porters, skycaps carrying luggage: $1 per bag*

*Doorman hailing a taxi: $1*

*Restaurant waiters: 10 to 20 percent depending on the level of service*

*Bartender: 10 to 15 percent*

*Room service waiter: Check the bill; a service charge is usually included. If not, 10 to 15 percent*

*Concierge: for special services, $5 to $10*

*Housekeeper: $1 per day (leave it on the dresser)*

*Parking valet: $1 to $2*

*Hairstylist, masseuse: 15 percent*

*Tour Guides: Optional, but $1 for a day and $5 to $10 for a week of touring is usual.*

*Shuttle Van Driver: Tip not necessary*

*Health Club Attendant: Tip not necessary*

many countries, the tip is included in the price of the meal. In the United States, the usual percentage may vary in different parts of the country.

# Handy Companions

Some terrific gadgets have been devised to help you feel and look cool and collected on the road. One valuable traveling companion is a compact clothes steamer to remove wrinkles in a hurry when you unpack; they really work. Just remember to have the right adapter plugs if you are traveling in a foreign country.

Other handy travel gadgets include inflatable hangers for drip-dry clothes; tiny sponges that expand in water when you find yourself without a washcloth; portable clotheslines and individual packets of laundry soap; portable alarm clocks; and tiny calculators that help you figure foreign currency rate in a flash. I love my Banana Republic unisex Gore-Tex hat that packs flat but can be popped into shape to ward off both sun and rain. Again, remember that folding umbrella. It's expecting too much to think a thundershower will wait until you're within convenient reach of shelter or an umbrella store.

Shop your own department store notions department, or browse through stores like Brookstone and Sharper Image for these and many other intelligent travel items. If you don't have access to a good selection, here are three mail-order companies that specialize in travel gear; write for their catalogs:

### MAGELLAN'S

Box 5485, Santa Barbara, CA 93150; (800) 962–4943. This company provides a 55-page comprehensive roster of useful accessories.

### TRAVELSMITH

3140 Kerner Boulevard, San Rafael, CA 94901, (800) 950–1600. Official outfitters for many top adventure travel operators, this enterprise's catalog features outdoor gear, luggage, gadgets, and many clothes in wrinkle-proof fabrics.

### CHRISTINE COLUMBUS

P.O. Box 2168, Lake Oswego, OR 97035; (800) 280–4775. This catalog is geared to women travelers.

..............................................................

# Staying Healthy

When you are tired or not feeling well, minor problems loom twice as large. To maintain a feeling of calm and control, it's wise to do what you can to minimize the fatigue of traveling and to take sensible precautions to keep yourself healthy.

Air travel is particularly tiring because seating space is tight. Experienced travelers make the best of the situation by asking for seat assignments as soon as they make plane reservations. To be sure that you enjoy the most leg room available on board, ask for a window or aisle seat. Always avoid the squeezed-in middle seats if you can. Aisle versus window is a matter of preference—the aisle makes it easier to leave your seat, the window provides a headrest for napping. Inflatable pillows contoured to support the neck are a smart investment to rest better on planes, trains, or buses and to leave your transportation without a stiff neck as a souvenir of your trip. Use the little pillow given out on the plane as a back support.

On most planes, the lower-numbered seats near the front of the cabin get the quickest meal service and the best chance of getting your meal of choice; sometimes the most popular dish is no longer available by the time the meal cart gets to the back.

However, this matters less now that so little food is served on planes. If you are taking a plane trip of less than four hours, remember to bring along a snack or sandwich unless you want to survive on a tiny bag of peanuts.

Rows 10 to 20 are often the best choice for a quick exit; on many planes they are closest to the door. If you are serious about getting the best seat for seeing the movie or stretching your legs, you can invest in the *Airline Seating Guide,* a reference that comes in U.S. and overseas editions. For information, contact Forsyth Travel Library, Box 2975, Shawnee Mission, Kansas 66201–1375; 800–FORSYTH.

As for jet lag, no one has solved the problem. Only time really helps your body clock to adjust when you cross several time zones. Some strategies may help to reduce fatigue, however. Begin a few days before departure to gradually shift your meal and sleep times to fit the new time zone. Adopt the new time immediately when you arrive at your destination, and spend time out of doors—daylight somehow seems to help adjust the body's rhythms. Avoid overeating or excessive drinking on the plane—as well as at your destination. Whether you are better off traveling by day or night depends a great deal on how well you sleep on a plane. Some travelers find that taking a mild sleeping pill helps them rest better and feel fresher at journey's end. In general, arriving at night is easier on the system because you have time to rest.

Don't leave your sunglasses and suntan lotion behind just because you are heading for a city; sight-seeing often puts you out of doors for long periods.

Bring along bandages and medication from home. Be sure to include remedies for the most common travel maladies such as headaches and diarrhea. You'll be thankful you did if the need arises when pharmacies are closed. Just in case you might need them in the middle of the night, remember to look for extra blankets or pillows as soon as you check into your hotel room. The middle of the night may be too late.

If you are traveling to countries where hygiene is a problem, you no doubt have been warned to drink only bottled water. Remember to avoid drinks with ice as well. Eat only cooked fruits and vegetables or those that can be peeled, and eat only meat that is well done. Many people even play safe by using bottled water for brushing their teeth.

Time for rest should be a must in your travel schedule. Travelers generally are better off seeing one less sight and getting more out of what they do see. Being tired is a special problem when you are alone. It magnifies the difficulties and gets you down, making you less willing to reach out to meet other people. Allow plenty of time for sleep and plenty of rest breaks in your day. If you are traveling to a high-altitude destination, remember to allow extra rest time until you adjust.

Be good to the feet that are doing extra duty getting you around. When you return to your room after tours of sight-seeing, elevate your legs to give them a rest. Even if you are a confirmed shower-taker at home, you'll find that a soak in the tub does wonders for a travel-weary body.

# P l a y i n g   S a f e

When you are traveling alone, safety in hotel rooms is a concern. Ask for a room near the elevator; don't accept a room at the end of a long corridor. In a large hotel, someone from the front desk should always escort you to your room when you check in. The employee should unlock the room door, check to be sure no one is in the bathroom, and pull back curtains over any sliding glass doors. Sliding doors should have a secure lock, preferably in the floor track. If not, ask for some type of rod to put into the track. The hall door should have a chain as well as a bolt lock and a peephole so that you can see who is outside the door.

Never hang the "Make Up My Room" sign on the door; it announces to the world that the room is unoccupied. To discourage intruders, do

# Safety Tips
## on the
# Road

- Use the peephole in your hotel room door to identify visitors. If you don't recognize the person, call the front desk to verify identification.

- Don't accept delivery of items or services you did not request; ask that the items be left at the front desk.

- When you ride in elevators alone, stand next to the floor button panel. If you sense any problem, press the button for the next floor and get off as soon as possible. Don't press the emergency stop button; it could leave you trapped inside the elevator waiting for assistance.

- When you leave your room, leave a light on and close the curtains if you plan to return after dark.

- Ask hotel personnel to point out unsafe areas on your street map so that you will take care to avoid them.

- Don't keep all of your cash and credit cards in one place; otherwise, you may be left without funds if a pickpocket strikes. Keep your main stash of cash and your passport (when traveling abroad) in a money belt or a safe travel pouch that can be worn out of sight.

- Have keys ready when you get to your guestroom door so you won't have to fumble for them in a corridor. Ditto for cash to pay for cabs or bus fare.

- Don't let a stranger touch your belongings. A common travel scam starts with spilling coffee or ice cream on a tourist and offering to clean it up. While the traveler is distracted, the thief or his partner is cleaning out his wallet. Another distracting ploy: a big "welcome to my country" hug at the airport; the accomplice comes up behind and startles the victim with a punch in the back so the hugger can get the loot.

the opposite—when you are not expecting the maid, hang out the "Do Not Disturb" sign as you leave the room and leave the radio or television playing softly.

It's also wise to check the location of the fire exit nearest to your room. A helpful booklet published by the federal government, "A Safe Trip Abroad," suggests that a room between the second and seventh floors is the best bet, high enough to prevent easy entry from outside but low enough for fire equipment to reach.

Chances are that nothing will happen to spoil your trip, but you'll sleep easier away from home if you take intelligent precautions.

# Worry Insurance

One final matter to think about before you travel is insurance. Most tour companies and several independent companies now offer trip cancellation insurance. The average cost is low compared to the price of a trip and can prove a worthwhile investment whenever you plan far ahead for a very expensive journey. Cruises, for example, offer sizable discounts for early booking, but if it's necessary for you to cancel your plans at the last minute, you can lose your entire payment without insurance. Insurance also includes coverage for any costs that may occur due to travel delays en route.

Your U.S. health insurance probably will not cover you outside the United States, but travel insurance is available. Access America, Inc. (800–284–8300), Mutual of Omaha (800–228–9792), and GlobalCare (800–821–2488) are among several organizations providing this service. Travel agents and tour operators can supply names of other groups who will provide coverage. If you are traveling to remote places, be sure that emergency evacuation coverage is included.

Holders of gold Visa, MasterCard and American Express cards also may be entitled to many travel benefits, from life insurance to car rental discounts to a help-line abroad with an English-speaking operator who can advise on medical or legal problems. It pays to check what your card offers, as it may be worth upgrading if you travel often.

# Driving Safety

Just you in the car? Chances are you'll be just fine, but don't take chances. Here are some tips to keep you rolling along safely:

- Keep the doors locked and the windows up. Use the air conditioner if necessary. Be extra-sure the windows are up when you stop for a light.

- Keep the gas tank full. When the gas level gauge reaches the halfway mark on your dashboard indicator, fill up. Don't wait for the gauge to read "empty."

- Park only on well-lit streets or parking lots. Check for loiterers when you get out, even in your own neighborhood.

- Have keys out and ready so you can get into the car quickly.

- Never stop if a stranger signals that something is wrong with your car— not even if two or three cars go by with the same message. They may be working as a team. Keep going to a service station to check it out.

- If you think you are being followed, head for the nearest police or fire station or a well-lit grocery store or gas station. Hit the horn hard in short, insistent beeps. If you can't find a place to stop, keep moving and keep beeping. You'll attract attention—maybe even the police, which is just what you want.

- If you have car trouble in the daytime, lift the hood and tie a cloth to the antenna or outside door handle to signal for help. In the nighttime, turn on headlights and emergency flashers and get back in the car and lock the door. If a stranger stops, lower the window slightly and ask him to call for help.

- If you are arriving at an airport late at night, stay at an airport hotel and get your car in the morning rather than trying to make your way to an unfamiliar destination on dark roadways.

# Be Ready for the Blues

Vacations serve a great many important functions. They are our best chance to rest from routine and revive the spirit, to hone old skills and acquire new ones, to learn about other life-styles and appreciate other cultures. However, many of us have the fantasy that vacations will be happy and exciting from beginning to end. That is not reality, whether you travel alone or with a companion.

Leaving familiar surroundings creates stress—pleasant stress, yes, but a strain nonetheless as you learn your way around a new place. You may not sleep as soundly, for instance, in an unfamiliar bed. Add the fatigue of unaccustomed exercise, and it's easy to understand why solo vacation emotions tend to be uneven, sometimes shooting from exuberant high to lonesome low. There will inevitably be moments when you may wish there were someone close to share a beautiful sunset or a wonderful experience.

The best way to cope when those feelings arise is to let your feelings out in writing—write to a friend back home or spill it out to your journal, the solo traveler's best companion. It's okay to write about your blues, but make a point of writing about the better side of the trip as well. It really helps to put good and bad in perspective.

One other suggestion: In addition to guidebooks, take along the most engrossing books you can find about your destination, either nonfiction or novels set in the locale you are visiting. You'll be learning and building excitement for the next day's outing even while you are distracting yourself from loneliness.

You will discover that traveling on your own will yield a bonus when you get home. With the knowledge and confidence gained as a successful traveler, you will be a more aware person—and you'll never feel quite as fearful or dependent on others again.

Probably none of us would choose to spend all of our vacations alone, but that does not mean that we cannot reap the special pleasures and rewards that come with solo travel. With the right preparation and an optimistic outlook, single can be a singular way to go!

# Appendix

## Travel Information Sources

### Other Books for Solo Travelers

#### Travel Alone and Love It:
#### A Flight Attendant's Guide to Solo Travel
SHARON B. WINGLER, CHICAGO SPECTRUM PRESS, EVANSTON, IL, 1996.

Practical advice on health, safety, packing, and traveling along with first-hand enthusiasm about the pleasures of solo travel.

#### A Journey of One's Own:
#### Uncommon Advice for the Independent
#### Woman Traveler
THALIA ZEPATOS, EIGHTH MOUNTAIN PRESS, PORTLAND, OR.

More practical advice, this time with emphasis on extended budget travel to offbeat destinations. Good suggestions on safety and socializing and first-hand accounts from women travelers.

#### Women Travel: Adventures,
#### Advice and Experience
EDITED BY MIRANDA DAVIES AND NATANIA JANSZ, ROUGH GUIDES, LONDON, 1993.

A compilation of adventuresome personal experiences, such as "Six Months in the Outback," or "Behind the Picture Postcards" in Ireland.

# Mail-Order and Retail Travel Book Sources

## THE COMPLETE TRAVELER
199 MADISON AVENUE, NEW YORK, NY 10016; (212) 685–9007.

## THE TRAVELERS BOOK STORE
22 WEST 52ND STREET, NEW YORK, NY 10022; (800) 755–8728 OR (212) 664–0995.

## BOOK PASSAGE
51 TAMAL VISTA BOULEVARD, CORTE MADERA, CA 94925; (800) 321–9785.

## FORSYTH TRAVEL LIBRARY
P.O. BOX 1975, SHAWNEE MISSION, KS 66201; (800) 307–7984.

# The Internet

If you have access to the Internet, you have a world of additional travel information at your fingertips. Books on all kinds of specialized topics can be ordered from Amazon.com., an on-line bookstore with more than a million titles.

Shawguides.com offers free the updated text of the most comprehensive guides published to cooking schools, art and craft workshops, and photography workshops and schools. Many of the operators listed in this book have current information on their programs under their own names on the Internet.

This is only the beginning of the vast resources to be tapped. Almost every state, city, and country now has a page on the Internet, which also carries Zagat restaurant listings and some guidebooks. You can browse through pictures of bed-and-breakfast inns, get transportation information, and even make reservations via computer. And you can ask for tips from travelers who have recently visited your destination.

......................................................

# European Travel

The European Travel Commission publishes a booklet, *Planning Your Trip to Europe,* that includes highlights of their twenty-six member countries and names and addresses of their U.S. tourism offices. To request a copy, write to European Planner, P.O. Box 1754, New York, NY 10185.

......................................................

# U. S. State Offices of Tourism

These offices can also supply contacts for tourist information in specific cities in the state.

Alabama Bureau of Tourism and Travel, P.O. Box 4927, 401 Adams Avenue, Montgomery, AL 36104; (800) ALABAMA or (334) 242–4169.

Alaska Division of Tourism, Box E, Juneau, AK 99811; (907) 465–2010.

Arizona Division of Tourism, 1702 North 3rd Street, Suite 4015, Phoenix, AZ 85004; (800) 842–8257 or (602) 230–7733.

Arkansas Department of Parks and Tourism, 1 Capitol Mall, Little Rock, AR 72201; (800) 643–8383.

California Division of Tourism, P.O. Box 1499, Dept. 200, Sacramento, CA 95812; (800) 862–2543, ext. 200.

Colorado Tourism Board, 1625 Broadway, Suite 1700, Denver, CO 80202; (800) 265–6723.

Connecticut Tourism Division, 865 Brook Street, Rocky Hill, CT 06067; (800) CT–BOUND or (860) 258–4355.

Delaware Tourism Office, 99 Kings Highway, Box 1401, Dover, DE 19903; (800) 441–8846; in state, (800) 282–8667.

District of Columbia Visitors Association, 1212 New York Avenue, NW, Washington, D.C. 20005; (202) 789–7000.

Florida Tourist Division, 126 Van Buren St., Tallahassee, FL 32301; (904) 487–1462.

Georgia Tourist Division, Box 1776, Atlanta, GA 30301; (800) VISIT–GA or (404) 656–3590.

Hawaii Visitors Information, 2270 Kalakaua Ave., Suite 801, Honolulu, HI 96815; (808) 923–1811.

Idaho Travel Council, 700 West State Street, Boise, ID 83720; (800) 635–7820.

Illinois Bureau of Tourism, 100 West Randolph Street, Suite 400, Chicago, IL 60601; (800) 223–0121 or (312) 814–4732.

Indiana Tourism Development, Indiana Division of Tourism One North Capitol, Suite 700, Indianapolis, IN 46204; (800) 289–6646.

Iowa Tourism Office, 200 East Grand Avenue, Des Moines, IA 50309; (800) 345–4692 or (515) 242–4705.

Kansas Travel and Tourism Division, 400 West 8th Street, Suite 500, Topeka, KS 66603; (800) 252–6727 or (913) 296–2009.

Kentucky Department of Travel Development, Capital Plaza Tower, 22nd Floor, Frankfort, KY 40601; (800) 225–8747.

Louisiana Office of Tourism, Box 94291, Baton Rouge, LA 70804; (800) 33–GUMBO or (504) 342–8119.

Maine Publicity Bureau, P.O. Box 2300, Hallowell, ME 04347; (800) 533–9595 or (207) 623–0363.

Maryland Office of Tourism Development, 217 East Redwood Street, Ninth Floor, Baltimore, MD 21202; (410) 767–3400 or (800) 543–1036.

Massachusetts Office of Travel and Tourism, 100 Cambridge Street, Boston, MA 02202; (800) 447–MASS or (617) 727–3201.

Michigan Travel Bureau, Box 30226, Lansing, MI 48933; (800) 543–2937 or (517) 335–1865.

Minnesota Office of Tourism, 375 Jackson Street, 250 Skyway Level, St. Paul, MN 55101; (800) 657–3700 or (612) 296–5029.

Mississippi Department of Tourism, Box 1705, Ocean Shrimp, MS 39566; (800) 927–6378.

Missouri Division of Tourism, Box 1055, Jefferson City, MO 65102; (800) 877–1234 or (314) 751–1433.

Montana Promotion Division, 1424 Ninth Avenue, Helena, MT 59620; (800) 541–1447 or (406) 444–2654.

Nebraska Division of Travel and Tourism, 301 Centennial Mall South, Box 94666, Lincoln, NB 68509; (800) 228–4307; in state, (800) 742–7595.

Nevada Commission on Tourism, Capitol Complex, 600 East Williams Street, Suite 207, Carson City, NV 89710; (800) NEVADA or (702) 687–4322.

New Hampshire Office of Vacation Travel, Box 1856, Concord, NH 03301; (800) 258–3608 or (603) 271–2343.

New Jersey Division of Travel and Tourism, C.N. 826, Trenton, NJ 98625; 800–JERSEY7 or (609) 292–2470.

New Mexico Tourism, 491 Old Santa Fe Trail, Santa Fe, NM 87503; (800) 545–2040; in state, (505) 827–0291.

New York Department of Economic Development, Tourism Division, 1 Commerce Plaza, Albany, NY 12245; (800) CALL–NYS or (518) 474–4116.

North Carolina Division of Travel and Tourism, 430 North Salisbury Street, Raleigh, NC 27603, (800) VISIT–NC or (919) 733–4171.

North Dakota Tourism Promotion, Liberty Memorial Building, 600 East Boulevard Avenue, Bismarck, ND 58505; (800) 437–2077.

Ohio Division of Tourism and Travel, Box 101, Columbus, OH 43266; (800) 282–5393 or (614) 466–8844.

Oklahoma Tourism and Recreation Department, 215 NE 28th St., Oklahoma City, OK 73105; (800) 652–6552.

Oregon Tourism Division, 775 Summer Street. NE, Salem, OR 97310; (800) 547–7842.

Pennsylvania Bureau of Travel Development, Chamber of Commerce Forum Building, Harrisburg, PA 17120; (800) VISIT–PA or (717) 787–5453.

Rhode Island Tourism Division, 1 West Exchange Street, Providence, RI 02903; (800) 556–2484 or (401) 277–2601.

South Carolina Division of Parks and Tourism, P.O. Box 71, Columbia, SC 29202; (800) 346–3634 or (803) 734–0122.

South Dakota Department of Tourism, 711 East Wells Avenue, Pierre, SD 57501; (800) 732–5682.

Tennessee Tourism Development, Box 23170, Nashville, TN 37202; (615) 741–2158.

Texas Tourism Division, Box 1272, Austin, TX 78711; (800) 888–8839 or (512)462–9191.

Utah Travel Council, Council Hall, Capital Hill, 300 North State Street, Salt Lake City, UT 84114; (801) 538–1030.

Vermont Travel Division, 134 State Street, Montpelier, VT 05602; (802) 828–3236.

Virginia Division of Tourism, 901 East Byrd Street, Richmond, VA 23219; (804) 786–4484; D.C. office, (202) 659–5523.

Washington State Department of Trade and Economic Development, 101 General Administration Building, P.O. Box 4250, Olympia, WA 98504; (800) 544–1800 or (206) 586–2088.

West Virginia Tourism Division, 2101 Washington Street East, Charleston, WV 25305; (800)CALL–WVA.

Wisconsin Division of Tourism Development, 123 West Washington Avenue, Box 7606, Madison, WI 53707; (800) 372–2737 or (608) 266–2161.

Wyoming Travel Commission, I–25 and College Drive, Cheyenne, WY 82002; (800) 225–5996; in state, (307) 777–7777.

# *Index*